Idols in the House

Ted Flynn

This book may not be reproduced in whole or in part by any means without the prior written permission of the publisher.

Written, compiled, and edited by Ted Flynn

Published by MaxKol Communications, Inc., © 2002

Cover by S. G. Graphics

Cover photograph: Anonymous

ISBN: 0-9634307-1-8

Published in the United States of America

Copies of this book may be obtained by contacting:
MaxKol Communications
P. O. Box 606
Herndon, Virginia 20172;
Telephone: (703) 421-1300; fax: (703) 421-1300;
e-mail: MaxKol@msn.com; web site: www.MaxKol.org.

Also by Ted Flynn:

The Thunder of Justice
Prophecy and the New Times
Key to the Triumph
Hope of the Wicked

Contents

Introduction   1

1   The True State of the Union   4

2   Perfuming the Pig   19

3   Are Your Servants Listening?   30

4   Sieg Heil!   43

5   The Deepest Needs of Man   58

6   The Sins of Judgement   73

7   The Culture of Death   96

8   Why Does That Monkey Glow in the Dark?   115

9   Endangered Species   122

10   The Great Idol   137

11   Come See, Grandpa   149

12   Throwing in the Towel   163

13   The Cohorts of Heaven Battle   184

14   Are America's Wings about to Be Clipped?   202

15   The Red Dragon Confronts America   220

16   Where's the Hope?   238

17   The Correct Response to Scandal   247

18   Coming Prophesied Events   264

Endnotes   273

Because of all the evil of the children of Israel, and of the children of Juda, which they have done, provoking me to wrath, they and their kings, their princes, and their priests, and their prophets, the men of Juda, and the inhabitants of Jerusalem. And they have turned their backs to me, and not their faces: when I taught them early in the morning, and instructed them, and they would not hearken to receive instruction. And they have set their *idols in the house*, in which my name is called upon, to defile it. And they have built the high places of Baal, which are in the valley of the son of Ennom, to consecrate their sons and their daughters to Moloch: which I commanded them not, neither entered it into my heart, that they should do this abomination, and cause Juda to sin. And now, therefore, thus says the Lord the God of Israel to this city, whereof you say that it shall be delivered into the hands of the king of Babylon by the sword, and by famine, and by pestilence (Jeremiah 32:32–36).

Dedicated to my parents,

Edward F. Flynn
&
Cynthia I. Flynn,

whose sacrifices created the opportunities

Acknowledgements

With everything in life, we are products of the many people and happenings that have touched us. It is for this reason that we are all like we are today. I've had a lot of help along the way with many good people touching my life.

First and foremost, I give a very warm and sincere thank you to Ron Westernik for his contributions of time, energy, data mining, thought, and broadening of scope in helping the book to evolve and hatch. It wouldn't have happened without you. In the end, we were finishing each other's sentences. Your time is an indication of your commitment to the Lord.

Many thanks to George Bossy for his friendship and help in getting me to think ideology. In addition, the insights and guiding hand of Seamus from Boston were invaluable and helped bring a balance to the themes. Thanks to Mike Loflin for the Scriptural themes, and to Paul and Leslie Regan for suggestions and understanding the big picture. The work was greatly enhanced by the editing and suggestions of Fr. Joseph Esper and Roger Raslavsky Many thanks to Tony Christ, the Saint Joseph Group, the Sheridans, and many others not mentioned. For all your help and support, I am eternally grateful.

Introduction

No matter where I go in the country, people ask me the same question, "Ted, how did we get here, what happened to us? How did we decline so quickly?" People across the country are suffering, hurt, fearful of what we have become and where we might be going. The events of 9/11 are like the final straws that broke the camel's back in a country already overburdened by divorce, crime, and addictions of every kind. Let me tell you from the outset that I am with you in these fears. I have listened to many associates and friends into the late evening hours and their concerns are universal.

The beating heart of this book asserts that a man, society or country, which does not pursue spiritual joys, will seek carnal pleasures and practice idolatry in its many fashions. Since we have abandoned much of the spiritual, especially over the last generation, America presently is reaping the bad fruits of our endeavors. It does not take a leap of faith for anyone to realize that our sorrowful situation is the direct result of decades of misguided and corrupt governmental and social engineering wedded to globalism and secular humanism. As history proves repeatedly, the world is full of proud, wealthy and cold-hearted people who are hell-bent to destroy the Judeo-Christian social order to achieve a deluded vision of utopia. The ultimate outcome of such endeavors typically results in the painful tribulation of the vast majority of a society. The late Fr. Malachi Martin, in his bestseller, *The Keys of this Blood*, asserted that "Willing or not, ready or not, we are all involved in an all-out, no-holds-barred, three-way global competition...for the first one-world system of government." Has anything changed? There are more civil conflicts worldwide between 'right' and 'left' wing opponents, or if you prefer, democratic-capitalists versus totalitarian-radicals and terrorists, than ever before. Religious corruption, apostasy and scandal are pervasive across all denominations. Economic turmoil and dozens of violent conflicts currently are in progress and extend throughout the continents stretching America's military and financial capabilities beyond our limits. Can this confusion go on indefinitely?

For Americans, all of the traditional social support mechanisms that we once knew, including wholesome families living in a well-ordered society, are passé. Let's face it; the way of life in the U. S. in 1960 has disappeared. How is it that we went from Ward and June Cleaver

1

raising their two boys in *Leave It to Beaver* to the adventures of Al Bundy, *Will & Grace*, and other entertainment media trash in one generation? If present trends continue, such programs will be tame years from now. Across the board there is no civility, nor a respect for authority of any kind. It was unthinkable years ago that one in two families would be affected by divorce; that parents wouldn't let a child walk a block to school for fear the child would be molested or kidnapped; that crime would be so widespread as to cause fear of walking the streets at night; that hardly any American families would be untouched by addictions to alcohol, drugs, or rampant promiscuity. In today's schools, teachers educate our children, even pre-adolescent youths, down to the first-grade level on how to conduct immoral sexual behavior and that homosexuality is an acceptable, alternative lifestyle. Thanks in part to multi-culturalism, many parents (and grandparents) teach their children that all religions are relatively the same, culturally inspired and are acceptable so long as such religions contain some sort of moral fabric or code that our society can tolerate. Through it all, most people stubbornly believe that these changes in our society just naturally evolved, that somehow or other they just happened. This book clearly demonstrates the contrary.

The tears and the pain of Americans are too numerous to mention. We see and feel them in our gut every day. We all know something is very wrong. It is for these reasons of abnormality that Americans are an uptight and anxious people. For example, we see anxiety even in the good times when the stock market is at unprecedented highs. Can you imagine the fear, anger, confusion and despair that will exist if the financial markets tank?

Acclaimed as the last great superpower, is America presently targeted by our enemies, externally and internally, to become the final victim in the near future of the globalists, who are determined to prove that our current mode of government is outdated and ineffectual? Has our nation imperceptibly been sabotaged over the last fifty-plus years by political, business, educational and clerical leaders who purposely by design, or through benign acquiescence, have created a cultural environment that is inherently corrupt both temporally and spiritually? Are Americans, like the Romans of the 4th Century, wedded to 'bread and circuses,' ignoring the ominous signs around us? Do we care what God thinks of our nation versus what we perceive ourselves to be? Did God allow the terrorist acts of 9/11 to happen as a warning for America's own good?

Idols in the House examines how our nation has dramatically changed in virtually every domain of our lives. It addresses directly the questions posed above and concludes that most Americans are quite comfortable with idolatry by many names and selfish interests. Many alarming facts are illustrated that make this assertion crystal clear. Worse still, as a nation we are quite unprepared for the ultimate, concluding step which the globalist leaders are unfurling before our very eyes. Wedded to practical paganism and growing barbarism, what many of us do not realize or fail to appreciate is that God will not allow mankind to build another 'Tower of Babel.' He presently is warning America through many means that our time is short. Divine Mercy is offered, but Almighty Justice may be necessary to save us.

This is not a dissertation about doom and gloom. Do not look to the evil around us that is the mantra of the press, but focus on what is good. This is the attitude that will make a life worth living. I do not cower or shudder over our current state of affairs in America or in the world, because I know that better times ultimately await us. There are justifiable reasons to have great hope. Yet, if there is a fire in the house, a fireman sounds the alarm before putting out the fire. It is only after the alarm is acknowledged that we can put out the fire, assess damages and begin repairs. Through the grace of God, if the reader has the fortitude to read this book in its entirety, and thereby becomes dissatisfied with the status quo, then perhaps we have achieved our objective; for this book is truly about America having a change of heart. The choice between the current state of affairs in our country versus what God desires is now upon us.

Dei perfecta sunt opera!

Ted Flynn
May 13, 2002

1

The True State of the Union

People are judged in eternity; nations are judged in time and on earth.

—Paraphrase of Saint Augustine,
The City of God

Along with December 7, 1941, the date of September 11, 2001, will live forever in American history as a "Day of Infamy." The great American Empire took a direct hit by a foreign power. Americans were virtually glued to the news for days as they watched the horror of our great symbols of financial and industrial might being reduced to rubble and smoldering ashes. All of a sudden, the last remaining superpower from the Cold War era looked vulnerable to the rest of the world. Did anyone perceive that it is a sign of a weakening nation when one's enemies use that nation's own technology to take potshots? There was no one in America without an opinion on what happened—or why—but how to solve the problem of terrorism was entirely another matter.

The range of emotions ran the gamut for all Americans and the international community. Arab students at several U. S. universities rejoiced in the student unions, and only when they realized that their reaction was being seen did they make a quick exit. But the point was clear: No one really knew what was in the heart of a fundamentalist Muslim. Trying to figure out the public persona from the heart of such an individual was an impossible task. Beyond the horrific acts themselves, what made this terrorist attack new was the profile of the attackers. As a group they were educated in European schools, travelling the world financially comfortable, joining health clubs, and drinking cappuccinos at Starbuck's. A doctor in one of America's finest medical institutions had arranged the airline tickets for the terrorists. Was it done knowing who they were?

Frustration is apparent on many levels as no one is really sure if more violence may be on the way. Several airlines went out of business in less than two weeks, and the largest airlines needed a guaranteed cash infusion of $17 billion from the federal government just to stay afloat. As a nation we were very fragile, and deep down everyone knew it. We suddenly felt vulnerable and uncertain. This was the reason for the anxious mood of the country. The battle required a new way of thinking and it would be a long struggle.

In the Greek story of the Trojan Horse, Odysseus unleashed soldiers upon the enemy after being wheeled inside the gates of the city. In America and the rest of the world, Islamic people, including extremists with ill intent toward America, were roaming inside the gates, all with the blessings of the immigration policies of the Western world. Paradoxically, the practice of multi-culturalism, religious relativism and due process made the U. S. different from a Muslim fundamentalist country where you could lose limb or life for exposing a Bible in public, a challenge for present day democracies to say the least. America was changed forever on 9/11 and living with the repercussions will be a normal state of life from here on out on many levels.

The tradeoff between freedom and security presently swings in favor of security for the majority of the American public. No better illustration of this shifting tide is the establishment of the new cabinet post in the Executive Branch of the federal government called Home Land Defense. A few political pundits ignored by the media questioned if this is simply the next strategic and sequential step towards the ultimate obliteration of the U. S. Constitution.

No one is attempting to minimize the pain and suffering from the recent attacks. Over 10,000 children are without a parent and the loss of life of very brave and selfless souls was very difficult to watch on television. But what does it all mean for us as a nation and as citizens of the great empire called the United States of America? Is there a bigger agenda to see?

Americans are focused presently on primarily one problem. It is the problem of inserting Islam into an American Christian heritage. The World Health Organization (WHO) estimates there are approximately 1,200,000,000 Muslims worldwide. If only ten percent abide by the strict fundamentalist Islamic view, that Christians are infidels, then there are 120,000,000 potential problems walking the streets of the world. If only five percent of the 1.2 billion are stridently anti-American, that is still 60,000,000 potential enemies. If only 2.5 percent would be willing to aid and abet a violent act, the number is still around 30,000,000. Journalist Barbara Walters spoke with some graduate students in Saudi Arabia and they said, "Yes, we're shocked and horrified. At first we thought we were watching a movie, but much of the Islamic world was in favor of what happened because of the United States' one-sided stance with Israel."[1] With this in mind, 2.5

5

percent is probably a realistic estimate. This is not a diatribe against the Muslim world, it is simply an illustration of the magnitude of the challenge now facing the United States of America.

There are legitimate reasons for the tensions in Israel stemming from the abuse, occupation, and humiliation of the Palestinian people. The U. S. has alienated Arab nations unnecessarily for over a generation through its export of pornography and filth. Due to the modern technology of television and the internet in Muslim countries, Muslims are now aware in real time of what goes on in the West Bank. It is going to take the direct intervention of God to somehow find a solution for Israel, for it is beyond human control. The hatred towards America will continue to increase in the Muslim world. The polls indicate that the Arab people do not hate Americans, but despise our foreign policies.

As security issues escalate, freedom will dramatically and steadily erode. Those unwilling to go along ultimately will be considered enemies of the state. Is security the real problem? This book is one attempt to shed light on America's fundamental problem and help remove the selective amnesia that shrouds American society. If America does not soon recognize the severity of its spiritual and social malaise, then America is destined for God's purification.

How to Look at an Issue

In any given situation there are only three ways to look at something: as I see it, as others see it, and as God sees it. It would be safe to say that there is not a shortage of opinions—anywhere. Every time we render an opinion it will always have a bias of self-interest, nationalism, culture, education, ethnicity, and a host of other factors. Where we stand on an issue is directly dependent on where we sit. However, opinions are oftentimes flawed because they tend to discriminate, particularly as they pertain to God's will. There is no shortage of opinion in the print and electronic media on the state of America. Now is the time to view the general state of America to see what the Lord may be trying to tell us.

Needless to say, people are doing more soul-searching now than prior to September 11. The day after the 9/11 attacks, churches were filled across America, no matter the denomination. The range of emotions ran the gamut from introspection to anger. Where is God in all of this? Has He abandoned us? Is this a God of wrath and anger? If God is a God of love and mercy, how could He let this happen? These are valid questions no matter the orientation or the belief system.

Depending on the predisposition of the person, including one's beliefs, attitudes, interests and opinions, there exist various paths of discernment and answers. For example, a Christian believer would recognize that the date, 9/11, is a symbol of a national emergency and would turn inward to find the mind of God, while the unbeliever would vent opinions of self-knowledge and reasoning. It is a classic example of how diverse segments of people search for answers to very complex issues and derive different and often conflicting answers. Ultimately, it becomes a public debate and unfortunately, those with power and money who profess self-serving insights tend to beat the loudest drum to the widest audience.

For example, two prominent secular humanists have conveyed publicly their beliefs on this subject. Look at Ted Turner, who posits that the terrorists who hijacked the planes are "brave but insane" that the terrorist acts had been caused by poverty. "Lots of people live under awful conditions, without any hope for a better life." Former Vice President Al Gore chimes, "More problems besides terrorism were also urgent: poverty, illiteracy, environment, diseases, corruption and political pressures are among them." Notwithstanding Turner's absurd commentary on bravery, Americans are apt to be empathetic to their commentary regarding the plight of humanity throughout the world. However, what neither one of these two men will admit publicly regarding their means to solve this tragic condition of humanity is their total disdain and disregard of God's justice and mercy. They would legislate more government programs with greater restrictions on civil liberties. This agenda includes, but is not limited to, abortion, eugenics, euthanasia, dumbed-down public education, legal and illegal drug propagation, self-amusement, and entertainment. It is not often in history that elite moneyed groups of people have marched in the streets for civil rights. The humanists have sought to change mankind with their own wisdom, while the man of God most often picks up a cross in spite of obstacles and asks God what He wants, for His ways are different.

This is because the ultimate goal of leading secular humanists (i.e. those who believe that man's progress is solely dependent on his own ability and merit devoid of God's Will or involvement) is to significantly reduce the worldwide population to less than ten percent of the current total worldwide, enslave us with 'bread and amusement,' and conserve the vast resources of the world to be controlled by a select, few 'gifted' leaders.

Just take a ride down to Elberton, Georgia, to view "The Georgia Guidestone," a mammoth set (twenty feet high) of granite monuments

(951 cubic feet weighing over 245,000 pounds) that espouse ten commandments for the coming "New Age of Reason." The commandments are presented in eight languages spoken by two-thirds of mankind: English, Russian, Hebrew, Arabic, Hindi, Chinese, Spanish, and Swahili. The new age commandments, shown below, inscribed on the monuments demonstrate a blasphemous disregard for God's Decalogue by American and world leaders who underwrote the multi-million investment in the property and its monuments. These commandments imply the mass destruction of over 90 percent of the current worldwide population, idolatry based on the new tolerance of multi-god worship, elimination of cultural distinctions, arbitrary balance of personal liberties with subordination exclusively to the state and social norms, divinization of personal vanity and the continued existence of a human life based solely on utilitarian value. In a sentence it is the spiritual suicide of every individual who is deemed worthy of existence in this new age of reason.

The ten commandments for the New Age:
- Maintain humanity under five hundred million in perpetual balance with nature.
- Guide reproduction wisely, improving fitness and diversity.
- Unite humanity with a living new language.
- Rule passion, faith, tradition, and all things with tempered reason.
- Protect people and nations with fair laws and just courts.
- Let all nations rule internally, resolving external disputes in a world court.
- Avoid petty laws and useless officials.
- Balance personal rights with social duties.
- Prize truth, beauty, love...seeking harmony with the infinite.
- Be not a cancer on earth...leave room for nature...

Each of the ten commandments above echoes the philosophy of Marx in *The Communist Manifesto*. They sound somewhat innocuous on paper, but require indoctrination, coercion and violence in the street to implement them. Devoid of God, they represent humanism in its highest, or should that be lowest, form. It is convenient for one's personal psyche and society as a whole to choose to ignore what is made manifest by people whose designs include our enslavement. The present government, media and commercial establishments are quite industrious and successful in convincing Americans that God must bless America. We have convinced ourselves that our might makes right, whether financial, industrial or military. A good illustration of this is President George W. Bush's State of the Union Address in January 2002. Clearly, the emphasis of the speech centered on the nation's military and industrial might. The strategies focused on the elimination of terrorism, state sponsorship of terrorism, homeland security, economic growth, job security and volunteerism. Juxtapose these strategic subjects of our national interest to the terror perpetrated on the unborn, the state sponsored/funded abortion, contraception and cloning, the widespread misuse and illegal use of drugs and alcohol, particularly by our youth and the growing resignation of society to such abuse, the ever growing violence within our schools, the introduction of promotion of homosexuality and the accommodation of promiscuity by the National Education Association (NEA) into our schools. Combine these with the significant economic growth of industries that aggressively promote vanity, pornography and promiscuity into our neighborhoods and homes all resulting in the aggressive invasion of sexually transmitted diseases and the total breakdown of the traditional family structure, all while government and the private sector ineffectually apply massive amounts of resources to stem the growing tide of crime, disease and social unrest that is a direct consequence of America's inability to understand or cope with the fundamental problems confronting us.

Here are some revealing statistics that our government doesn't communicate in its State of the Union, as reported by Dr. James Dobson at a Spring 1998 Council for National Policy meeting. In 1997 the Republican-led Congress, House and Senate, gave $900 million to Planned Parenthood to take the abortion message around the world. In spite of twenty-five years of condom distribution in America and over $3 billion spent on safe sex promiscuity programs, America now faces two major epidemics from traditional sexually transmitted diseases: syphilis and gonorrhea. In 1998 alone, Congress gave $200 million for safe sex promiscuity. It remains a failed policy, because wherever teen sex is taught, pregnancy rates increase. Those who wish to put their faith in government policies should take note that President George W. Bush decided to recognize families "'in various forms,' including unmarried cohabiting couples and homosexual partners." Bush's representatives allied with European delegates at the U. N. General Assembly's Special Session on Children in May 2002 to overturn the traditional U. N. definition of family: married heterosexual parents and children.[2]

Meanwhile there has not been one hardcore pornographer indicted in America since 1993 because President Clinton and Janet Reno eliminated the Obscenity Task Force. The National Endowments for the Arts was given $99 million to offend people of faith by promoting lewd art. Talking about tax policies, the marriage penalty tax still discriminates against the traditional family.

Recall that the people of Germany refused to acknowledge truth even when it came out in the trials of Nuremberg that they knew what was going on inside Germany. The sin was progressive and ultimately destroyed that nation. The buildup against the Jews in Germany and Europe was gradual. First, the Brown Shirts began to mobilize and intimidate. Second, the ante went up when Jews were prohibited from holding government jobs, the windows of Jewish-owned buildings were broken during Kristallnacht. Third, even when Jews were being herded into boxcars like diseased cattle, many still refused to believe that Germans could do that to their citizens. Many Jews who remained were in a state of denial that this could all be happening. The American people today are so dumbed down that they refuse to look at what has happened in the last forty years, twenty years, and even the last five years in America. Human nature doesn't change.

The sign outside of the Auschwitz death camp during liberation says it all. "When they came for the mentally retarded, I said nothing. When they came for the infirmed, I said nothing. When they came for the elderly, I said nothing. When they came for the Jews, I said nothing. When they came for me, there was no one left to speak. Signed, a Catholic priest."

There is no way to justify a terrorist act, but now that the deed is done, it must be asked in an honest and courageous way: Is there culpability on our part in the eyes of God that would allow a people or a nation to harm us? Why did God allow it, and how are we responsible? What should our next response be? How will God react to our response?

Culture Wars

Let's examine how we arrived where we are. Was it by accident, or by some form of immutable process which no one has defined? To many older people in the world, few can believe the moral slide came so fast. One decade America seemed good and virtuous, the next it seemed morally bankrupt. If one believes there is a God in Heaven, and an Evil One who seeks to destroy, the statements below will make sense.

We have not arrived at our state of malaise by accident, but are here as a direct result of a specific and calculated set of political strategic principles. The communist experiment has been by all accounts a seemingly miserable failure. Even at the height of the Cold War, the U. S. S. R. was like a Third World country. All had been sacrificed socially so the military industrial complex could be built. The writings of Marx, Engels, and Trotsky varied, but collectively their style of takeover requires violence. The communists have always been men in ruthless pursuit of nothing but absolute power. Kiev/Rus has had a thousand-year history of Christianity. Lenin's contemporaries tried to virtually eliminate Christianity from the land stretching from St. Petersburg to Vladivostock, an area encompassing eleven time zones— from Finland to the Bering Sea off Alaska. As the gulags filled up with dissenters, the system broke down, taking a dramatic turn in November of 1989 with the collapse of the Berlin Wall. Even Mikhail Gorbachev, in a meeting with Pope John Paul II in the Vatican, lamented that the mistake of the Soviet communist strategy had been the attempt to completely eliminate Christianity (rather than merge it gradually into a one-world religion as espoused by his organization, Green Cross International). Did the communist system actually collapse, or did it simply change in outward appearance?

Karl Marx had a disciple by the name of Antonio Gramsci who was an Italian communist around the time of Mussolini. After Mussolini took Rome in 1922, Gramsci fled to Russia. Gramsci was an astute observer who knew that the Soviet style of communism in every phase would be seriously challenged. He reasoned that a system based on generational violence would be hard pressed to endure. With only approximately three percent of the Russian people joining the Communist Party, Gramsci concluded it was the Christian Russian soul that prevented the Russian people from embracing the Communist Revolution. The people did not respond to fear. "The [Western] civilized world had been thoroughly saturated with Christianity for 2,000 years and a regime grounded in Judeo-Christian beliefs and values could not be overthrown until the roots were cut."[3]

Americans need to appreciate that for communism to emerge victorious, Marxists had to de-Christianize the West. To understand world history over the last 70 years with all the destruction around us, one must appreciate this point. To not believe it, or to miss it, will prevent an individual from correctly interpreting modern history. To understand what has happened since the Russian Revolution, it is essential to recognize the point of Gramsci's strategy. The socialist approach is less violent than the communist strategy. It attracts people of like mind generationally, with patience and an ideology. It is very effective. This is what has happened in the West. The ideological war has been seemingly won by this thinking, at least for now. When this is understood, one will more clearly understand how America and the West have fallen so rapidly. Gramsci's genius was to deconstruct the systems in the West. To achieve his long-term goals, this deconstruction could only work if done incrementally.

Gramsci returned to Italy realizing the Soviet system under Stalin would be a reign of terror that would not produce the type of socialism he envisioned. He then became a leader of the Italian Communist Party and Mussolini threw him in jail. What came out of that jail cell was a new blueprint for a less violent, more calculated takeover that until then no one had ever tried. It is the system of thinking arising from this blueprint that has captured the hearts of the people in the U. S. and the West without us even realizing it.

The philosophies and strategies of Antonio Gramsci are arguably the most important in the 20th Century concerning the spread of communism and socialism throughout the world. It centers on gradual, yet progressive, indoctrination and acceptance by the masses of socialist ideals and programs. Although his ideas were not immediately understood or agreed on by the communists, the socialists and Fabians of England and the United States embraced his thinking as a way to create a newer and more just world for all. The socialist approach to social change is one of infiltrating the existing system and changing it from within even if it takes several generations. This gradual change is the reason that the symbol of the Fabians is the turtle. Socialists believe the communists are in too much of a hurry and cannot change society as quickly as they would like, that they are too violent and sudden in their tactics, thus not winning the hearts of the people. Changing hearts is what is necessary for the revolution to succeed. In his book, *The Death of the West*, Patrick Buchanan presents in cogent form how simple the battle plan for the culture war is.

> ...In the West there was a proper relation between the state and civil society, and when the state trembled a sturdy structure of civil society was at once revealed. The State [in the West] was only the outer ditch, behind which there stood a powerful system of fortresses and earthworks.[4]

Rather than seize power first and impose a cultural revolution from above, Gramsci argued, communists in the West must first change the culture; then power would fall into their hands like ripened fruit. But to change the culture would require a "long march through the institutions"—the arts, cinema, theater, schools, colleges, seminaries, newspapers, magazines, unions, and the new electronic medium, radio. One by one, each had to be captured and politicized into an agency of revolution for 'social justice and welfare.' Then the people could be slowly educated to understand and even welcome the revolution.

Gramsci urged his fellow communists to form popular fronts with Western intellectuals who shared their contempt for Christianity and bourgeois culture and who shaped the minds of the young. Message to the comrades: "It's the culture, stupid!" Since Western culture has given birth to capitalism and sustained it, if that culture could be subverted, the system would fall of its own weight. On the cover of his 1970 runaway bestseller *The Greening of America*, the manifesto of the counterculture, author Charles Reich parroted Gramsci perfectly:

> There is a revolution coming. It will not be like revolutions of the past. It will originate with the individual and the culture, and it will change the political structure only as its final act. It will not require violence to succeed, and it cannot be successfully resisted with violence. It is now spreading with amazing rapidity, and already our laws, institutions, and social structure are changing in consequence....
>
> This is the revolution of the new generation.[5]

Now that they had a formula that showed it could work in the street, not only on paper, it was time to go to work—and go to work they did. With the combination of a Hegelian doctrine of man serving the state, and a social plan to change Western civilization, the method of indoctrination and changing the system from within has brought the U. S. to where it is today. The Gramsci strategy has been a colossal success. Just take a look around at the impact of the National Education Association, the intrusive path government has taken, and the destruction of the family to the point where the father has been reduced to an Al Bundy or Homer Simpson—the village idiot. Part of the de-Christianizing process has been that those with an agenda have put people of like minds in positions of power and influence in order to create a new mentality in society. The New World Order has spiritual as well as physical dimensions. An agenda has been promulgated and enforced, and if you focused your attention on material well-being, you missed the revolution.

In 1958, Aldous Huxley, in his book *Brave New World Revisited*, quotes a character called the Grand Inquisitor, from one of Dostoyevsky's parables, as saying: "In the end the people will lay their freedom at the controller's feet and say, 'Make us slaves, but feed us.'" Huxley gives us a date when changes could occur. He writes: "The 21st Century will be the era of World Controllers." Then he tells us why these "controllers" would not fail: "The older dictators fell because they could never supply their subjects with enough bread, enough circuses, enough miracles and mysteries. Under a scientific dictatorship education will really work—with the result that most men and women will grow up to love their servitude and will never dream of revolution. There seems to be no good reason why a thoroughly scientific dictatorship should ever be overthrown."[6]

The genius of people like Gramsci and Huxley is that the takeover of society would be carried out so well, so gradually, and so subtly that people wouldn't even know it had happened. The reason that so many people today ask, "How did all of this happen over the last 40 to 50 years?" is because it was engineered to happen that way. As Dostoyevsky wrote, "The world controllers will make us love our servitude." In 1931, Josef Stalin said that the Soviet Union had two major enemies. First was the Roman Catholic Church, which he said the Soviets were well on their way to destroying. Second was the moral foundation of America. To destroy that, they would have to target the media, entertainment, and education. He said, "If we can do that, we will take over America and never fire a shot."[7]

God's *If...Then...* Clause

How does God counter such diabolical strategies? What is God trying to say? *If* we can safely say that everything goes through the permissive will of the Father, and the hairs on our head are numbered before we are born, *then* we must have the courage to ask ourselves individually and corporately as a nation what message the Lord is trying to communicate. Individuals often oversimplify and hastily select manageable sets of facts because one cannot embrace history in all of its complexity. The eternal word of God, however, is a constant and has stood the test of time, whether or not one has the courage and faith to admit it.

God offers Holy Scripture as a means of communication. We can see what God says at one point in time, and then we can see the action coming to fruition exactly as He, Yahweh, said it would. This method of conditional outcome is all throughout the Old Testament typically conveyed by God through the prophets as an "If…then" clause. *If* My people do this, *then* I will…. For example, "*If* my people who are called by my name humble themselves, and pray and seek my face, and turn from their wicked ways, *then* I will hear from heaven, and will forgive their sin and heal their land" (2 Chronicles 7:14). There is little doubt to the believer reading Holy Scripture that there are conditions that must be met if we are to stay in the good graces of the Lord. He is a loving God, a merciful God, but also a just God. A follower of the Lord, once shown the light, has the requirement to adhere in its totality to the message. In any such situation, an unbeliever typically is unable to discern correctly the message or will of God and responds accordingly. There is simply no other response because the frame of reference is based solely on personal reasoning and self-interest. Notwithstanding a higher order of perceived understanding and intelligence, when push comes to shove the unbeliever acts like any other animal focused on survival and preservation of the species. They have only their own internal thoughts and wisdom and current social norms and expectations to value. To look at the Lord's conditional message requires accepting an entirely different set of criteria to evaluate based on faith in God alone, not the animal instinct.

This new tension crystallized when Jesus confronted the Jewish Scribes and Pharisees with a clear set of rules for all political and social dialogue. The wisdom of Christ is not the wisdom of man, and the contradiction between the two is very dramatic and emotional. Yet, the Lord in His infinite love will never force His will on anyone. It is a simple yet profound truth. It is explicitly tied to one of Christianity's great mysteries, man's free will. If the heart is predisposed to God's teachings, then He will pour out mercy and graces. Circumstances oftentimes are strong enough to bend a man's will in His favor, but it is never certain what man will do. Until one is ready to mortify one's own will and unite it with God's, one will never find an enduring purpose for existence.

Some people just refuse to listen to what He is saying no matter the circumstances. For example, at the time of the Crucifixion of Jesus, next to Him were two thieves. Less than hours from death with complete presence of mind, Jesus offered both of them a way out. One said, "Truly You are the Son of God." Jesus replied that before the day was out he would be with Him in paradise. Both were given the same opportunity. At death, one said 'yes' and stole Heaven at the last moment because of his contrite and humble spirit. Yet the second thief remained unwilling to submit to Divinity even with the Son of God right next to him. This is a stark example of the point that some people, no matter the circumstances, are unwilling to go along with the agenda of Heaven. These decisions by the two thieves characterize what free will offers: spiritual health and eternal happiness in Heaven, or spiritual suicide with the ultimate destination of Hell. It is just as true for us today as it was for the thieves crucified with Christ. Some people are simply unwilling to submit to the will of God no matter what is going on around them. Some people take their pride to the grave and beyond.

How does this apply to America? Since 1960, America's leaders, with the concurrence of the general population, have progressively spurned God's grace. America's heart is hardened toward God. Today, Americans typically view the Judeo-Christian God as antiquated, needing renovation or some type of renewal which relegates Him to a benign group of role models (with other competing gods) for the sake of community and individual social development. It follows that Americans pay lip service to the will of the one true God. We have abandoned or degraded the Judeo-Christian principles subscribed to by our Founding Fathers, preferring instead to spend our nation's time and effort to maintain and expand our superior might, intellect and financial clout because we believe that these material interests are all that matters to our individual and collective success. Accelerating the deconstruction of our nation's reliance on God, our nation's leaders invited people into our country who do not share our way of life nor conform to our beliefs, attitudes and interests. Under the guise of multi-culturalism, this initiated the development of a misguided and unhealthy view of tolerance.

Therefore, the strategy to promote this multi-culturalism begins with kicking the Judeo-Christian God out of the classroom in the United States by the tribunal known as the Supreme Court in 1962, thereby saying publicly under the guise of separation of Church and State, that we do not want Supreme guidance for our children. Yet, Abraham Lincoln, in his Presidential Inaugural Address of March 4, 1861, warned Americans, "I do not forget the position assumed by some that constitutional questions are to be decided by the Supreme Court.... At the same time, the candid citizen must confess that if the policy of the Government upon vital questions affecting the whole people is to be irrevocably fixed by decisions of the Supreme Court, the instant they are made...the people will have ceased to be their own rulers, having...resigned their Government into the hands of the eminent tribunal...."[8]

The issue was not separation of Church and State, but separation of State from God as a strategic sequential step towards unraveling of the Constitution and ushering in a New World Order. For generations,

God was the key to our success and good fortune as a nation, and it was submission to Him that made us a great nation. As a result, the first step towards the downfall of our children would be to imitate the pagan and sometimes barbaric practices of perverse multi-cultural beliefs. A new religion, promoted as a philosophy, would be introduced called relativism, which would know no truth. Relativism became the key strategic capability for arguing any case in the media, courts or in the legislature. With it came the elimination of a moral compass of right and wrong. The door was now left wide open for any doctrine and dogma to be taught to children. Relativism became a moral and civil sledgehammer having free reign to rear its ugly head in all types of education. Capturing the minds of the young became a strategic objective of these efforts, leading to the uprooting and removal of traditional values, beliefs, and even history from the classroom. It was now only a matter of time before the downfall went into a free fall.

With the Ten Commandments expelled from our public facilities, including the schools, and with the prohibition of contraceptive drugs declared unconstitutional by the Supreme Court, all hell seemed to break loose. Dress codes unraveled, sex education promoted promiscuity, searches of lockers became unconstitutional and suddenly drug, tobacco and alcohol abuse soared. Not surprisingly, violent crimes and sexually transmitted diseases and unwanted pregnancies became their fruits. The next logical step in the deconstruction of our nation then arrived.

In 1973, the Supreme Court voted that a woman could rip a baby out of her womb and have it paid for by the tax dollars of citizens. It was most magnanimous of our leaders to be so generous, and so kind of our fellow citizens to impose their immoral behavior and its ramifications on the rest of the country, thereby institutionalizing a collective sin. Simple logic would say that the Creator of that child's conception would not bless such a heinous action. The most precious being on earth, made in the very image and likeness of God, could now be murdered because the pregnancy was inconvenient to a lifestyle; besides, it is all about personal choice and has nothing to do with God's law impressed on our hearts. Abortion is not only the law of the land, but the federal, state and local governments continue to actively enforce court decisions that effectively strip pro-life activists of their civil rights. Compounding the growth of this "Culture of Death" is our Government's agenda to promote on a global basis, abortion and contraception through the use of substantial federal funds, tax sheltered philanthropy and foundations, and United Nations programs. That America is a post-Christian society is manifested clearly in its

17

implementation and enforcement of abortion legislation. Heaven cannot and will not bless a nation with these views.

The moral breakdown is everywhere. On March 19, 2002, Bill Moyers was interviewing Mr. Robert Bartley, Senior Vice-President of *The Wall Street Journal*, on PBS television. Moyers asked, "How did the Enron debacle happen, what were its causes?" Bartley didn't give a typical financial answer speaking about off-balance-sheet partnerships. He said, "Enron happened because there has been a moral breakdown in America over the last 40 years or so." No matter the field of occupation, the system of order in the United States is collapsing because we have a broken moral order.

Charles Habib Malik, Ambassador to the United Nations from Lebanon, member of the U. N. Security Council in 1953–54, and President of the 13th Session of the United Nations General Assembly in 1959, summed it up when he conveyed the following during his farewell speech to the U. N.: "The good (in the United States) would never have come into being without the blessing and power of Jesus Christ.... Whoever tries to conceive the American word without taking full account of the suffering and love and salvation of Christ is only dreaming.

"I know how embarrassing this matter is to politicians, bureaucrats, businessmen and cynics; but, whatever these honored men think, the irrefutable truth is that the soul of America is, at its best and highest, Christian."[9]

For all the cynics, remember that the Lord is slow to anger, great in power, and yet rich in mercy. We all have stories and the session could be called "Can you beat this one, or how bad is it?" So the question is, "Based upon historical perspective, can the Lord bless or indefinitely tolerate such a wayward people who refuse to be obedient to His laws?" The answer seems obvious. The question is: What's next?

2

Perfuming the Pig

Tell a lie often enough and people will soon believe it.
—Tyrants throughout history

Has man's search for acceptance and appropriate use of definitive, objective truths become confused and irrational? If so, has this problem transcended the physical world to the moral and spiritual realm? Why does western society, particularly the United States, promote and enforce what is increasingly evident as the "New Tolerance," forsaking adherence to fundamental Judeo-Christian truths, morals and virtues, and scorning such absolutes and the messengers with a religious zeal? For today's new tolerance agenda is not about separation of Church and State, but rather the separation of the state from God. This is the equivalent of perfuming a pig. America has bought the lie. The pig is the lie that we are sold or fed year after year. Like the ancient Jews, after prosperity and success, we think we do not need God. Because we have no God, we have no absolutes. Therefore, society has totally lost the concept of right and wrong. Every area in life today has been perfumed to the point where truth is distorted. Relativism has won. For instance, after the destruction of the Twin Towers, a photograph was taken of three white firemen raising the flag in a way reminiscent of the six Marines hoisting the flag on the top of Mt. Suribachi on Iwo Jima during World War II. The press immediately wanted to alter the photo to include a woman and a black man. Day by day, the attempt of relativism, secularism, and multi-culturalism is to distort reality. The mounting lies each year have distorted the reality of Scripture and the American past to the point where people can no longer even find the truth. Lies on top of lies have confused and betrayed all of America. You cannot pick a topic in America today where this is not the case. Families have been virtually destroyed because of the effects of a humanistic ideology. A young girl needs a permission slip to go on a school field trip, she cannot buy tobacco, but in many places she can get an abortion without her parents' permission. If people question these things, they are considered intolerant and extreme. When God is out, anything can and will come in. Gramsci's philosophy has worked in spades. Give credit where it is due. His plan has been pure unadulterated genius and has given birth to the piglet. The piglet is now a huge 900-pound snorting pig roaming around at will in the halls of Congress and schools.

It is an agenda which insists on the public withdrawal, including government enforcement via laws and regulations, of any objective moral or virtuous reasoning or faith that proclaims an absolute truth. Of course, Christian faith is profoundly absolute and therefore viewed with disdain—and ironically, intolerance—by all who profess and insist on the new tolerance. This is illustrated by the case of Shannon Berry, a first grader at Bayshore Elementary School in Bradenton, Florida. A teacher pulled aside and reprimanded Shannon and a classmate for talking about Jesus one day during recess. This conviction against absolute truth pervades beyond America as attested by the United Nations, which declares that "Tolerance...involves the rejection of dogmatism and absolutism."[1] For a New World Order to emerge globally, faith must be done away with in its present form. A state faith must emerge and take the place of a Christ-centered faith. The faith of the New World Order will rely heavily on the state's enforcement of personal freedoms.

Historically the laws and civil codes of western society relied on God's standards as conveyed to his people and recorded in the Bible. Our laws used to be God's laws. Yet presently, the new tolerance culture trivializes and distorts the truth about the Bible through relativism. Father Bill McCarthy, who leads the Mother of Unity ministry in Moodus, Connecticut sums it up well in his essay *"The New Tolerance, How Much Tolerance Can We Tolerate?"* He describes how America "used to be a nation under God" but now behaves quite like a pagan culture void of Judeo-Christian ethics, morals and virtues. We not only have thrown God out of our classrooms, courts and public arenas, we have removed His Decalogue, the Ten Commandments, from our hearts. Perhaps evolutionist Richard Dawkins, named "1996 Humanist of the Year" by the American Humanist Association, put it best when in a speech he compared the threat of AIDS and "mad cow" disease to the threat posed by the Christian faith. According to Dawkins, the Christian faith is "one of the world's great evils, comparable to the smallpox virus but harder to eradicate."[2]

Fr. McCarthy utilizes as a reference the best-selling book by Josh McDowell and Bob Hostetler entitled *The New Tolerance: How a Cultural Movement Threatens to Destroy You*. This informative work explains the "cultural metamorphosis" our society is undergoing, with suggestions for encountering and neutralizing the threat to one's self, family, community and church. In the book McDowell begins by defining what tolerance used to mean, that is, to recognize and respect others' beliefs and practices without sharing them or to bear or put up with something not especially liked. This form of tolerance is intolerable to society today and McDowell coins it "negative tolerance." McDowell defines the new tolerance as "positive tolerance", which says this: Every individual's beliefs, values, lifestyle and truth claims are equal. McCarthy apparently agrees with McDowell and adds, "...no matter how sinful, pagan, or destructive...." This has dangerous implications. Not only is our society building an anti-Christian mind set, but there is also a definitive potential for government abuse to enforce what is popular in society regardless of what is morally or ethically right before God. For example, in May of 1994, Congress passed a law making it a federal offense to block an abortion clinic. Pamela Maraldo, then-President of Planned Parenthood, commented to the press, "This law goes to show that no one can force their viewpoint on someone else." The self-contradiction is obvious: All laws force someone's viewpoint.

Personal Freedoms and Responsibility

If secularism is not an ideology, which in turn becomes a religious view being enforced by a judge in a state, then how could a priest be in jail for exercising his Constitutional rights? Federal Judge Richard Arcara sentenced Father Norman Weslin (founder of the Lambs for Christ), to five months in federal prison. His crime: kneeling in silent prayer on a public sidewalk outside an abortion mill. In Judge Arcara's opinion, four hours of public prayer deserved five months in federal prison. Father voluntarily surrendered on November 5, 2001. Meanwhile New York State's 2nd Circuit Court of Appeals ruled that Judge Arcara's Buffer Zone is unconstitutional. Father Weslin said, "If Jesus wants one of His priests in prison while the evil is going on...that's what I want." Father Weslin's trial, sentencing, and incarcerations are examples of raw judicial power and sheer political persecution. Father Weslin was given the prison assignment of picking up cigarette butts! He was not allowed to bring his Rosary and Liturgy of the Hours prayer book into prison.[3]

Without a moral compass based on Judeo-Christian truths, public policy to legislate morality will swing forever with the tide of public assent or dissent. In a debate on "Legislating Morality" a narrator introduced to his participants the thought that all the thousands of laws have a moral framework to try to guide behavior towards a morally acceptable goal. Former Governor Mario Cuomo replied, "When you say morality.... You mean the right conduct, there are some things a community will decide are right conduct, whether you like it or not. And even though a hundred percent of you don't agree, they're going to say these are the rules that we need to insist upon in order to maintain a well-ordered community." Charles Willie, Professor of Education and Urban Studies at Harvard University, clarified that morality is the property of the individual, and ethics has to do with groups, and we should not confuse the two. He views the complementary vs. confrontational aspects between ethics and morality as the real issue in trying to determine how to deal with public policy issues. Whether it is abortion, physician-assisted suicide, public smoking, flag burning, affirmative action, welfare reform or school prayer, Willie admits he has no answer because "my only answer is that negotiation is eternal."[4]

Our society's acceptance of the new tolerance and its parallel descent into paganism and barbarism is likened by McDowell to the Borg from *Star Trek: The Next Generation*. The Borg cannot tolerate or coexist with other life forms or cultures. Therefore they take, use or assimilate all things of value and destroy any individual or world that is anathema to their beliefs or needs.[5]

McDowell asserts in his book that with the emerging acceptance by society of the new tolerance, "...there are no absolutes—that all truth is relative; right and wrong differ from person to person and from culture to culture.... Under the aegis of the new tolerance, our society has created a new civil right: the right neither to be offended, nor even to have to listen to competing truth claims."[6] There is no standard to discern between competing views or claims. *Since there are no such standards, morals adapt to the subjective consensus of the masses.* In 1991 and again in 1994, pollster George Barna asked a random sampling of adults, and then a sample of Christians, whether they agree with the statement, "There is no such thing as absolute truth; two people could define truth in totally conflicting ways, but both could still be correct." His results: In 1991, 67 percent of all Americans, and 52 percent of Christians agreed. In 1994, those numbers increased to 72 percent and 62 percent, respectively.[7]

Those who profess the new tolerance view claims of truth as merely opinions culturally derived. With the demise of the search for and use of objective or absolute truth, mankind is becoming increasingly lax in the discipline needed to observe and discern moral and spiritual truths. Man is losing his ability to utilize the God-given tool to acquire knowledge called rationality. Or as Ingrid Newkirk,

President of People for the Ethical Treatment of Animals said publicly, "A rat is a pig is a dog is a boy."

Similarly, Charles Darwin starts out saying early on in *The Origin of Species*, "Let us assume." By the end of his famous voyage on HMS *Beagle*, "Let us assume" had been used so frequently that the tadpole had become a whale, and the chimpanzee an upright professor with a soul and the gift of reason. (Thus, the famous witticism, "When you assume, you make an 'ass' out of 'u' and 'me,'" might have to be updated by replacing "ass" with "monkey.") Yet, Wernher von Braun, the "Father of the American Space Program," stated in an article published in May of 1974:

> One cannot be exposed to the law and order of the universe without concluding that there must be design and purpose behind it all.... The better we understand the intricacies of the universe and all it harbors, the more reason we have found to marvel at the inherent design upon which it is based...
>
> To be forced to believe only one conclusion—that everything in the universe happened by chance—would violate the very objectivity of science itself.... What random process could produce the brains of a man or the system of the human eye?
>
> They (evolutionists) challenge science to prove the existence of God. But must we really light a candle to see the sun?... They say they cannot visualize a Designer. Well, can a physicist visualize an electron?... What strange rationale makes some physicists accept the inconceivable electron as real while refusing to accept the reality of a Designer on the ground that they cannot conceive Him?...
>
> It is in scientific honesty that I endorse the presentation of alternative theories for the origin of the universe, life and man in the science classroom. It would be an error to overlook the possibility that the universe was planned rather than happening by chance.[8]

If there is no absolute truth, the scourge of relativism never ends.

An effective tactic used to promote the new tolerance is the Orwellian system, called "Newspeak," that uses name calling and labeling of any opposing view with emotive words such as hatred, cruelty, fanaticism and bigotry. An example where this is particularly effective is in categorizing people who express disagreement with the homosexual lifestyle and its effective treatment as being "homophobic." The homosexual activists are not looking for tolerance;

they are looking for affirmation that they are right. They are trying to get more rights over time so they can effectively legislate themselves above everyone else, and so they can become an elite group in society that is legally untouchable. According to the National Association for Research and Therapy of Homosexuals (NARTH), these activists repeatedly play on the compassion of society by perpetrating the myths that:

❖ Homosexuality is normal and biologically determined.
❖ Homosexuals cannot change, and if they try, they will suffer great emotional distress and become suicidal.
❖ We must teach our children that homosexuality is as normal and healthy as heterosexuality. Teens should be encouraged to celebrate their same-sex attractions.

NARTH directly challenges the false claims and myths of the homosexual activists, showing that scientific research indicates no biological or genetic cause for homosexuality. Rather, the research suggests that social and psychological factors are strongly influential, including problems in early family relationships, sexual seduction, and societal influences and pressures. Furthermore, psychotherapists around the world report substantial healing of homosexuals, with their homosexual feelings greatly diminished; many go on to lead married or celibate lives typically experiencing a deeper and fuller sense of themselves as male or female as they grow into their heterosexual potential. The keys to change are *desire, persistence* and a willingness to investigate the *conscious and unconscious conflicts* from which the condition originated. Lastly, NARTH shows that scientific research supports age-old cultural norms that homosexuality is *not* a healthy, natural alternative to heterosexuality. Research shows that homosexual teens are especially vulnerable to substance abuse and early, high-risk sexual behavior. The teen years are critical to the question of self-labeling, so the facts must be presented in a fair and balanced manner. It is a sad state of our society when homosexual activists ignore and struggle against the right-to-treatment for other homosexuals who yearn for freedom from their attractions simply to promote their deluded agenda.[9]

Media Bias: A Lot of Perfume
If one wants to observe Satan's great strategy, it would be readily apparent in the manipulation of minds through the liberal media. The

minds of the American public are so bent out of shape that they no longer have the ability to use reason and logic. To find truth is an effort. People who speak of Satan's direct influence in human affairs are often marginalized. There are several layers of evil, with the first and strongest being a direct influence by Satan himself on those who share his views and willingly submit to them. Another level down are those who simply go along with the worldview of secularism. A great problem surrounding people speaking on issues right of center—often called conservative—is that they cannot explain the spiritual nature of the fight raging in the world. At the spiritual level, the battle is for the soul of man. At the physical level, it is played out on television, in the press, and in the classroom. The left relishes in words like wacko, nutcase, extremist, and a litany of other pejorative "newspeak" terms for those who do not share their views. However, the point often missed is that secularists, humanists, and those of that ilk share a common ideology that is not Christocentric. When a doctrine is not based in Christ, it is less than perfect; with time it becomes increasingly perverted.

Nowhere in America is the liberal agenda shoved at people morning, noon, and night more consistently and continuously than through the media outlets. The reformers knew the places to go were television and newsprint. In his book, *Bias*, a former network news correspondent, Bernard Goldberg, wrote that the news vilifies anything that is considered conservative. This ex-insider in the news business wrote that anyone who doesn't agree with the liberals is presented as a right-wing nut. Goldberg's book has sold nearly a half-million copies, but has not been mentioned on ABC, NBC, or CBS news. Goldberg believes *Bias* is the first non-fiction bestseller in modern times that has failed to get a single minute of notice on the major networks. In 1990, *Los Angeles Times* media critic David Shaw stunned everybody with a four-part series on press coverage of the abortion issue. His conclusion was that the American media was so strongly pro-choice that it cannot bring itself to report on the issue fairly. There was no other press coverage of this series, though many admitted privately that it was true. Bernard Goldberg saw firsthand that feminists in the newsrooms would not stand for the abortion issue to be aired without a pro-choice bias.

No matter the issue of social policy, Americans are given the liberal view of the press, of whose members the vast majority is pro-choice, pro-homosexual, and pro-liberal in nearly every sense of these terms. Over 90 percent of correspondents in America are unchurched. They are a bunch of 'pros' who don't believe—so why should we expect God's perspective from the press? Antonio Gramsci was a revolutionary genius, for one of his main precepts was the need to control the reporting of information to people. It has worked quite well in the U. S. A.

The End of the Supernatural

The broad acceptance of the new tolerance complements secular humanism, which makes man view the universe egocentrically; that is, man *is* the measure of all things. From a religious perspective, man views himself as sufficient unto himself, severely discounting if not outright omitting the idea of Grace or Divine Will. As a result, today's society is increasingly fatalistic, seeing all things as being subject to an immutable process driven by cause and effect. Our actions do not depend on our own wills, but on inevitable forces and random chances over which we hold no control. The direct consequence, though furiously denied by its victim (for example from a philanderer to a homosexual, from a corrupt politician to a terrorist, from an abortionist to a corrupt bio-ethicist) is the elimination of right and wrong.

The method has worked through the generations at the hands of big government: We will be your savior; man is best when man serves the state; society is best when man serves the state. This is the philosophy of the utopia of Plato, metamorphosed to Hegel, to Ruskin, to Modernism. It should be noted that "utopia" comes from the Greek *utopos*, which means "no place." If people with no moral and spiritual convictions are given the choice of freedom or security, they will take security every time. When a person wants security and freedom, he will get neither.

When the communists moved into a country, the first thing they did to take control of the people was to remove symbols of faith. They knew that once these were removed, culture could be dominated over time. Why? Because those symbols remind us of the supernatural and draw us to God, Who leads us to think individually, and Who leads us into a relationship with Him, and through Him with each other, above and beyond statism. Once the sense of God, and the consequent knowledge of right and wrong, is extinguished, people can be manipulated through verbal and social engineering.

Our country is experiencing the collapse of justice, the loss of conviction, the further fragmentation and individual privatization of what constitutes "faith." This ultimately bears bad fruit, which includes not only the tyranny of the individual, but the disintegration of human rights, the dominance and overemphasis of emotions or feelings, the exaltation of nature, and the decent into extremism. As Omar

Bradley, one of the most popular generals of World War II said in his address on Armistice Day, 1948, "We have grasped the mystery of the atom and rejected the Sermon on the Mount.... The world has achieved brilliance without conscience. Ours is a world of nuclear giants and ethical infants."[10]

As absolute truths regarding our Judeo-Christian faith fragment, increasingly individuals disconnect from one another in public displays of shared faith and values, preferring as individuals to go it alone. Notwithstanding the fact that religious faith remains the major social connection for Americans, churchgoing has declined steadily. Robert D. Putman, Harvard University sociologist, cites pollsters who claim that half of the nation's churches have fewer than 75 members. These churches are dying at the rate of 50 every week in America. Meanwhile, formal church membership shrank ten percent between the 1960's and 1990's with those Americans identifying themselves as having "no religion" whatsoever climbing from two to eleven percent. Recent polls estimate that historical over-reporting of weekly church attendance ranges as high as 50 percent, effectively erasing the post–World War II boom in religious participation. Mr. Putnam reveals, "the fraction of the population that spent any time on religion at all fell by nearly one-half." He notes that religious dropouts have come at the expense of people who were modest practitioners of their faith. The result, he concludes, is that the country is becoming clearly divided between devout observers of faith and the entirely unchurched.[11]

We are all responsible for the state of the nation. That is how a democracy works, where the voice of the people prevails. Our attention must be directed on the role of the courts in the disordering of our liberty and the associated by-product of the disintegration of human rights. Our nation's contract with its people assures that "we the people," through representative institutions of republican government, must deliberate and decide how we ought to order our life together. Our government derives its just power from the consent of the governed. Is it not an interesting coincidence that on July 4, 1997, forty United States religious leaders declared that the consent of the governed has been thrown into question? They viewed the American experiment in ordered liberty as deeply troubled and asked God to continue to bless our country for the benefit of us and our future generations, provided we keep faith with the founding vision of our country.

In America today we can see the protracted negotiations around morals and ethics over disputed public policies that are influenced, and if necessary coerced or usurped, by a growing community devoid of inspiration by the divine revelation from God. Reflecting on the past century's tribulations that directly correlate to the rise of secular humanism and misguided tolerance, one can easily foresee that continued progression in this society of these types of corrupt philosophies would yield enormously tragic results for our country in the 21st Century.

Hilaire Belloc, the famous and influential Christian historian, predicted in a 1931 book that our civilization was slipping back not only into paganism, but also barbarism, and especially the institution of slavery.[12] No better example of slavery exists than the subordination of the unborn to the exclusive, individual self-interest of the mother-to-be or to the scientist who wishes to harvest brain stem cells [or any other part of an unborn child] with the financial help and approval of the government. Educational institutions and their educators, philosophers and ethicists are reengineering public knowledge and truth on the subject of what is life. To quote Peter Singer, Chairman of Princeton University's Center for Human Values, "Many of our moral institutions are formed for religious reasons, which were once strong but are now outdated." Claiming to be an ethicist, he further comments, "Killing a defective infant is not morally equivalent to killing a person. Sometimes it is not wrong at all…. No infant has a strong claim to life as a person."

Belloc coined this emerging civilization as the "New Paganism." He predicted that mankind will find gods to worship, but they will be evil gods as were those of the older savage paganism before it began its advance towards Christianity. He asserts that the New Paganism despises reason, and boasts that it is attacking beauty. (Regarding the latter claim, just look at the debate over the funding for the National Endowment of the Arts and the type of artwork that is funded by the American government.) It is a pagan society that believes "art" is a photo of a Crucifix in a glass of urine. The New Paganism delights in superficiality, and conceives that it is rid of the evil as well as the good in what it believes to have been superstitions and illusions. A good example of this is the secularization of Christmas and Easter, with the accompanying emphasis on impious self-gratification, while in the meantime virtually every local community has some form of government restriction on public display of religious scenes, instructions, e.g., the Ten Commandments, and religious acclaims. The chief pagans today are well groomed, educated at the best schools, belong to beautiful clubs, and leave for work with a tie, a briefcase, and a Palm Pilot. It is for these reasons that their philosophies are so insidious.

One can only conclude, like Belloc, that men do not live long without gods; but when the gods of the New Paganism come [thanks in large part to the new tolerance] they will not be merely insufficient, as were the gods of Greece, nor merely false; they will be evil. One might put it in a sentence, and say that the New Paganism, foolishly expecting satisfaction, will fall, before it knows where it is, into Satanism.[13] As the Lord warned through the prophet Jeremiah (32:32–36), those who set false idols in the house can expect to experience Divine judgment. This warning is of particular relevance and urgency for America today.

God judges nations not by their military or economic power, but by their fidelity to His laws. In God's justice and mercy, tolerance is subordinate to Truth. Recall the pronouncement of God's conditional blessings or curses. "Now if you will hear the voice of the Lord your God, to do and keep all his commandments, which I command you this day, then the Lord your God will make you higher than all the nations that are on the earth. And all these blessings shall come upon you and overtake you: yet so if you hear his precepts.... And turn not away from them neither to the right hand, nor to the left, nor follow strange gods nor worship them. But if you will not hear the voice of the Lord your God, to keep and to do all his commandments and ceremonies, which I command you this day, all these curses shall come upon you, and overtake you" (Deuteronomy 28:1,2,14,15).

3

Are Your Servants Listening?

Speak, Lord, for your servant hears.

—1 Samuel 3:10

When Isaiah prophesied to the nation of Israel, it had been increasingly disobedient for over 250 years. The pattern of the nation was fairly well established, much as it is with us. Israel accumulated wealth, prominence, and dominance over its enemies and it was only a matter of time before the arrogance of the nation led to the thinking that Yahweh was but one of many gods. In their pride, the Israelites began to reason that it was through their own might that they were victorious, rather than seeing their good fortune as a blessing of the one true God. Their wealth and victories over their enemies had made them feel invincible. In their alliances and conquests, they began to assimilate some of the cultural and religious traditions of their partners and former enemies. With prosperity, the relaxation in faith, and the introduction of multi-cultural traditions, the Israelites began to worship other gods besides the God of Israel—for example, Baal. Baal is a false god standing for anything other than the One True God. One time it is a golden bull, and other times a pagan god with or without a name. Baal can be manifested in anything at any time. Think of today's obsessions. There are people today who worship money, vanity, careers, sports cars, fashion, golf, or government. Our society has no end of amusement and distractions with its endless litany of entertainment. The people of Israel had ignored the pleas for repentance of all the prophets sent by God. Scripture says, "And they worshipped abominations, concerning which the Lord had commanded them that they should not do this thing. And the Lord testified to them in Israel and in Juda by the hand of all the prophets and seers, saying: Return from your wicked ways, and keep my precepts, and ceremonies" (2 Kings 17:12–13).

But the chosen people ignored the requests of Yahweh, and so "light afflictions" plagued them as a nation. "And they hearkened not, but hardened their necks like to the neck of their fathers, who would not obey the Lord their God" (2 Kings 17:14). The people illustrated the common theme of the history of the entire Bible and all of civilization—they ridiculed the prophets who came to give them the word of God, which could bring them back to a wholesome and prosperous lifestyle. What could help them they openly mocked. Indeed, "They followed vanities, and acted vainly.... And they forsook all the precepts of the Lord their God...and they delivered themselves up to do evil before the Lord, to provoke him. And the Lord was very angry with Israel" (2 Kings 17:15–18).

Not convinced by Yahweh's light afflictions, Israel was then invaded by its enemy Assyria in the provinces of Zebulun and Naphtali. Damage was localized. God clearly tried to get the attention of His people. Israel remained belligerent. God then raised the ante. Israel received a second wake-up call, and this one was somewhat more severe. Two nations whom the Scriptures call the "enemies of Israel"—the Syrians and the Philistines—combined forces for a second attack. According to Isaiah, this attack came both "from the east, and...from the west" (Isaiah 9:12), completely surrounding Israel. This time their attack was totally devastating.

Now we come to the essence of it all. Is the Lord initiating the purification and chastisement of the United States of America, with the 9/11 event being a sequential step towards America's atonement or downfall? How should we look at the pain of those who lost loved ones? Were the planes hitting the Twin Towers and the Pentagon meant to have a more meaningful purpose for the United States? These are questions that require an attentive heart and courage to answer. Although there was considerable pain after the attacks, there was temporary and substantial good surfacing from that day as well. Church attendance soared immediately afterwards, but in only several days returned to previous rates. There was more talk about family values and people were temporarily more attentive to what mattered most. Groups like the ACLU were eerily silent as the country searched for answers that are only to be found in the ways of God. People began questioning the meaning of life in more serious ways. In terms of the potential devastation, it could have been a lot worse.

One week after the attack, television was back to normal programming. Seven days after the Twin Towers, two homosexuals were married on prime time television. The day after the attack, Congress sang God Bless America on the steps of the Capitol, and the very next day passed legislation for the District of Columbia offering health benefits to same-sex partners. This is a sign that the last 40 years have made America schizophrenic. The United States doesn't really know what God intends or we would not act like that. America's faith has been reduced to a state faith. The people were waving flags like no time since World War II, yet Americans could not see beyond national pride with a humble and contrite heart. Flag sales went into the millions, yet not one political leader asked if God was sending a message. No one questioned whether we gave Satan room to maneuver. No one asked if America had veered off course with our hundreds of thousands of internet sites of pornography, and the 40-plus million children aborted since *Roe v. Wade* legalized abortion. What about the rejection and wholesale abandonment of divinity in public schools, offices and the marketplace? Where is the public penance for the horrible education taught to a generation of children prevented from learning what God has ordained them to know so a life can be lived more abundantly? Where is the outcry for forgiveness as more children today are being born into homes where they are starting out with two strikes against them, because their parents have long abandoned what God has asked? The societal indices grow worse each year, and this book will illustrate that fact in alarming detail. We know in our hearts the truth, but do not have the courage to speak it for fear of what people may think of us. This fear creates a specter piercing our soul, suggesting that something greater and more horrible may be on the way because of our inability to listen, learn, and act.

A Stiff-Necked People

This is a hard message to hear and most will reject it. America is not concerned with God's divine principles, but rather with man's natural reasoning. The Lord speaks another language, which is why the wisdom of the world for natural man does not conform with the Lord even though He is always the answer. This much is certain based upon the wisdom of the ages: If we do not listen, the Lord will send worse things to get our attention. As harsh as it sounds, it is often necessary to cut off a cancerous limb to save the body. There are eighteen Muslim nations with 1.2 billion people. Estimates for the population of the People's Republic of China range anywhere from 1.5 to 1.7 plus billion. The Lord does not lack in creativity or imagination in regard to ways to get the attention of a people with a hard heart. War, weather, disease, pestilence and famine, all seem to be at His disposal based upon historical precedent.

Again, in Isaiah 9:11–13, an illustrative story is told for the benefit of God's chosen people. "And the Lord shall set up the enemies of Rasin over him, and shall bring on his enemies in a crowd.... And the people are not returned to him who has struck them, and have not sought after the Lord of hosts." There is no doubt in the history of man that the Lord used enemy nations to chasten His people. The means are many, but the intent is always the same—to purify. At the beginning of World War II, Germany was a country in complete apostasy. After the Allies' last act of firebombing Dresden, and with many of their major cities in ruins, *only* then did they cry out to God for help. When reduced to rubble and ashes, their churches filled again.

In Ecclesiastes 3:1, God teaches, "All things have their season, and in their times all things pass under Heaven." As an act of mercy, God in His infinite wisdom offers the best possible combination of warnings, trials and tribulations in their appropriate sequence and time to allow man to recognize his guilt and avoid unnecessary ordeals. As we continue our journey through biblical history with Isaiah, we see what happens as Israel's pagan enemies are used as an instrument of God's justice. "Woe to the Assyrian, he is the rod and the staff of my anger, and my indignation is in their hands. I will send him to a deceitful nation, and I will give him a charge against the people of my wrath, to take away the spoils, and to lay hold on the prey, and to tread them down like the mire of the streets" (Isaiah 10:5–6).

Here then is the possible Divine scenario for our nation. All of our actions have commensurate repercussions. The enemy attacked and the Israelites watched as their cities went up in flames. But the people still were haughty and proud. "And all the people of Ephraim shall know, and the inhabitants of Samaria that say in the pride and haughtiness of their heart: The bricks are fallen down, but we will build with square stones: they have cut down the sycamores, but we will change them for cedars" (Isaiah 9:9–10). Israel missed the point and said, "We will find new building materials." Look at the recent public debate in New York City regarding the World Trade Center area. Talk continues that the city will use its financial and industrial might to build a new set of skyscrapers, possibly the same ones or even taller. In other words, like Israel, once the battle was over, we will do it our way, "we will build with square stones." We have a better way. We will just rebuild and use even better materials. Like Pharaoh of Egypt in the Old Testament, America remains stubborn. Remember that until Pharaoh submitted to the will of Yahweh, the plagues continued ten times for Pharaoh and his nation, ending with the death of his own son.

The contention of this book is that the faith of the United States has been reduced to something much worse than secular humanism—the phrase of the 1960's, 1970's, and 1980's. America has been reduced to practical and theoretical atheism. The United States pays lip service to the Ten Commandments, which is why we can sing *God Bless America* on the Capitol steps one day and fund abortion the day after. One day we ask God for help with everyone on street corners with lit candles, and the next day do nothing differently with our lifestyle than the previous day. Is it a sign of spirituality to hold a candle on a sidewalk for the victims of tragedies? Something is very wrong with that equation. Only a nation in severe denial and steep decline has a thinking process like that. For those who think that the God of the Old and New Testament is different, they should be reminded of the verse from Hebrews 13:8 that says, "Jesus Christ, yesterday, and today; and the same forever." The Lord does not change His ways to conform to the thinking of our world.

In no way is there an attempt here to minimize the good deeds of the Americans throughout the country in times of crisis. Nor is the thinking a cynical view. It is the prudent recognition of the difference in perspective as seen by the Eyes of Heaven versus where America thinks it is spiritually. When a nation reaches a stage of a haughty spirit and hardness of heart, the Lord resorts to a progression of therapy (prophecy) and surgery (chastisement) to cure spiritual malaise. The Lord repeatedly sends his prophets to our land and we ignore, ridicule and persecute them. Believers can be confident that a series of chastisements is now upon us, because "the Lord God does nothing without revealing his secret to his servants the prophets" (Amos 3:7). Has not the federal government already told Americans that further acts of terrorism will occur? It even has color-coded schemes depending on the threat. Yet our nation's leaders continually fail to make the right moral decisions in times of crisis. The story of civilizations like ours has shown that the single greatest reason cultures and great empires perish is that the leaders fail to heed God's advice. Abraham Lincoln called for a national day of prayer and repentance to seek the mind of God for mercy to heal the land during the Civil War. This is necessary for us now. We are facing the same issues Israel did so many times in the Old Testament. In no way do we operate with full knowledge concerning what is happening around us. There are simply too many probabilities; in history, as in science and politics, relativity rules, and all formulas should be suspect. It's just not always easy if we operate on our own wisdom. However, there are patterns that exist if we look at civilizations preceding ours. The past is prologue to the future, and shows that civilizations perish for moral reasons.

Americans should not foolishly believe that our public profession of faith in God, expressed by proclaiming "God Bless America," is a "get out of jail free card" or a chastisement avoidance invocation. In the Old Testament both Judah and Jerusalem refused to believe they could be brought down. Yet, the Lord said to Isaiah, "Shall I not, as I have done to Samaria and her idols, so do to Jerusalem and her idols" (Isaiah 10:11)? God was saying, "Are you different to be judged outside of My law? Are you exempt?" Recall also in the first book of Samuel in the Old Testament when the Levites brought forth the Ark of the Covenant to the Israelite troops in the field who were about to engage in battle with the Philistines. God would not come to the aid of the Israelites. They were slaughtered en masse and the Ark captured during the battle. This should be a sobering thought to all Americans.

No one in his right mind would argue that it would be foolish for a nation to defend itself when attacked. There is the principle of a just war and the case was sufficiently made regarding 9/11. To achieve the desired end, however, this nation must first conform to the word of God on the spiritual and physical plane. Otherwise, America ultimately will know suffering, poverty, and defeat, because physical might and just provocation are insufficient in themselves and subordinate to the will of God. Unfortunately, believers can only conclude that the root cause of why an outside, pagan enemy successfully committed these terrorist acts, killing thousands, remains essentially unanswered by the collective conscience of Americans. The issue is not to wave the flag, but to become children of God.

Lessons of Biblical History

America urgently needs to reform her collective conscience if we wish to protect ourselves from future perils and sustain our prosperous way of life. Aside from modern day prophets, Americans must recognize that God speaks to each of us personally through the age-old and proven method of prayer. To read is to learn about God, but to pray is to know God. In the stillness of our souls His voice communicates one on one. If we pay sufficient attention within the quiet recesses of our heart, we are able to discern when He speaks and what He tells us. This is an immutable fact. Only atheists would claim otherwise. The question is, "Do we have the courage to follow through with what we have heard?" Will we let the tares of self-doubt and public opinion in their many forms quench what has been said? Should the media through radio, television and print be our primary portal for genuine advice? Advice from the media, confidants and friends should be subordinate to the peace and comfort which God presents to an attentive soul. For this reason Jesus said to the believers, "You are the salt of the earth" (St. Matthew 5:13)—meaning a preservative. In addition, He said to "be the light and not hide the lamp under a bushel."

Only a believer who prays often acts in Christian love can rejuvenate a dying culture, because the light of life that God in His infinite mercy has placed in them becomes a testament that Jesus assures us could pierce any darkness. For this reason, it was people like Saint Francis of Assisi who brought light to a dead church culture in the Middle Ages.

God is sending America a warning par excellence. He speaks publicly, manifesting His growing anger through various worldly events. He also speaks privately to each one of us in our hearts about the corrupt lives we lead and our blasphemous indifference to reestablish an intimate relationship with Him as our only God. But are we listening?

God Withdraws His Grace and Removes His "Protective Hedge"

Americans have become lackadaisical, forgetting it is the Lord who lifts up a nation, and the Lord Who tears it down. When God's people belligerently turned away from Him, Isaiah conveyed God's plan for chastisement. Presented below is Isaiah 5:1–7, which states the problem of man's independence from God and the totality of His justice.

> I will sing to my beloved the canticle of my cousin concerning his vineyard. My beloved had a vineyard on a hill in a fruitful place. And he fenced it in, and picked the stones out of it, and planted it with the choicest vines, and built a tower in the midst thereof, and set up a winepress therein: and he looked that it should bring forth grapes, and it brought forth wild grapes. And now, O you inhabitants of Jerusalem, and you men of Juda, judge between me and my vineyard. What is there that I ought to do more to my vineyard, that I have not done to it? Was it that I looked that it should bring forth grapes, and it has brought forth wild grapes? And now I will show you what I will do to my vineyard. *I will take away the hedge thereof, and it shall be wasted: I will break down the wall thereof, and it shall be trodden down.* And I will make it desolate: it shall not be pruned, and it shall not be digged: but briers and thorns shall come up: and I will command the clouds to rain no rain upon it. For the vineyard of the Lord of hosts is the house of Israel: and the man of Juda, his pleasant plant: and I looked that he should do judgment, and behold iniquity: and do justice, and behold a cry.

Note the verse where God's hedge of protection is taken away due to national sin. There is a lot being said here about the very nature of God and how He judges and punishes those with hard hearts. See the progressive nature of how God deals with the people. There are mini-judgments, not just one big swift one that can devastate the people. He gives us enough time to make choices. If we do not hear, He tries again with something that will make us take notice. This is why, many times, the only way for people to recognize God is through a lost job, some calamity, or the death of a person close to them. Many times parents are brought to their knees because of a difficult situation with their children. (This does not mean, of course, that all family difficulties are the result of parental irresponsibility or sinfulness; good people—even including some of the saints—have also experienced difficulties with their children.) When Isaiah spoke of the vineyards being destroyed he was speaking to an agricultural economy that clearly understood the repercussions of clouds with no rain. As mentioned, the Lord has His ways to bend the will of man to align it more with the direction He wishes His people to move. The discipline He gives us is because of His love for us. As the Creator, He knows what works best for us in the short, medium, and long run. Proverbs says the "beginning of wisdom is the fear of the Lord." Fear is so often mistranslated in spirit and tone, but is actually the "awesome respect" for God. A car runs best on gas, not on molasses. We run smoothest on His ways, not always on what we think is best for us. As we saw earlier with the loss of the Ark in First Samuel, wars are permitted as a punishment for the sins of mankind. God has showered America with graces like no other nation in all of history, and like civilizations preceding ours, we are now wise in our own eyes. As a nation we have defiantly told God, "We have our technology and do not need You. We travel into space. We have created life in a test-tube. We have even solved the genetic code with super computers. We have the expertise and know-how to design our own children to our image and expectations through genetic engineering. We have our satellites to speak to the world just by picking up a phone, and we fly around the world to exotic destinations in less than a day. We have our creature comforts, so why do we really need You?" September 11, 2001, showed just how fragile the world, politically and financially, really is. The prosperity and self-indulgence can evaporate in the twinkling of an eye. "Alas! alas! that great city Babylon, that mighty city: for in one hour is your judgment come" (Revelation 18:10).

Themes of the Fall

In Psalm 78, Asaph recalls Israel's history which is filled with God's provision, His leadership, His numberless miracles, and the way generation after generation God provided for His people. This is the story of the Bible. It is the story of all creation that God provides in abundant ways when there is obedience. In Psalm 79:8, the Psalmist cries out, "O God of hosts, convert us: and show your face, and we shall be saved." Then Psalm 80 carries the prayerful words of restoration as a result of heeding God's words.

Are we different from the great civilizations that have preceded the great American empire? We may think so because of the limited distance our periscope can see. But the eyes of the Lord are eternal and can see the past, the present, and the future. Our wisdom is based upon pride and foolishness. The Mesopotamians, the Phoenicians, the Greeks, the Romans, the Spanish, the French, and the English Empire sailing the seas for spices and herbs, all rose and descended in the exact same ways. They grew proud and haughty as a result of their own might and prowess. One thing is certain looking at history. There is only one absolute and all in the end will approach Divinity with bended knee. Most history is guessing, the rest is prejudice.

Although to a person without spiritual eyes it all possibly would appear a big jumble, a mish mash of ideas, thoughts, occurrences, people and events, to someone watching the rise and fall of civilizations, and watching history evolve and repeat itself, a discernable flow of similar events does occur, and for precisely the same reasons. These reasons are at the end of the rope for the great empires of the world, which disintegrated due to rejecting the natural laws of God and the commandments of Yahweh. As much as many historians, policymakers, and social scientists may wish to complicate the story of man, the prophet Jeremiah speaks very directly about how and why a nation is judged, and what happens when the nations are subjected to the cup of God's fury.

> For thus says the Lord of hosts the God of Israel: Take the cup of wine of this fury at my hand: and you shall make all nations to drink thereof, unto which I shall send you. And they shall drink, and be troubled, and be mad because of the sword, which I shall send among them. And I took the cup at the hand of the Lord, and I presented it to all the nations to drink of it, to which the Lord sent me: To wit, Jerusalem, and the cities of Juda, and the kings thereof, and the princes thereof: to make them a desolation, and an astonishment, and a hissing, and a curse, as it is at this day.... And

you shall say to them: Thus says the Lord of hosts the God of Israel: Drink, and be drunken, and vomit: and fall, and rise no more, because of the sword, which I shall send among you. And if they refuse to take the cup at your hand to drink, you shall say to them: Thus says the Lord of hosts: Drinking you shall drink: For behold I begin to bring evil on the city wherein my name is called upon: and shall you be as innocent and escape free? You shall not escape free: for I will call for the sword upon all the inhabitants of the earth, says the Lord of hosts. And you shall prophesy unto them all these words, and you shall say to them: The Lord shall roar from on high, and shall utter his voice from his holy habitation: roaring he shall roar upon the place of his beauty: the shout as it were of them that tread grapes shall be given out against all the inhabitants of the earth. The noise is come even to the ends of the earth: for the Lord enters into judgement with the nations: he enters into judgement with all flesh; the wicked I have delivered up to the sword, says the Lord (Jeremiah 25:15–18, 27–31).

A Divine Template for What America Can Expect

Whether we approve or not, God sends blessings and curses. If you read Deuteronomy, Chapter 28 and beyond, you can clearly see that the covenant God made with His people involves blessings and curses:

The "Blessings"

Now if you will hear the voice of the Lord your God, to do and keep all his commandments, which I command you this day, the Lord your God will make you higher than all the nations that are on the earth. And all these blessings shall come upon you and overtake you: yet so if you hear his precepts, blessed shall you be in the city, and blessed in the field. Blessed shall be the fruit of your womb, and the fruit of your ground, and the fruit of your cattle, the droves of your herds, and the folds of your sheep. Blessed shall be your barns and blessed your stores. Blessed shall you be coming in and going out. The Lord shall cause your enemies, that rise up against you, to fall down before your face: one way shall they come out against you, and seven ways shall they flee before you. The Lord will send forth a blessing upon your storehouses, and upon all the works of your hands: and will bless you in the land that you shall receive. The Lord will raise you up to be a holy people to himself, as he swore to you: if you keep the commandments of the Lord your God, and walk in his ways. And all the people of the earth shall see that the name of the Lord is invocated upon you, and they shall fear you. The Lord will make you abound with all goods, with the fruit of your womb, and the fruit of your cattle, with the fruit of your land, which the Lord swore to your fathers that he would give you. The Lord will open his excellent treasure, the heaven, that it may give rain in due season: and he will bless all the works of your hands. And you shall lend to many nations, and shall not borrow of any one. And the Lord shall make you the head and not the tail: and you shall be always above, and not beneath: yet so if you will hear the commandments of the Lord your God which I command you this day, and keep and do them, and turn not away from them neither to the right hand, nor to the left, nor follow strange gods, nor worship them. **But if you will not hear the voice of the Lord your God, to keep and to do all his commandments and ceremonies, which I command you this day, all these curses shall come upon you, and overtake you.**

The "Curses"

The "curses" categorized below are a few examples of God's chastisement on a stubborn and proud people:

Curse on cities and rural communities: Cursed shall you be in the city, cursed in the field (Deuteronomy 28:16).

Drought and disease: May the Lord set the pestilence upon you, until he consume you out of the land, which you shall go in to possess. May the Lord afflict you with miserable want, with the fever and with cold, with burning and with heat, and with corrupted air and with blasting, and pursue you till you perish (Deuteronomy 28:21–22).

Curse of madness: The Lord strike you with madness and blindness and fury of mind. And may you grope at midday as the blind is wont to grope in the dark, and not make straight your ways (Deuteronomy 28:28–29).

Curse of divorce: May you take a wife, and another sleep with her. May you build a house, and not dwell therein. May you plant a vineyard and not gather the vintage thereof. May your ox be slain before you, and you not eat thereof. May your ass be taken away in your sight, and not restored to you. May your sheep be given to your enemies, and may there be none to help you. May your sons and your daughters be given to another people, your eyes looking on, and languishing at the sight of them all the day, and may there be no strength in your hand (Deuteronomy 28:30–32).

Curse on the children: You shall beget sons and daughters, and shall not enjoy them: because they shall be led into captivity (Deuteronomy 28:41).

Foreign ownership of business: The stranger that lives with you in the land, shall rise up over you, and shall be higher: and you shall go down, and be lower. He shall lend to you, and you shall not lend to him. He shall be as the head, and you shall be the tail. You shall serve your enemy, whom the Lord will send upon you, in hunger, and thirst, and nakedness, and in want of all things: and he shall put an iron yoke upon your neck, till he consume you (Deuteronomy 43–44,48).

Breakdown of the family: The man that is nice among you, and very delicate, shall envy his own brother, and his wife, that lies in his bosom, so that he will not give them of the flesh of his children, which he shall eat: because he has nothing else in the siege and the want, wherewith your enemies shall distress you within all your gates. The tender and delicate woman, that could not go upon the ground, nor set down her foot for over much niceness and tenderness, will envy her husband who lies in her bosom, the flesh of her son, and of her daughter, and the filth of the afterbirths, that come forth from between her thighs, and the children that are born the same hour. For they shall eat them secretly for the want of all things, in the siege and distress, wherewith your enemy shall oppress you within your gates (Deuteronomy 28:54–57).

Return of plagues: The Lord shall increase your plagues, and the plagues of your seed, plagues great and lasting, infirmities grievous and perpetual. And he shall bring back on you all the afflictions of Egypt, which you were afraid of, and they shall stick fast to you (Deuteronomy 28:59–60).

What is most unusual about this is the number of verses dedicated to the blessings versus the curses. There are fourteen blessings and He says, "Everything you put your hands to I'll bless." Then he gives a laundry list of over 100 curses if the people of Israel disobey Him.

41

There is importance to the disproportionate number here and one can rest assure it is rooted in the simplicity of obedience to His Word. When there is disobedience, life gets more difficult and the Lord has immeasurable ways to bend the minds, hearts, and wills of His people. Notice the change to curses in the fifteenth verse that the Lord speaks in Deuteronomy, Chapter 28. One is reminded here of the adage that in homes of joy and happiness there is always the same story. In unhappy homes there are many different stories.

It seems life is more simple and peaceful on the obedience side of the equation. To bring this to a New Testament theme, the Lord says in Galatians 6:7–8, "Be not deceived, God is not mocked. For what things a man shall sow, those also shall he reap. For he that sows in the flesh, of the flesh also shall reap corruption. For he that sows in the spirit, of the spirit shall reap life everlasting." What is of the spirit is spirit, and what is of the flesh is flesh, and never the two shall meet.

God is a just God, and justice must be served on His level of understanding, not ours. For us to understand the times in which we are living, we must seek God's mind, not that of natural man. It is for this reason that there is so much disagreement in trying to come to a conclusion on many matters. Few interpret with the mind of God, using the Scriptures as the major point of reference. It is the Lord Who grants favors, and as He said to the prophet Jeremiah, "For I know the thoughts that I think towards you, says the Lord, thoughts of peace, and not of affliction, to give you an end and a patience. And you shall call upon me, and you shall go and you shall pray to me, and I will hear you. You shall seek me, and you shall find me: when you shall seek me with all of your heart. And I will be found by you, says the Lord: and I will bring back your captivity, and I will gather you out of all nations, and from all the places to which I have driven you out, says the Lord: and I will bring you back from the place to which I caused you to be carried away captive" (Jeremiah 29:11–14).

This book examines the true state of the union of America and concludes that our nation is not what we believe it to be. As a result of our corrupt existence, America is presently in a transition state from God's warnings to His justice. Our response must be swift, decisive and rooted in our faith in God and His Only Begotten Son, Jesus Christ. The remedy, like many medicines, may be difficult to swallow, but the stakes are high enough to warrant our fortitude and our willingness to persevere—no matter what it costs.

4

Sieg Heil!

*Everything can be taken from a man but...the last of
the known freedoms—to choose one's attitude in any
given set of circumstances, to choose one's own way.*
                                    —Victor Frankl,
                              Man's Search for Meaning

It could be argued that the rise of the Third Reich under Hitler was
one of the greatest events of barbarism in the 20th Century. What
happened inside China with Mao or in Soviet Russia with Lenin and
Stalin had very broad implications, but did not see American deaths to
the extent the war with Nazi Germany did. Ideologies of yesterday
have meanings, which will manifest themselves in social, military, and
economic ways tomorrow. So how did a Christian nation like Germany
allow the wholesale slaughter of millions of people, including their
own? Is there validity to the theory of "the errant German gene" or is
the philosophy of thought more pandemic of man? Is it "the German
thing," or is there a difference in Stalin slaughtering 25 million
Ukrainians? Pol Pot? Mussolini? Mao after his long march killing an
estimated 50 million "dissenters," depending on your source? If it were
a lesser number, it would still be a large number of deaths. What
changes in the soul of man that allows this to happen? Is modern war
and death different from previous ages? The methods of death are
different, but the heart of man remains the same. If God is "the same
yesterday, today, and forever," does Satan change his agenda? When all
is said and done, the battle is a spiritual one, where the cohorts of
Heaven and Hell fight for control of the soul of man. Satan seeks to
destroy; God in His love wishes to bless us love and renew the earth on
our behalf. Since the angels fought in Heaven and a third were thrown
from the sky, therein lies the heart of the battle. Where Satan is the lust
of the eye, lust of the flesh, ego, and the pride of life, God uses
humility, the subjugation of the flesh, and no worldly honor. Virtue
and vice are opposite on the spiritual scale. Can the slaughter of people
happen again like it did during the reign of Hitler? The answer is it will

happen again, the only issue is where and when—with the how irrelevant.

A Heart of Light or Darkness

As King Solomon stated, "Nothing under the sun is new" (Ecclesiastes 1:10). It was said that Solomon was the wisest man to inhabit the earth. The Lord said, "Behold I have done for you according to your words, and have given you a wise and understanding heart, insomuch that there has been no one like you before you, nor shall arise after you" (1 Kings 3:12). To achieve such a lofty and sublime title and be called this wise by God Himself, one would have to logically assume that there is an element of grace and not solely a self-determination in such words by the Almighty. A basic question must be asked from a historical perspective, and that would be, "Has human nature changed over the millennia?" Have morals changed? Is man a different creature today than yesterday? Education has spread, but intelligence and wisdom don't seem to change much based upon history. A cynic remarked that "you mustn't enthrone ignorance just because there is so much of it." However, ignorance is not long enthroned, for it lends itself to manipulation by the forces that mold public opinion. It may be true as Lincoln supposed that "you can't fool all the people all the time," but you can fool enough of them to rule a large country.[1]

The synthesis of philosophies over the course of modern history evolves like light through a prism. An immediate divergence occurs with discriminating emphasis along distinct subjects pertaining to economic, spiritual, physical, and psychological needs. Typically, the rationale for each need is woven by the philosopher into a weave of "isms" where man seeks to attain a utopia valued primarily on one need to the diminution or exclusion of another. However, unless the needs of man are all met as ordained by Almighty God, the weave unravels. No matter how hard a man wants to fight God, and no matter how long he continues, the Lord's presence will be the driving force in history long after we are gone. No matter how much we deny or reject, the very beginning of the Bible starts with the words, "In the beginning God created heaven, and earth" (Genesis 1:1). No matter how many musings on which man wishes to wax philosophical, all will stand before the throne of God and give an account of their lives. Our resources, our intellect, our pride, our brilliant career will be judged, and in the final analysis, we will all be humbled by Divinity. Some acknowledge the truth quietly and quickly in their lives, others endure a lifetime of pain before they submit to eternal Truth. Some remain belligerent even to the point of committing spiritual suicide. There is no avoiding the Truth. Those who deny it invariably will confront those who acquiesce to the Truth. Such confrontations typically become violent.

From the earliest family in history there was something more than an argument, there was murder. Cain killed Abel to have something more. Is pride altogether different from competition? Competition is the wheel of man's very existence, which makes the world go around. When there are not enough resources to be spread among the people, violence erupts. When food is plentiful, peace is more likely—but by no means guaranteed. As long as one has more than another, there will be competition and thus war. There are wars in the world because there is war in the heart of man. War is a culling process which eliminates the weak. Weak nations are invaded and conquered. Therefore, a military system being superior or at least posing a significant threat to its neighbors is capable of sustaining itself as a sovereign nation.

Is there a spiritual reason for man's existence? When looked at by a Karl Marx where man is only an economic unit, the answer is no. If it is a service or a utility to be used by the state for Hegel, the answer is no again. If it is to ponder philosophical niceties and come to the conclusion of a deist, the answer is still no. Camus and Sartre gave mankind nothing other than a life with no answers, thus leading to despair. Walking the streets of Paris today, their impact is felt. Unless the philosophy and ideology of a person seek the meaning of life's greatest and truest purpose, variations of sadness, emptiness, and despair will prevail. Lack of hope will prevail under such circumstances no matter the person. Only when the person cries out, "I am not in control. I want a purpose, a meaning, a reason to know, something bigger than my earthly existence," then and only then can a change take place. Only when we are emotionally and physically capable of saying, "I can never endeavor to understand with my finite intelligence," can we grow and become a new creation. This is a deep mystery in an abyss of mercy, which human intelligence cannot understand. One cannot fully appreciate the beauty of God's mercy unless one has experienced the misery of sin. But what the intelligence of man cannot understand, the intelligence of love, the love of the spirit, does. It understands and confidently penetrates the mystery, which is God, and the mystery of the relationship of the soul with God. This is what God wills. When man allows that to happen through the grace of the Redeemer, only then will there be an abundant life. Only when we move in the light of Him Who created us, do we find purpose.

Every day, through free will, we choose light or darkness, a life of joy or a life of pain. It's a daily choice, whether we articulate it or not.

As history unfolds, the soul giving itself to God is involved in the ongoing war in the heavens choreographed and danced on the world stage in so many ages by so many people. Those who have the spirit give life; those who do not cannot give what they do not have. The history of the Old Testament revolves around Yahweh. The history of the New Testament revolves around Jesus Christ. Jesus is salvation, and until a soul looks to Him who is The Way, The Truth, and The Light, there is no peace of soul. He is the life of the soul, which is dead until The Light enters. Only He is the great Physician, and all need a doctor and medicine. He is available. After the pomp, the circumstance, the physical beauty, the arts, the estates, the accumulations, the births, weddings, and deaths, all that is left is your faith and your deeds on earth. The great divide in recorded history is "Do you love Me?" All else passes in the twinkling of an eye. As Blaise Pascal said about the exercises in self-gratification, "It is like licking the earth." The struggle remains that some say 'yes' while others in the fallen state never acknowledge the greater truth. This is the dividing point of humanity—the desires of the flesh or the spirit. There is no neutral ground. You cannot love both God and mammon.

The circumstances around the rise of barbarism will be similar in the near future to what they were in the past. Why? Because when the people fall away from a higher ideal of doing good—a moral code—the die is cast for that nation. That is the one-sentence synopsis of civilizations. The moral tone of a nation governs the nation. Polemicists, intellectuals, and historians can argue otherwise, but it is true. Due to bad economics of the Weimar Republic, Germany had policies detrimental to an ethical and moral behavior of its people. Economic and social policy took precedence over religion or faith. Nations may consider themselves righteous in their own eyes, but is this how Heaven sees them? How does Heaven view America? Do we measure up? If we measure ourselves up against a pagan nation we probably look pretty good. Should that be our measuring stick? Or do we look before the bright light of God—as He should judge us? A painting from a master looks impeccable from a distance. As one approaches and looks closely, one can see the imperfections and the brush strokes. How is it that a country once a chief part of the Holy Roman Empire laid siege to an entire continent? There are many valid reasons for the progression in thinking that led to this. Listed below are several factors influencing the German people as a population moving to extreme and radical views:

❖ Embedded in its culture for generations was an anti-Jewish mentality. Martin Luther's writings had some vehemently anti-Jewish passages. As the founding father of the Lutheran faith, Luther's views helped an ideology take root in a nation's intellectual and cultural thought.

❖ The Aryan mentality of racial purity had been developing as the state became the dominant focus as spirituality declined. New Age spiritualism had crept in since the late 1880's, including the views of Madame Blavatsky, Annie Besant, and Alice and Foster Bailey. The intellectual elite of England offered the Weimar Republic an apparent way out of economic distress by presenting socialist policies. In other words, rather than dig deeply for a moral solution on sound moral principles, extreme patriotism or nationalism reared its ugly head—the thread we have seen in all of Scripture. Alice Bailey was the reigning queen of the New Age movement until her death. Foster Bailey ridiculed the Christ of the Bible and heralded the false gospel of the New Age christ saying, "The Christian doctrine that He comes as a Christian to save us from hell and for some distant judgment date is a hangover from humanity's childhood days."[2] Alice Bailey was born of high social standing in Manchester, England, in 1880. After a bitter divorce, she transformed herself into a master teacher of the occult. Because this group of spiritualists believed in anything and everything, the door was open for chaos in Germany. These views took root beginning in approximately the mid-1880's, and Germany embraced them. Appealing to the senses rather than to the Cross, Germany evolved over the next sixty years into a nation capable of the Holocaust. As it worshipped Baal, it moved to Asherah, the Old Testament god of fertility and flesh, exactly as previous civilizations did. Asherah has different names depending on the ethnic group that worships her. Asherah is more than the goddess of fertility and lust; she is also the goddess of destruction and incest. No matter how we say it, she is the goddess of abortion and vice. Following the views of New Agers is beyond the scope of this book, but a review of the lives of Bailey, Aleister Crowley and Besant is like an evening swim in a sewer. Nudity, debauchery, drug addiction—anything went in the cabarets of Berlin and elsewhere where this thinking permeated the culture. Culture doesn't appear overnight, nor do the beliefs of the people. Views incrementally grow and change people's opinions. Germany didn't march into Poland ready to take on the world in 1939 based on just six years of ideology and preparation.

❖ The full-scale collapse of traditional Christian belief continued unabated. Secularism led to an abandonment of faith. The clergy embraced a secularist philosophy rather than the Cross of Calvary, and the sacrifice of Christian morality led to a nationalist and super-patriotic mentality.

❖ Adapting the geo-political objectives of their English cousins, leading German intellectuals were wedded to Masonry and organized by the Thule Society (which gave rise to the Nazi party); for example Klaus Haushofer promoted economic and political strategies void of Christian ethics and filled with pagan Teutonic/Aryan imagery and eastern mysticism. These philosophies and strategies became the foundation and driving force behind such tactics as Aryan purification (eugenics), Lebensraum ("living space"—the acquisition by force of Slavic territories), the Anschluss (unification of Germany with Austria) and the creation of the SS ("Schutzstaffel" or "state security"), drenched in the Japanese warrior code of Bushido.

❖ The marginalization of clergy was fomented throughout Germany. Social and political progress gave rise to Nazism. Nationalism took on a more extreme role to the point of the exclusion of others. Anyone not contributing to the state, such as the infirmed, mentally handicapped, elderly, or less than perfect, were considered expendable. Toward the end of the cycle, the clergy in Germany were imprisoned or murdered if they spoke against the state.

❖ Philosophical thought from art, science, and social sciences permeated the schools and culture. Germany developed its view based upon a romantic evolution that moved violently away from Christianity. Nowhere is this more powerfully shown than in the writings of Georg W. F. Hegel (1770–1831) and Friedrich Nietzsche (1844–1900). Germany cannot be understood in Nazi thinking until these two men are recognized for the philosophical thought they generated throughout the nation. The Rousseau's, Voltaire's, Sartre's, Camus' and other philosophers created an ideology to last for generations. The Nazi mentality did not spring up overnight, it evolved intellectually and emotionally for generations. The same process is true for America and other countries today. We are today what we were yesterday, and we will be tomorrow what we are today.

Georg Hegel

Georg Hegel was Germany's most influential political thinker during the 19th Century, and his philosophy has exerted an immense influence on modern thought in general. Not only political theory, but the disciplines of ethics, historiography, aesthetics, biblical studies, and theology have absorbed Hegelian assumptions. Central to Hegel's thought was his concept of history, which is expressed by the terms *dialectic* and *dialectical*. History is understood to be the unfolding process whereby one force or idea, identified as thesis, is confronted by an opposing force or idea, the antithesis. Out of the clash of thesis and antithesis arises a third force, that of synthesis, which itself becomes a new thesis.

As this concept came to be applied to theology, we see that Hegel's idea of God is an interesting distortion of the biblical picture. In Scripture, God transcends nature and is actively involved in the affairs of mankind. He reveals His eternal nature and purpose in and through human events—action which itself constitutes history. For Hegel, the transcendent nature of God is denied, and "God" is identified with history itself. Deity becomes wholly "immanent," or "in the world" and is indistinguishable from the historical process itself. History is the unfolding of the universal "Absolute Spirit," which is constantly in the process of realizing itself. History shows the evolution of Spirit, marching ever onward to the fulfillment of its potential, with human institutions as the primary vehicle of this realization.

To the extent this theological viewpoint impacted Christian thought, its influence was such as to militate strongly against historic Christian understandings of man, nature, God, and human institutions. The most radical difference, of course, is rooted in the matter of revelation. Christianity affirms a "once for all" revelation of the moral will and purpose of the God Who transcends the world and judges it. In Hegel, and in subsequent theologies influenced by him, we see an understanding which virtually identified Deity with the world itself. Such a conception can retain no admission of biblical miracles, for there can be no manifestation of God apart from the natural course of events. This Hegelian immanentism, or an outlook rooted entirely in this world, was adopted by German biblical scholars and provided the framework for the conclusions of German 'higher criticism" of the Bible. Under the "process" view of God, the centrality of the Bible for

Christian faith declined—for if history itself constitutes the exhibition of Spirit working out its own potentialities, then no single historical event or person can finalize a divine revelation. Hence, the New Testament must be viewed, at best, as a tentative authority, a small part of the larger picture of thesis, antithesis, and synthesis.

If one accepted Hegel's view of God and history, the biblical record had to be explained and addressed in terms other than those affirmed by Christian orthodoxy. To put it simply, if Hegel's concept were true, then the things that the Bible says happened could not have happened in any actual sense. Thus, began a process in which Christian understandings were gradually detached from any basis in literal fact. Building upon a Hegelian base, David Strauss, in his *Life of Jesus* (1835), denied all supernatural events in the life of Jesus and asserted that the story of Christ was an imaginative and mythological matrix of symbols embodying truths about human existence. Another Hegelian theologian, A. E. Biedermann (1819–1885), drew a distinction between the "Christ principle" and the "Jesus of History," thereby segregating Jesus from Christ, while implying that there could be a "Christianity" substantially free of historical evidences and the biblical record. The word Christ became something defined merely as a symbolic concept related to man's evolving religious consciousness, rather than in accordance with the biblical presentation of Jesus. As we will see, these principles were to be used eagerly by Nazi ideologues in their desire to discredit the witness of the Judeo-Christian Scriptures.

Moreover, Hegel's notion that human institutions are the primary vehicle of the evolving absolute spirit exalted one institution above all others—the State. The State was, for Hegel, the very institutionalization of Divine Spirit in human life and was to be revered above all other institutions. Below is a summary of the Hegelian concept of the state:

> In Hegel's special formulation—the Hegelian dialectic—the state is the higher synthesis which evolves from the clash of thesis and antithesis. The state synthesizes individual will and collective will, power and justice; it combines both moral right and physical force, freedom and authority. In fact, according to Hegel, freedom can fully exist only in a national state, and only in the state can moral purpose be fulfilled.[3]

Robert Nisbet calls Hegel "the preeminent philosophical influence in the glorification of human progress as attainment of national power" and the "transmutation of freedom from a state that has individual autonomy and rights as its essence to one in which the true measure becomes not autonomy or independence for the individual but his willing participation in a centralized absolute structure of power."[4]

The groundwork was laid for questioning the authenticity and relevancy of Scripture. The state would become the central player in man's affairs. Man is best when man serves the state. This is the extension of Plato's *Utopia* where there are three entities: a governing elite, a military, and a working class. Professor John Ruskin of Oxford had similar views based upon Plato which is how Cecil Rhodes formed his views for an intellectual elite which became the Rhodes Scholars— all financed by his South African mineral mines. The theories of Hegel were not new. Man will be more useful as a utilitarian creature of the state. Hegel often referred to the state as "the divine will," where man's inherent worth is serving the state. Germany is best understood concerning psyche and maniacal nationalism in the following statement by Hegel. It needs no explanation:

> The Nation State is Spirit in its substantive rationality and immediate actuality; it is therefore the absolute power on earth.... The State is the Spirit of the People itself. The actual State is animated by this spirit in all its particular affairs, its Wars and its institutions.... The self-consciousness of one particular Nation is the vehicle for the...development of the collective spirit;...in it, the Spirit of the Time invests its Will. Against the Will no other national minds have rights: *that* nation dominates the World.[5]

To separate Lutheranism from nationalism becomes more difficult. They had morphed into one, with nationalism in time subjecting the church to its views. Faith came to play less of a role and the same model of history played out again as it has so many times before. In England this happened when King Henry VIII wanted to divorce his wife because his glands were winning the internal war, and the aristocracy perceived the opportunity to split the state from the Church and seize the Church's property and wealth. The Church said divorce was not permitted, so King Henry decided to form a new church. In today's parlance, Henry continued to divorce on whim, and in essence became a serial killer. Take away the concept of the Cross, of suffering as redemptive, a wariness of "isms" and new philosophies or old thinking regurgitated in another point in place and time, and the society will unravel—slowly and surely. It is another form of Baal worship— in this case, the worship of the state. Take Jesus off the Cross and anything can and will happen. Abandon the simplest elements of faith, and society is doomed. What will the historians write in 30, 40, 50, 100 more years about the American empire that in 1962 by order of the Supreme Court of the land expelled God from the classroom, where years later teachers in public high schools lost their jobs by simply having a Bible in the classroom? Secularism is a faith and an ideology. In all probability, it will take more bloodshed in our schools to bring the Bible back into the classroom.

Friedrich Nietzsche

Adding gasoline to the fire was the rugged individualism of Friedrich Nietzsche (1844–1900). Take a strong people always seeking its place in history and a collective thinking of state superiority, and you have a powerful mixture:

> Adolf Hitler is known to have visited the Nietzsche archives in Weimar on numerous occasions, and, as William Hubben observed, he "was made to serve the ideology of national-socialism, and an extensive popular literature grew quickly that added the philosopher to the long line of spiritual ancestors of the new political faith."[6] Writing of Nietzsche in the midst of World War II, Erich Kahler referred to him as "the man who started this revolution that threatens the foundations of the world of man."[7]
>
> Nietzsche is most well-known for his declaration that "God is dead," a statement uttered by a madman in a parable that appears in his work *The Gay Science* (1882). The character in the parable expresses Nietzsche's view that the Christian God revealed in the Bible had become unworthy of belief and incredible for modern man. The death of the "old" God was, for Nietzsche, a reason for gratitude and great expectation. An admirer of the Enlightenment, which had established an anti-supernaturalist, rationalist, and skeptical point of view in religious matters, Nietzsche carried forth the Enlightenment's anti-Christian bias. His polemic against Christianity was accompanied by an equally intense criticism of existing institutions and systems. This is not difficult to understand, in that Christianity underlies the historic worldview and society of the Western world. For Nietzsche, the death of the Christian God meant the abandonment of the entire Western system of life itself, moral and institutional. This abandonment left man with no metaphysical obligations or certainties. There is a radical autonomy attributed to man in Nietzsche, which forthrightly rejects the biblical tradition that sees man as existing under the reality of

an absolute moral law to which all are responsible. In Nietzsche, humanity becomes its own lawgiver and source of morality. No recognition is given to any transcendent power over man's moral conscience. He employed the concept of the "Superman" to express this autonomy, a being risen to superiority through the realization of values that reflect direct opposites of the traditional Christian virtues such as meekness, kindness, and sacrifice. The Superman comes with power, and the force of will, overcoming the "inferior" and "life-denying values" of the Christian faith. This is expressed in his book, *The Antichrist*:

> What is good? All that heightens in man the feeling of power, the desire for power, power itself. What is bad? All that comes from weakness. What is happiness? The feeling that our strength grows, that an obstacle is overcome. Not contentment, but more power; not universal peace, but war; not virtue, but forcefulness. The weak and ineffective must go under; first principle of *our* love of humanity. And one should even lend one's hand to this end. What is more harmful than any vice? Pity for the condition of the ineffective and weak— Christianity.

> Christianity should not be beautified and embellished: it has waged deadly war against this higher type of man; it has placed all the basic instincts under the ban; and out of these instincts it has distilled evil and the Evil One: the strong man as the typically reprehensible man, the "reprobate." Christianity has sided with all that is weak and base, with all failures; it has made an ideal of whatever *contradicts* the instinct of the strong life to preserve itself.... Christianity is called the religion of pity. Pity stands opposed to the tonic emotions which heighten our vitality: it has a depressing effect.[8]

The complex, obscure, and often contradictory character of Nietzsche's writings raise barriers to any attempt at systematizing his philosophy. Nevertheless, the impact of three major ideas was overwhelming, these being the death of God, the inherent potential of humanity to raise itself to a higher state through spiritual and cultural struggle, and the idea of the great man (the Superman). As one observer has remarked, the attempt on the part of Western civilization to act collectively on Nietzsche's premises was a major contributor to the modern crisis.[9]

These philosophies over time became the bedrock of German ideology which evolved into the concentration and death camps across Europe. It is very important for Americans to realize that ideas and philosophies devoid of Christian ethics can be dangerous to a civilization. The philosophers laid the foundation where man became the center of a world without Jesus Christ, God of the Universe. The spadework was complete; the German land and people were now in Satan's grip. This is neither a polemic nor history book on Germany, but is meant to show that a philosophy of thinking evolves, and over time, as a nation abandons the Cross—no matter how perverse—not only can happen, but is destined to happen. Once nationalism took precedence over faith, the marginalization, persecution, and martyrdom of committed Christians was on an accelerated path. Once the voice of God was silenced from the pulpits, clergy spoke out in fear of their life. See below the sermon of Cardinal Clemens Count von Galen:

"This ghastly doctrine tries to justify the murder of blameless men and would seek to give legal sanction to the forcible killing of invalids, cripples, the incurable and the incapacitated.... And so we must await the news that these wretched defenseless patients will sooner or later lose their lives. Why? Not because they have committed crimes worthy of death, not because they have attacked guardians or nurses as to cause the latter to defend themselves with violence which would be both legitimate and even in certain cases necessary, like killing an armed enemy soldier in a righteous war.

"No, these are not the reasons why these unfortunate patients are to be put to death. It is simply because that according to some doctor, or because of the decision of some committee, they have no longer a right to live because they are 'unproductive citizens.' The opinion is that since they can no longer make money, they are obsolete machines, comparable with some old cow that can no longer give milk or some horse that has gone lame. What is the lot of unproductive machines and cattle? They are destroyed. I have no intention of stretching this comparison further. The case here is not one of machines or cattle which exist to serve men and furnish them with plenty. They may be legitimately done away with when they can no longer fulfil their function. Here we are dealing with human beings, with our neighbours, brothers and sisters, the poor and invalids...unproductive—perhaps! But have they, therefore, lost the right to live? Have you or I the right to exist only because we are 'productive'? If the principle is established that unproductive human beings may be killed, then God help all those invalids who, in order to produce wealth, have given their all and sacrificed their strength of body. If all unproductive people may thus be violently eliminated, then woe betide our brave soldiers who return home, wounded, maimed or sick.

"Once admit the right to kill unproductive persons...then none of us can be sure of his life. We shall be at the mercy of any committee that can put a man on the list of unproductives. There will be no police protection, no court to avenge the murder and inflict punishment upon the murderer. Who can have confidence in any doctor? He has but to certify his patients as unproductive and he receives the command to kill. If this dreadful doctrine is permitted and practised it is impossible to conjure up the degradation to which it will lead. Suspicion and distrust will be sown within the family itself. A curse on men and on the German people if we break the holy commandment 'You shall not kill' which was given us by God on Mount Sinai with thunder and lightning, and which God our Maker imprinted on the human conscience from the beginning of time! Woe to us German people if we not only licence this heinous offence but allow it to be committed with impunity![10]

For the Nuremberg Trials of Nazi officials after World War II, millions of pages of supporting evidence were used in the cases against those in the dock, including an outline prepared by the O. S. S. (the forerunner of the C. I. A.) called, "The Persecution of the Christian Churches." For the conquest of the world, the Nazis knew they needed to destroy Christian ideology. Though conservative Christians supported the positive aspects of the National Socialists, such as their fight against communism and their movement to repudiate the Versailles Treaty from the end of World War I, they could not reconcile themselves officially with the racist or aggressive military aspects of Nazism, or with the requirement of the subservience of church to state. According to Baldur von Schirach, the Nazi leader of the German youth group later to be known as the Hitler Youth, "The destruction of Christianity was explicitly recognized as a purpose of the National Socialist movement" from the start, though "considerations of expedience made it impossible" to follow this tack until power had been solidly established.

The Nazis simply lied to the churches when making deals with them. The Protestants were much easier to handle as their administrative centers were located within German borders. This eased plans "to capture and use the church organization for their own purposes" and "to secure the elimination of Christian influences in the Evangelical Church by legal or quasi legal means," according to the outline.

The Roman Catholic Church posed a far more difficult problem. A Concordat was signed in 1933 between the Holy See and the Reich. "In return for the retreat of German Catholicism from the political scene [the disbanding of the Christian Democratic Party], the Church was guaranteed, by international treaty, freedom for Catholic organizations," states the outline. Hitler demanded "a pledge of loyalty by the clergy to the Reich government" and patriotic allegiance of Catholics to the Reich.

Soon after Hitler's dictatorship began, the Concordat's provisions were systematically violated, leading to Pope Pius XI's 1937 condemnation of Nazism. Gestapo and street mobs were now often raiding and vandalizing churches. Priests and other religious leaders who spoke against the regime or its tactics were arrested and sent to concentration camps. "Still, in a society where the entire Jewish population was being automatically condemned without public protest, care was taken to manipulate public perceptions about clergymen who fell into Nazi disfavor. 'The Catholic Church need not imagine that we are going to create martyrs,' the outline reported Robert Wagner, the Nazi Gauleiter of Baden, as saying in a speech. 'We shall not give the Church that satisfaction. She shall not have martyrs, but criminals.'"

Once the Nazis had established total power, however, it was clear that all churchmen who spoke against the Reich would be in great danger. "After 1937, German Catholic bishops gave up all attempts to print" their pastoral letters and instead "had them merely read from the pulpits," says the outline. Then the letters themselves were confiscated, the confiscations taking "place during Mass by the police snatching the letter out of the hands of the priests as they were in the act of reading it." In the same year, 700 Protestant ministers who joined in a manifesto against Nazi tactics were arrested. Dissenting statements of the clergy were no longer being tried in the courts. The outline reports that statements "injurious to the State would be ruthlessly punished by 'protective custody,' that is, the concentration camp."[11]

So much more could be said, as the issue of German guilt and what allowed the Holocaust to happen inside a Christian nation is one of the most studied subjects in the 20th Century. Many Holocaust survivors and family members have turned to psychology as a profession because of the pain inflicted on so many. How could a people allow such a thing to happen? The Nuremberg Trials showed the world that quite a few German people knew what was going on. While they did not know all the details, they knew enough that they should have tried as a nation to stop it.

The American government with its social programs has become an idol for generations of Americans. People are dependent on government largess rather than the Providence of God. Edmund Burke, the outstanding orator, author and leader in Great Britain during the time of the Revolutionary War, wrote in a 1791 "Letter to a Member of the National Assembly":

> What is liberty without wisdom and without virtue? It is the greatest of all possible evils; for it is folly, vice, and madness, without restraint.
>
> Men are qualified for civil liberty in exact proportion to their disposition to put moral chains upon their own appetites....
>
> Society cannot exist, unless a controlling power upon will and appetite be placed somewhere; and the less of it there is within, the more there must be without.
>
> It is ordained in the eternal constitution of things, that men of intemperate minds cannot be free. Their passions forge their fetters.[12]

Once the state is supreme, the people gradually move away from truth. Philosophical thought has an impact for generations. The battle is to control the mind. The culture, art, military, social norms, politics, economics, and finance will turn in a negative direction once Baal is introduced, accepted, and nurtured.

5

The Deepest Needs of Man: To Love and Be Loved

The heavens show forth the glory of God, and the firmament declares the work of his hands.
—Psalm 18:2

No matter the oceans we sail, the lands we traverse, or the skies we fly, man forever searches for happiness. Americans especially are most cognizant of this fundamental desire. We are nursed in our childhood and throughout life on a simple but most memorable declaration by our Founding Fathers who unequivocally declared, "life, liberty and the pursuit of happiness." The pursuit of happiness is engrained in the psyche of American culture. George Washington, our first president, in his farewell address said, "Of all the dispositions and habits which lead to political prosperity, religion and morality are indispensable supports. In vain would that man claim the tribute of patriotism, who should labor to subvert these great pillars of human happiness, these firmest props of the duties of men and citizens."[1] Indeed, faith and morality are the source and foundation of our pursuit for the common good.

We spend an inordinate amount of time attempting to capture the rewards of happiness. Haute couture, the cinema, cuisine of all sorts, coastal living, a sleeker and faster car, a lower handicap, a trimmer body, a bigger and better something—they all point us to what should make us happy. Regarding money and accumulated wealth, if money makes people happy, it would make sense that all people with money would be jumping for joy every day. But, if we take a good look around, it doesn't seem to work that way. To illustrate the point, Barney Welch, a Caring People Award honoree, seemed to sum up the "money thing" best: "I'm in a unique situation. I would work for millionaires on the farms, so I'd see them in the day and the poor at night. I'd see both sides of the coin, and I'm not sure I see any more contentment on one side than the other." We are not necessarily espousing poverty here. The deeper issue is the inordinate desire for more and more and more. Enough never seems to be enough for most men. When big John D. Rockefeller was asked how much is enough, he replied, "Just a little bit more."

If we are true Christian believers who pursue our faith in love and humility, we will hopefully be told to enter the Gates of Heaven with the invitation, "Well done, good and faithful servant." God in His infinite wisdom insures that the body loses its luster as we age, in part to awaken our conscience, as if our conscience were peering from a distance through the valley of the shadow of death to see the light of God's pending judgment. As if taking commands from the Seat of Judgment, nature seems to say, "Take your eyes off of yourself and your worldly possessions; for you shall soon perish!" The point is we must realize that in the end, all we bring with us is a portfolio of our fidelity to the commands of God.

In his pride Satan said, "I will not serve." Encased in Original Sin, fallen man in so many ways echoes the voice of Satan by his sins of omission and commission. There is no fear in the new law of Christ. We fail to realize that we are grasping at straws or attempting to hang onto something beyond our grasp. Because of our fallen nature, we refuse to accept the fact that the deepest things in life are mysteries. Man is incapable of piercing the veil of creation's mystery unless God grants the grace of understanding. Therefore, until man says, "Yes, I want to know You and mortify myself to Your will," this selfish urge to lust for complete knowledge eats away at one's immortal soul. It is no accident that the forbidden fruit in the Garden of Eden came from the Tree of Knowledge.

Modern man's foolish pursuit for complete knowledge as a prerequisite for happiness illustrates the great paradox that challenges us today. Technology and science have not advanced the state of man's soul but in many respects have retarded it. The cardinal sin of pride universally reigns, instilling the fraudulent belief that man can solve his own problems, so why should he need an antiquated Redeemer? The modern-day Tower of Babel is the exploitation of technology and science to raise man's self-image and material prestige as the measure of success and happiness. These are our new gods. Was the fall of the Twin Towers in New York on a spiritual level with the towers of idolatry and materialism which have consumed us? Are they the modern-day bull of the Old Testament? No better example of this is the unraveling of the genetic code. The goal is one of eugenics, which is simply the 21st Century's remarketing of age-old idolatry, discrimination and enslavement. Eugenics deals with the control of human reproduction and hereditary attributes. It places a utilitarian value on all life and is devoid of God. Cloning is Satan trying to reach the stature of God to create life without God.

The prior centuries of immigration into the U. S. that began with the weak and tired piling into New York via Ellis Island had its run of prosperity and righteous living. Immigrants shared the American value system. Modern day ethicians teach, or at a minimum imply, that such immigration policies propagated undesirable attributes as a cultural 'contagion' across the country causing disease, poverty, crime, fear and confusion. Now the Hegelian debate of "Is it the environment or heredity that determines the fate of an individual?" can be addressed through social engineering policies and genetic modifications enforced by government fiat to establish a new generation of the ideal man, or, in a word, utopia.

Meanwhile, John and Jane Q. Public are afraid of their own shadow, afraid of their neighbors, and virtually unwilling to leave their living rooms, because of the fear of the unknown. The media indoctrinates them with the ideas that their traditional values and institutions are antiquated, convinces them that their fears are justified, and tells them that the new social engineering, science and technology will ultimately allay their fears. They turn inwards to their home as a symbol of security, something that is at least controllable as the rest of the world passes them by and makes them irrelevant. Despair sets in because the future seems vague and uncertain. Hope becomes a victim to the immutable process driven by science and technology, as an increasingly hedonistic society questions the value of their lives. In all of this they forgot that God can dispel all fear and can bring them enduring peace and happiness. The older generation, seeing the social programs of F. D. R. apparently work to suit their needs after World War II, put their faith in government—and that, too, has failed them. They, too, are fearful. Over the last 40-plus years, Americans have turned away from faith and sought material gain as a measure of success and happiness. We are incapable of discerning where our true happiness lies. Practicing Christians know this, which is why they act differently than the general population and why they are ridiculed for it. The call of Christ is what sets them apart. When Christ calls a man to Him, He bids him to come and die.

The Search for Meaning

In youth, elders taught us that our purpose is "to love God with our whole heart, mind, and soul, and to love Him in this life and the next." Yet, as we get older our reasoning disregards this fundamental truth. Inevitably conflicts ensue on a material plane as each of us competes for our self-defined set of objectives. Like a species of animal we build alliances based on common attributes and interests, forming communities and states to defend ourselves. All of this clamor and activity without any higher goal other than self-preservation and self-content actually breeds discontentment. Searching for meaning becomes an afterthought or a by-product of our actions. Nevertheless a war rages for the hearts of men, which many of us fail to appreciate because we are preoccupied with the wrong things. Peace can only come from God and is often pursued elsewhere in vain, as the world is incapable of giving it. Until we resign ourselves to the fact that Jesus is Lord and King of the Universe and stop trivializing His will, there will be no peace. If we want peace, we need to take God seriously. Have you ever noticed that man achieves something great, like the cure for a disease, man receives the adulation? When there are problems or conflicts, God is always blamed.

As an observer over many decades of people's lives, I have noticed exceptional people live truly virtuous lives rooted in the gospel message, while others are insensitive or cavalier to spirituality in general. The latter spend little effort on spiritual formation. What is most striking over a twenty-five-year observation of friends, colleagues in the workplace, and general acquaintances, is the stark contrast in the thinking, attitude, family life, and a litany of other issues. There are great differences in outlook on life, raising of children, generosity, the view of their own possessions, how they spend their time, what they consider important, honesty, view of the afterlife, and other things too numerous to mention. The differences are profound, as believers become more deeply rooted in their faith and responsive to what Heaven is asking from them. Thus, as views between the believer and unbeliever become more divergent, the culture war escalates and plays out in every area of society. America is presently very polarized politically because of the vast differences in spiritual views. The U. S. is now emotionally unstable. This was clearly seen in the Bush/Gore election, as one witnessed that the candidates had very different moral perspectives and ideas on the way the U. S. should be run. The election results showed the extent of the culture war in our midst.

A Christian tries to adhere to a higher set of principles, a higher calling to be "perfect as God is perfect." The prize is not here on earth; as Jesus says, "My kingdom is not of this world" (St. John 18:36). Jesus came to fulfill the law, not abolish it. A new standard was being set with a new ingredient—the Holy Spirit. It was no longer a cloud of smoke and a fire by night which would tell the people where and when to move. The enlightenment of grace would now burn in the hearts of men and could be obtained by simply asking. Jesus also never advocated through judicial means; His agenda was a changed heart. If Jesus wanted to play a political role, He might have held meetings with Pontius Pilate to legislate laws for the Hebrew people. He didn't. When there is a changed heart, people become good; when people become good, families and nations become good.

The message of the New Covenant is so simple, even intellectuals can understand it. It supersedes all religious institutions, governments and economies. There is no better example of this than the events surrounding the birth of Jesus Christ. Mary, His mother, was a virgin in her early teens and understood that being pregnant and out of wedlock could at a minimum cause her great suffering and anguish. Yet, in the simplicity of her Immaculate Heart she overcame any doubts and said, "Yes." The story of man's redemption was written in the night's sky as the Magi followed the star called "Messiah" which lit up Bethlehem and all Israel. Herod, fearing for his political survival in the Roman Empire, went on a rampage against the innocents. Imagine the slaughter of all male newborns for fear a kingdom may be lost!

The intellectual and contentious elite, the Sanhedrin, must have had a first when they sat together to break bread while conspiring to murder Jesus. It did not matter that they knew the prophecies of Isaiah, Haggai, Jeremiah, and others, which foretold a new Messiah, a new King, and a new Lord. Jesus was a threat to their wealth and power. They realized that He came to upset the status quo, and the new paradigm would make them servants of the people, not served. They thought any support or decision in His favor would potentially bring hardship and ruin to their existing institutions. Jesus brought a new way of thinking that wasn't rooted in the caste system of the ancient world. In the end, all would stand in front of the throne of the Judge with only the faith, love, and deeds they had done while on earth. What made matters worse was Jesus' insistence that the playing field would now be level, no matter the birthstone. This is the equivalent of a modern-day socialist movement to redistribute income. One day He was curing the son of a Roman Centurion, the archenemy of Israel, and the next He was talking to a half-breed Samaritan—a woman, no less. To make matters worse, He would be seen with the most notorious prostitute in all Israel, Mary Magdalene. Of noble birth, a sister to His good friend Lazarus, and a sister of respectable Martha, Mary had disgraced her family. Sleeping with infidel Roman soldiers was unforgivable and more than the lawgivers could handle. Jesus dared to be different, emphasizing that love and mercy have a role every bit as important as justice. He then proved it on the Cross.

The new standard would not be the old laws, which no one could obey. The new law did not set as its objective a promised land for a worldly nation and financial wealth to sustain it and propagate a race. The new law would be obedience to Divine Truth, obedience to the Truth that the Eternal Father had written in the soul for all hearts to know right from wrong. The debate over the subject of a resurrection would soon end. No grave has been guarded before or since. Eternal happiness in unity with God is offered to all who believe. Being tutored by the great Gamaliel, or other teachers of the day, would not be required of the disciples of Jesus. Loving as He loves would make one a member of His group, no matter what one's shortcomings. The new law was love and bearing one another's burdens.

The destiny of man was no longer directed by a rigid set of rules. Rules on top of rules crushed the people, which is why the prophecy from Deuteronomy was fulfilled with Jesus on the Cross. In the mind of God, Who created each one of us, is the wish of the Father: a destiny of love, of peace, of glory—the holiness of being His children. That destiny was present in the Divine Mind when Adam was fashioned from dust, and will be present until the creation of the soul of the last man. Love, peace, and eternal happiness—these are profound words so difficult to advance in daily living. Before us stands the confrontation between two kingdoms. On the one hand we have a friendly King and Shepherd Who guides and protects us. Across His kingdom's borders is the enemy, perched like a lion waiting to devour us. Our Friend teaches us the rules and the means to keep us contented. He calls us and we hear His voice, which is Love and Peace.

The Battle for a Changed Heart

Man will always be confronted by the hostile powers of Satan, flesh and riches. The flesh is the pomp, the enticement of the world, the adulation of the crowd, the riches, the feasts, the honors and powers obtained from the world. Satan, the master of the flesh and of the world, speaks on behalf of the world and the flesh. Satan, too, has his rules. As prince of this world, Satan is given as much power as we allow, power dependent on whether we follow or ignore the laws of God. It is our doubts and disobedience that give Satan room to maneuver, causing the hedge of God's protective grace to be removed. Satan lurks in the dark prowling for the ruin of souls, so we can either let him in or barricade him out. As the flesh often traps our "ego" as a magnet adheres to iron, it is easy to follow a path of vice unless grace intervenes. The seducer says, "Come in and fear not." When the dirty deed is done, he extorts a hundredfold for the help he has given. Before you know it, you become ensnared in his vice. This is the power of sin. Sin becomes our master, enslaving us with chains and leaving us in a heap of smoldering ash after it uses us. From the great liar, everything is promised, but the return is temporary and addictive and the payment painful and unrelenting. If the cycle is not stopped, we become but battered flesh dying under its blows. "For the wages of sin is death" (Romans 6:23). Sin is like a disease that can break out from only one germ in the blood, but the germ multiplies and further corrupts the body. Man's fall into sin always begins with what appears to be an innocuous occurrence—a lapse in conviction or a lessening in standards. Then compliance with, and an even worse desire for, evil increases. One becomes accustomed to compromise in matters of conscience, neglecting one's duties and obedience to God and thus by degrees falls deeper into corruption. If the compromise continues as the conscience becomes cold, it leads to total rejection of God and total immersion into idolatry. This is the downward spiral of sin into spiritual suicide.

The lures of Satan are strong, judging by the metro section of any newspaper in America. The carnage of sin and vice are around us all day. If we can bear the daily martyrdom, then Mercy will come. In the end we know a great prize awaits us. Only One can still have mercy on that revolting misery, which the flesh, one of the masters, now loathes, and at which the other master, Satan, throws the arrows of his revenge and contempt. All men have different tolerances for the pain caused by sin.

Mercy, as the only One, passes by, bends down, picks us up, doctors us, cures us, and says, "Come. Do not be afraid. Do not look at yourself. Your wounds are but scars, but they are so numerous that you would be horrified, as they disfigure you, but do not look at them. I look at your good will. Because of your good will you are sealed."

Therefore, Jesus says to us, "I love you; let Me help you lift high your cross and follow Me." Jesus then takes us on a journey to His kingdom. Only then can we appreciate that Jesus is Mercy incarnate. Through the power of the Holy Spirit we discover the rules we did not want to follow. Now comes the single most important decision in a person's life. *Whom do you want to follow?* Here, we make a conscious decision to follow either the flesh or the Spirit. If we choose the latter, then the peace of God will follow. It is now free will's turn. How we respond is determined by the weight of our pride versus the state of divine grace in our soul, and only God knows the outcome of that decision.

Was it destiny imposed by God on that person, or did each person choose it for himself? It was chosen by the heart of the person to serve God or Satan. The gift of free choice remains always with us. Do we daily choose to forgive when wronged, or do we let it cause progressive damage, breeding alienation, bitterness and separation? In the end, civilization is broken into the groups that bind wounds and those who inflict them. The believer is called to a standard of forgiveness, putting balm and soothing ointment in a world where the vast majority abides by rules of an eye for an eye and looking out for No. 1. The cumulative response of every individual in society becomes the answer that ultimately decides the outcome for the entire nation or civilization. In the time of upheaval in the world today, the more perfect way is to bind wounds, not inflict them.

If there is a third power confronting man's nature, it may be gold, the inordinate pursuit of mammon, "filthy lucre" as Jesus called it. When the elders tried to trap Him, Jesus gave a one-sentence reply: "Render therefore to Caesar the things that are Caesar's, and to God the things that are God's" (St. Mark 12:17). The Jews further stiffened to this new King of the Jews because the best answer would have been, "We desire a new king to rule over us with political sway, not a leader of the lowly." Judas probably had this in mind, and never seemed in lockstep with Jesus. The enticements of gold have been a struggle of the ego, the flesh, and pride since the beginning of man. Bread is a great thing, and woman an even greater one for those longing for food or pleasure. To be acclaimed by crowds is a very great thing for man. How many crimes are committed for those things? But gold is a key that opens, a circle that joins; it is the beginning and end of ninety-nine percent of human actions. For the sake of bread and woman man becomes a thief. For power he will become a murderer. For gold he becomes an idolater. It was Satan himself, at the end of Jesus' fast when He was about to begin His public ministry, who tried to lure even Jesus with these enticements, offering Him all the kingdoms and power of the world, which were and are his to give, if Our Lord would bow down and worship him (St. Luke 4:1–13). As prince of the world, Satan does have authority if we give it to him.

It is precisely at that moment of rejecting the world's enticements that man becomes more like God. This is when the angels come. Here is a decision. For many, after a life of luxury and vice, there may be a decision. We all have tolerance for pain and the needs to satisfy the flesh. For each of us they are different. The degree of the pursuit of flesh, mammon, and sin determines the length of suffering and pain— hidden or in the open. No man is free until that decision is made. To the degree of the pursuit of virtue will come a complementary quantity of peace and contentment that will have a hundredfold return. That is the promise. Happiness can never be guaranteed in this life, but it can be in the next. Man misses this point until he submits his will. Until man submits his will to God, he will never find out what God's destiny is for him. He will never find the treasure chest unopened at his feet. He will never know God's best.

Jesus was a son of the law, and abided by the law in His family and as a Man. He didn't repeal the law, but gave it light and strength so that it could be fulfilled in a perfect way. It would be hard to read the New Testament without asking, "Where is the other half?" Jesus came to fulfill the law through His Divine Mercy. The fear of the Tabernacle, which the whole of Israel had for centuries, would be wiped away. Gentile, Greek, Jew, saint and sinner could equally approach Jesus and find Mercy.

America Is Being Purified

Should America be judged as God judged Israel so many times? The creation of this book began with heavy research into the Holy Scriptures on the themes of the judgment, purification, sin, national pride, suffering, victory and defeat of nations. What was noticed, after hundreds of stories and passages were looked at closely, is that this *is* the story of mankind and the reflection of all civilizations. You cannot read the Old Testament and not see that the story revolves around Israel, any more than you can read the New Testament and not see that Jesus is the central focus of activity. Book after book, the trend seems to be: God favors man, man abuses the favor, God warns him to change, man says no, God purifies. Over time, man comes back to his senses as he wallows in the ashes, God shows mercy, and the cycle starts over again. It's human nature.

This is a simplified version in the vernacular, but it is, in essence, the cycle of God's relationship to Israel, and it has also been the history of civilizations preceding ours. The cycle seems to have the mark of God's mercy written on it. God is mercy, and His mercy is justice.

Primary Signs that Judgment Is Near

Is America about to experience justice and judgment? One can say without equivocation that Heaven is begging for our attention through circumstances, calamities, weather, prophets, and nearly everything spoken of to Israel in Scripture. The data in our midst indicates as strongly as possible that the chinks in our moral armor justify God's judgment. Relativism has obscured truth, and the knowledge of right and wrong today is murky at best. What are the primary signs that judgment is near?

Confusion

The mysteries of God will never be totally understood by man, whether it is the Incarnation or the mystery of Divine Mercy and Love. If we refuse to accept these mysteries with humility as an act of faith, we are destined to corrupt what remains of our faith. We cannot subordinate God's will and His creation to our level, which is the goal of much of science and the humanities today. This is the primary cause of our collective confusion. We are following the wrong people. Psychotherapy, psychiatry, sociology, academics, and others all seem to be providing a solution for man that at best is incomplete, and at worst doesn't work. By supplanting God's mystery of creation with understanding based solely on human knowledge, logic and precepts, we deny our very souls of essential truth. Under such circumstances truth can be understood only by reason; otherwise it is rejected. The soul that rigidly adheres to the province of free will scorns the supernatural, slowly starving from a lack of Divine Grace. What follows is quite predictable—if man cannot grasp through reasoning and material evidence, then the subject is dismissed outright.

A stark contrast and debate unfolds among the religious and the laity regarding 'antiquated' traditions within the Church versus the necessary 'modern' renovation, reformation and renewal that is increasingly devoid of God's teachings. It is a sign of a haughty and corrupt race. Today there exists a shipwreck of our faith that previously sustained us in times of trial in the past. Notwithstanding our public acclamations and any protestation to the contrary, America is now a post-Christian society. Absolute Truth, once the bedrock of our society, has been quarried away. In a slick way through verbal engineering and social manipulation, true doctrines are not denied openly, but shoved into a spiritual closet in such an equivocal fashion that they become seriously compromised by error. It is the equivalent of having an enemy inside the gate. The institution called 'the church' is a mere shadow of its former self, no longer entrusted to Jesus Christ, but to manmade precepts. There is little power coming from America's pulpits. The Church is experiencing a *de facto* schism that will become more open. Many will split from the Roman Rite and its dogmas and the "American catholic church" will have its followers. Diocese by diocese, scandals will rock the foundation of the Church, and its best properties will be sold to the highest bidder to pay the enormous legal costs. Surgery is often required before a patient can start the healing process. The Church is now very sick, just like the rest of society.

Wholesale Abandonment of God and What Is Holy

There has been a nearly wholesale abandonment of what is considered good and holy. If a person is attempting to fulfill Divine commands concerning what is good and virtuous, then he is often mocked, marginalized, and vilified—especially in the workplace. The Lord had commanded, "Be you holy, because I the Lord your God am holy" (Leviticus 19:2). As the prayer life goes, so goes the person. Once the Divine inspiration is gone, there is generally an attempt to engineer a new social order based upon man's law rather than the way of Jesus. You can tell where a person's motivation comes from by merely listening. If it is the rhetoric of a political revolutionary without speaking of love, fasting, prayer, obedience and the commandments, you've hitched your wagon to the wrong train. There is an abdication of spiritual fundamentals, and this person will never pluck the desired fruit.

Unfortunately, it is often the misguided or corrupt clergy who facilitate the charge with a new interpretation or rationale to tickle the ears. Seldom is holiness present. Many of the American clergy refuse to fight militantly with spiritual armor, preferring instead the secular entrapments of prestige and financial security. The leadership often prefers the spirit of the world, accepting its way of life, sharing its values, listening to its propaganda, and adopting its mentality. The way of holiness and the Cross is abandoned.

The Church's agendas often mimic or mirror the secular world. It should be noted that the pro-life movement in America has followed such an agenda. Unwittingly, most pro-life leaders have fought the abortion battle on Satan's turf. The most effective tools God offers the faithful are prayer, fasting, the Eucharist and penance. This beast has not, cannot, and will not be slain with legislation. It is not to say that the Christian is not called into the political arena, but there has not been a mass exploitation of God's weapons in this movement. Further complicating this matter is a certain element of pride, where the leaders want their mailing lists, their legislative agenda, and their will to be done. It has been a failure to unite the leaders under one roof. Miniscule issues divide them, but the ego of position, place, and authorship cause a greater division with few positive results. The facts surrounding the "Culture of Death" make this assertion abundantly clear.

Division

The faithful have been set one against the other and have argued over many issues that do not matter. Each group believes it has a purer strain of truth, and is engaged in an attempt to defend the truth as they see it. Division occurs and the body is weakened. The most dangerous are those who proclaim unity but have their own agenda as they dissent interiorly. The result is a lifeless body. The gospel cannot be divided. The division leads to open battles where the sheep scatter, get lost, and are eaten up by wolves. Human pride has so deeply divided the Church, it shows with certainty that God's judgment is forthcoming. The Church is witnessing its Crucifixion and is now approaching the summit of Calvary. The warning of the Third Secret of Fatima confirms this. We are at the stage where Jesus is being stripped of His garments as scandals in every denomination are being exposed. No one seems immune to the apostasy. Without steadfast conviction and repeated demonstrations of love and humility, our Christian faith can never be in a superior position to maintain virtue, nor can it avoid corruption—let alone act as leaven in the world. No denomination is exempt from the institutional rot in our midst. All is laid bare for God and the rest of the world to witness.

Persecution

Relativism, rationalism, and every other type of 'ism' have caused truth and the Church to suffer. Government decrees and secularism have choked practically all religious piety out of the Church. The persecution was subtle at first, but recently the spirit of the world has so deeply infected the clergy that the salt has become stale, and their vitality has been paralyzed. Heresy, that is false doctrine, and apostasy, that is lost faith, deeply wound the present Church. It makes one think about Christ's scourging at the pillar. A believer is inclined to believe that, indeed, in the words of Pope Paul VI in 1972, the "smoke of Satan" has entered the Sanctuary of our Church. Contrary to many misquotations, it is the Sanctuary, not the Church that is threatened. There is a big difference. The enemies of the Church are operating at its summit. The Gospel is seldom heard as the clergy are fearful of offending the laity. Concerns of politically correct thinking and financial security inebriate the thinking of the corrupted in the Church hierarchy and deflect them away from their responsibility to be good shepherds. An intoxicating "feel-good" doctrine is preached instead, so no one is offended. Those who speak openly in a constructive but critical fashion are often put to pasture in the hinterlands. Within religious orders, many superiors marginalize those who attempt to learn sound Catholic tradition as part of their vocational development. In many seminaries, such aspiring postulants are indoctrinated thoroughly in modern theological error. When a seminarian questions or objects to such teachings he is dissuaded or encouraged to leave, if not outright evicted.

The result is a weak clerical institution in America with severely declining vocations and a divided laity. One segment increasingly looks to participate in priestly functions to dispel or ameliorate the growing anxiety associated with the lack of effective pastoral leadership and service. Accelerating the clergy's malaise is the growing publicity of occultism, homosexuality and pedophilia that has demoralized the faithful priests and alarmed the parishioners and civil authorities. As a result, the dioceses affected will see further loss of vocations and financial contributions. The state will intervene in Church affairs. Leaders of all faiths will be tried in secular courts.[2]

General Douglas MacArthur, the Supreme Commander of Allied Forces in the Pacific during World War II, recounted: "History fails to record a single precedent in which nations subject to moral decay have not passed into political and economic decline. There has been either a spiritual awakening to overcome the moral lapse, or a progressive deterioration leading to ultimate national disaster."[3]

The signs of evil around us are everywhere. The sign of some sort of divine intervention is in our midst. There is a flood of impiety, impurity, and incurable disease. Violence and hatred are exploding, misfortunes are occurring, wars and threats are spreading. It seems few can read the signs of the times. Anxiety and fear are in nearly every home, as people are victims of widespread sin. Through the means of social communication, experiences of life contrary to those indicated by God's holy law are being proposed to poor and defenseless children everywhere. Each day we are being fed with the poisoned bread of evil and given to drink of the polluted spring of impurity. Evil is shown to us and proposed as something good, sin as a value, and transgression of the law of God as a way of exercising autonomy and personal freedom. We are losing consciousness of sin as an evil, and injustice, hatred and impiety cover the earth and make it an immense desert, deprived of life and love.

Unless there is a change of heart in America, a very bloody ordeal will take place. The heart of Christ is pierced again and again. It is bleeding, transfixed with deep wounds, and immersed in a sea of sorrow. Mankind is spending days in a state of complete unawareness, indifference, and complete incredulity. Heaven has warned us with extraordinary signs, buried us with signs As God buried Israel, warned Israel, loved them and gave them the opportunity to repent.

The faithful are deeply wounded by a plague of infidelity and apostasy. As Saint Paul wrote, the day of the Lord will not be at hand until "the man of sin be revealed, the son of perdition, who opposes, and is lifted up above all that is called God, or that is worshipped, so that he sits in the temple of God, showing himself as if he were God" (2 Thessalonians 2:3–4). Complete and worldwide apostasy is making it possible for the son of perdition to emerge and rule. People will cry for security when disaster is widespread. On the surface, things look normal and calm with things running smoothly. Underneath the veneer of civility is a rage of discontentment. The lack of faith has spread the apostasy everywhere. What we see as Americans is actually on a worldwide basis. The loss of faith is on a universal basis. Those who believe fight for their families to remain faithful. The apostasy is not localized. The disunity and strife are everywhere.

The primary reasons for the loss of faith are: the spread of errors taught in seminaries and schools to the young, the open rebellion against the Magisterium of the Church in its splendor, and the bad example of pastors who have allowed themselves to be possessed by the spirit of the world and propagators of spiritual and sociological ideologies rather than be messengers of God—victim souls for the Gospel. When the Church reaches this stage, it must be purified by fire. Disunity, division, strife and antagonism are everywhere in the Church. The forces of atheism have infiltrated within it and are on the point of breaking up its interior unity and darkening the splendor of its sanctity. Satan has entered the very summit of the Church through willing souls who tear apart the defenseless. The heart of Heaven weeps because of the hardness of hearts so closed to the gospel message. Our roads will be smeared with blood while we live in obstinate unconsciousness.[4] "The Son of man, when he comes, shall he find faith on earth" (St. Luke 18:8)?

When Jesus walked the earth, it was only the humble of heart that could understand Who stood before them. It was all in Scripture, but the pride and hubris from a hardness of heart prevented the established church of Israel from accepting Him. Only a few found their way to Him Who had stature, including Nicodemus, the night apostle ventured out only under the cover of darkness, and Joseph of Arimethea who provided resources and a burial plot. At the foot of the Cross were only one apostle, John, plus a small remnant of women that included Mary, His mother. In difficult times those following Jesus remain few. As we walk away from the sun, our shadow lengthens, and our deepest needs become further obscured.

6

The Sins of Judgment

You stiff-necked and uncircumcised in heart and ears, you always resist the Holy Ghost: as your fathers did, so do you also. Which of the prophets have not your fathers persecuted?

—Acts 7:51–52

Now let's investigate the critical issue at hand. "If God is a merciful and loving God, then why do people suffer so much?" This is a question for the ages, and unless one sees with spiritual eyes, it's foggy at best. As much as part of the answer lies in the free will of man, the other half of the equation is that one must ask, "What does God want? What does God expect from us?" Why are nations judged? Yahweh says that He is the precipitator of wrath. Societies by the multiple hundreds have been judged by means of the voice of the prophets, weather, calamities, pestilence, and geophysical events of every kind. The anger was so great at one point a flood wiped out the world by water save a single family righteous before God. Sodom and Gomorrah suffered a similar fate by extinction.

The cycle of deterioration is progressive and steady, following the same steps generation after generation, since time began—which is the single thread weaving throughout this subject. It starts with the pride of man wanting to be independent and being rebellious toward a superior authority. If the rebellion continues over time, a hardness and callousness of heart develops where man feels it is best to rely on his own human instincts, doing that which is best in his own eyes. Then, the innocence of youth is lost and an independent spirit drifts away from a moral code.

Judaism had a moral code independent of the state. A ruling body of moral leaders called the Sanhedrin was the group enforcing a moral code. Yahweh gave the Jews 613 laws to live by, establishing the moral foundation for the existence of the state. With hubris and pride, the people of Israel were often disobedient, and God had His ways to rein them in. Sometimes they complied, other times the forceful means of military defeat was needed.

This is precisely why the Christian church operated so well for nearly eighteen centuries. A moral code of a higher calling asks its believers to comply with its system of order based on natural law and God's commandments, rather than consensus or compliance within a social confederation to an ever-changing set of secular rules. The state is simply a formal recognition of codified laws belonging to a social contract rooted in Judeo-Christian principles of justice and mercy. The recognition becomes institutionalized and gets its power from the voting elect. In such a society, the Church complements the state, guiding political leaders and the public-at-large. Given the fallen nature of man, the Church must take the added responsibility—at the risk of marginalization—of constructively criticizing the state, its leadership and the public, and if necessary take initiatives privately and publicly to curtail any injustice. This includes the establishment of the Church property as a 'sanctuary' for the oppressed, and encouraging civil disobedience and the demand for public penance where appropriate.

When society's morals are corrupted, man essentially ignores Church teachings and guidance, looking inward while using flawed reasoning. Contention develops between Church and State. The immoral society turns to the state as the remaining and only alternative means to provide satisfaction. Then the Church is persecuted. God sends His prophets. Man ignores the advice and the chastisement ensues.

In Sodom, as in other civilizations, the moral decay was simply due to rampant sin—a complete disregard for God. Whether we speak of previous civilizations or our own, nations perish for the same reasons. Whether through spewing ash, lava or fire, infesting the land with insects, shutting down the skies creating drought, or making a spear for battle from molten metal rather than wood, Heaven has its ways.

Possibly the most poignant example in the Old Testament about the destruction of a people is the story of Sodom and Gomorrah. Very early in the Scriptures we see the destruction of Sodom (Genesis 19), the home of a vile and wicked people. We know that homosexuality was so rampant that the men of the city stood outside the door of Lot's home and demanded the messengers of God be given over so they could have sexual relations with them. Even though Lot had daughters, the inhabitants of Sodom wanted the men. Lot offered his daughters because he knew his visitors were from God. In the history of mankind, Sodom is a graphic example of how a society becomes perverse. Yahweh speaks, "I will go down and see whether they have done according to the cry that is come to me: or whether it be not so, that I may know" (Genesis 18:21). So after the decision is made to destroy, Abraham has a nephew by the name of Lot in that city. Abraham stands before Yahweh and intercedes for the people and asks, "Will you destroy the just with the wicked? If there be fifty just men in the city, shall they perish withal? And will you not spare that place for the sake of the fifty just, if they be therein" (Genesis 18:23–24)? Then the boldness of Abraham is shown as he continues to negotiate the number down. Abraham, unsure of how just the people are, says, "Seeing I have once begun, I will speak to my Lord, whereas I am dust and ashes. What if there be five less than fifty just persons" (Genesis 18:27–28)?—then forty, then thirty, then twenty, and finally Abraham stops the negotiation at ten. The Lord said, "I will not destroy it for the sake of ten" (Genesis 18:32). Abraham then returned home. Only Lot, his wife, and two daughters left the city (Genesis 19:16). The two would-be sons-in-law who were to marry his daughters were invited, but thought that Lot was joking (Genesis 19:14). History shows it was no joke. So who knows the mind of God?

Ezechiel asks the Lord why He destroyed Sodom. He gives Ezechiel (16:49) five reasons:

> "Behold this was the iniquity of Sodom your sister, pride, fullness of bread, and abundance, and the idleness of her, and of her daughters: and they did not put forth their hand to the needy, and to the poor." Verse 50 continues by saying they "committed abominations before me: and I took them away as you have seen."

There is little left to the imagination as to why God destroyed Sodom. Psychotherapy can give us all sorts of niceties and verbal equivocations so the parties may not have to get too introspective, but the answer for sin is judgment.

A Nation's Moral Life Is the Foundation of Its Culture

As the root of debt is sensuality, the root of a homosexual lifestyle is idolatry—something other than God and in this form Baal and Asherah, other gods. The homosexual community can say whatever it likes, but homosexuality has been and always will be a perverse lifestyle. Over the last generation, homosexuals have influenced legislation to incrementally and surely become more of an accepted group. Hollywood has become their greatest friend, and the media—so infiltrated with homosexuals—pushes their agenda. Years ago, it was unthinkable for the state to allow homosexuals to adopt children. Year after year, television has assaulted families and made them think that if they do not accept the homosexual agenda, they are the ones who are extreme. Traditional families have been made to think they are the ones who are wrong. On March 13, 2002, *Prime Time* with Diane Sawyer interviewed Rosie O'Donnell. For two hours, ABC shoved the homosexual agenda at the American public. ABC is owned by Disney and Michael Eisner, who heavily promote the homosexual lifestyle through the media and entertainment. Eisner openly boasts of the great number of homosexuals on the Disney payroll. Again, the lie the American people are told is that this lifestyle is normal. It points back to the old adage, "Tell a lie often enough and people will believe it." This was a favorite tactic of tyrants like Lenin, Stalin, Hitler, and Mao to gain political acceptance.

Once a person leaves the worship of God and His commandments, there is a progressive drift to immorality, which ultimately ends up in perversity. Playing the sin all the way out, it ends up in death to others or ultimately death to self. No nation, culture, or church has a monopoly on these vices (as each denomination would like to believe about the other); they come in many shapes and forms and are universally a problem for mankind. Those who say that America is not a potential target for severe judgment as a result of idolatry are simply living an *Alice in Wonderland* existence totally devoid of a historical or scriptural reality. Looking at the data and social indices presented in other sections of this book, one should ask, "Does America deserve purification?" Are the terrorists hitting the Twin Towers and the Pentagon an example of an enemy being *allowed* by God to wake up America? To elaborate, the sins of Sodom were:

Pride

How much can be said, no beginning nor no end? As Proverbs 16:18 says, "Pride goes before destruction: and the spirit is lifted up before a fall."

All of mankind is subject to pride or self-conceit since the moment that Adam and Eve fell from grace. One particular aspect of this vice is that Christians are likely to recognize this failing in others, yet never see it in themselves. There is no vice in mankind which is more unpopular, yet so confused by its association in the affirmative sense with admiration and praise. The following is from what is considered one of the great works of C. S. Lewis—*Mere Christianity*. Lewis, the famous 20th Century author and professor of Medieval and Renaissance literature at Cambridge University, writes elegantly on pride, the greatest sin of man, which is the root cause of so many problems throughout the history of civilization.

In *Mere Christianity*, Lewis calls pride "The Great Sin." Christians typically identify pride as one of the "capital sins" which oppose virtues that help mankind grow in sanctification. Such a vice tends to lead to other and greater sins including avarice, envy, wrath, lust, gluttony, and sloth. C. S. Lewis affirms this view by noting that Christian teachings view pride as an "essential vice, the utmost evil...the complete anti-God state of mind."[1]

It was pride and self-conceit that corrupted many angels who became devils, because they viewed themselves as gods and refused to serve the Lord's will. Pride was the instrument of the serpent that convinced Adam and Eve that, "No, you shall not die the death.... You shall be as gods, knowing good and evil" (Genesis 3:4–5).

Pride, therefore, is covetous and driven by self-conceit. It never gets enough pleasure only in acquiring things. It is essentially competitive, causing great joy in having more than others have. There is a simple litmus test. C. S. Lewis suggests that if you want to find out how proud you are, simply ask yourself, "How much do I dislike it when other people snub me, or refuse to take any notice of me, or shove their oar in, or patronize me, or show off?" Each person's pride is in competition with every one else's pride. Jesus said, "Judge not, that you may not be judged, for with what judgment you judge, you shall be judged: and with what measure you mete, it shall be measured to you again. And why see you the mote that is in your brother's eye; and see not the beam that is in your own eye? Or how say you to your brother: Let me cast the mote out of your eye; and behold a beam is in your own eye? You hypocrite, cast out first the beam in your own eye, and then shall you see to cast out the mote out of your brother's eye" (St. Matthew 7:1–5). So, it is the comparison that makes us proud: the pleasure of being better than the rest. Whether it is wealth, intelligence, good looks, power, athletic ability, or whatever. As a result a proud man will look down on others and is incapable of seeing something that is above him. Pride makes us forget that whatever is good originates and belongs to the Creator. The things of which we so often boast are not ours, but God's. We so often consider ourselves better than our neighbor because of some talent, ability, or circumstance which God placed at our disposal. He could just as easily have given these things to those who are at present less gifted.

The Fullness of Bread

There would be two ways to look at this subject as God would view it. One would be a spiritual fullness, the other physical. Our fullness of bread is the filling of our appetites with secularism and the illusion of modernity and all of its comforts. In Revelation 2, Saint John is beginning to talk to the seven churches that have contemporaneous spirits in all Christendom. In Revelation 2:4, the first spirit of the church in error, the Lord says, is that "you have left your first love." When we leave our first fidelity, a nation fornicates. Destruction is now predictable. Take a good honest look around to see what occupies the time, expense, and energy of America, and be intellectually and emotionally honest in deciding if we measure up to a standard requested by God. Yes, we all fall short, but some nations fall shorter than others. Has the faith been passed from one generation to the next? Does the excessive smorgasbord of entertainment and the relentless and mad pursuit of pleasure crowd out a divine agenda? Yes, we are a generous nation to the rest of the world, however, our own fornication, pride and fullness of pleasure drives out much of the good. Yes, we left our first love breeding a society fostering the roots of violence. If there is violence in a mother's womb, would we not expect violence in our streets?

Idleness/Abundance

The youth today paint and pierce themselves because they have no purpose in life and thus amuse themselves with inane behavior. People who know why they are here, and who recognize their personal responsibilities, do not shave their heads in sculptured forms with eight different tints. Several months ago this author was with a husband and a wife in their late sixties lamenting the lack of spirituality of their children and grandchildren. The grandmother was amazed by what her daughter, now a middle-aged woman, didn't know. Over dinner, I listened as she blamed the parochial school system. It was obvious the party to blame was not a fifth grade school teacher, but her. The nursing ground of saints is the dining room table and she failed to teach them. The school system is an easy and visible target, but the primary responsibility of teaching the faith to children will always remain with the parents. There is no doubt the school system is broken, and often people in the Church have betrayed the trust of the people. But parents are to be the primary teachers. Television has not only made Americans obese, it has made us listless. People lament they don't have time to teach their children, but from 12:00 to 10:00 p. m. on weekends, they have time to watch sports, not to mention all the inane sitcoms during the week. America is spiritually lazy. If time is not used wisely, idleness can become a sin.

The youth today, pampered and spoiled way beyond any previous generation, are buried by the mass media and the entertainment industry in trite material idolizing false role models. Traditionally, the youth would aspire to be like their parents and other worthy heroes in society. Today, American youth have few role models worth aspiring to. With the breakdown of the family, and the encouragement of the media and entertainment industry, the youth look to the likes of the Beastie Boys, the Back Street Boys, Mariah Carey, Michael Jordan and Britney Spears to emulate. Pro sports and entertainment figures of every sort are viewed as gods of our age. With baseball players making $20 million a year, the emphasis in America is clearly on sports. Each sport has similar salaries in the millions per year. Judging by posters in the rooms of American kids, sports figures and rock stars are the idols of youth.

What follows is the accelerating decline of the moral character of an entire nation of youth soon to become adults. Data on the church, family, addictions, and other material show us where our affections are as well as how we spend our time. How we spend our time and what we spend our money on are good barometers of who we really are—as people and as a nation. Forgotten by the vast majority of Americans is the old adage, "The family that prays together stays together." Americans of every age have time for anything and everything, it seems—everything but prayer.

Neglecting the Needy and Poor

America is often generous in its charity, but for the wrong reason. Americans gave our proxy to the U. S. government to redistribute wealth, conditional on acceptance of secularism. No better example of the flaw in this method is the public funding and enforcement of contraception, family planning and abortion. The most poor and needy, the unborn, are worse than ignored—they are crucified on the cross of self-interest. The net effect is the Church is left with a substantial shortfall in charitable time and money. Along with a dramatic decline in church attendance, contributions are significantly down and per capita contributions are well below the guideline set for tithing, or from percentages of the previous generation. Exacerbating this financial chasm is the lack of substantial charitable time given by the laity to activities beyond church education and ministries.

A nation absorbed in feeding its own materialistic appetite finds little time for the needs of others. Persons living life with the view that other people are important will find time for the needy and the poor. They will find time for political causes demanding justice. People with a view of the Lord's kingdom being elsewhere will take this step in the journey more seriously. People need to become more important than creature comforts such as leather seats, a gourmet meal, and points shaved off a handicap. The proper balance of relaxation and recreation is necessary for peace of soul, but obsessions to the point of abdicating personal and spiritual responsibilities are another matter. When a person expresses a view of wanting prayer in the classroom, or God's presence in his life, the government steps in and enforces secularism—meaning no religion. On the other hand, sex education is taught down to the first-grade level in many schools, thus exposing children to things they can't handle at such an early age. This results in the loss of youthful innocence and corruption at an early stage of life. Secularism is a religion because it is a view of the world without the mind of God. A world devoid of God is the ideology of the antichrist and is in direct opposition to the gospel message. The way a nation helps those in need is an indication of its spirituality and faith.

A Closer Look at Pride—the Greatest Sin

As a pervasive and dimensional attribute of any capital sin, pride has extended its corrupt influence and its bad fruits beyond the individual to every family and nation since the world began. It is enmity. It is the spirit of rebellion. Pride violates the two greatest commandments of "loving God above all things, and your neighbor as thyself" by pitting man against God and man against man.[2]

Yet, how is it that people say they believe in God and appear to themselves and others to be very religious? Could it possibly be that they are worshipping an imaginary or false God? Such people convey a belief that they are nothing in the presence of this phantom god, yet they imagine with delight his approval and higher esteem of them versus the rest of mankind. They give a penny's worth of humility to their god and dump a ton's worth of pride on their fellow men. Some deluded souls, e.g. highest-level Masons, even believe that they will become "Ascended Masters", reincarnated or rulers of other worlds and kingdoms. Perhaps these are poor souls referred to by Christ as being able to cast out devils in His name, only to be told that at the Final Judgment He will say, "I do not know you." Whenever our religious life convinces us that we are better than our neighbor, rest assured that it is not God, but the devil, who has inspired us.

Whereas other vices are the devil's influence on our animal nature, pride comes directly from Hell. It was Satan's first choice to corrupt mankind in the Garden of Eden. Its roots are entirely spiritual. How often can you recall a parent, teacher, manager, or friend appeal to your pride or self-respect? Many poor souls have overcome a bad habit or attitude, believing such behavior is beneath their dignity. The devil revels in such misguided efforts. C. S. Lewis coins this demoniac strategy as the "Dictatorship of Pride." It is as if the devil is a medical charlatan who convinces you that he can cure your ills only to introduce terminal cancer into your soul. Rest assured that pride is a spiritual cancer, which consumes the very possibility of love, contentment or even common sense. Pride is devoid of trust in God and His mercy and justice. Pride not only causes envy for things others have, but ultimately despair in things that God denies.

We must be careful not to confuse pride with praise or warm-hearted admiration given appropriately to others as an instrument of giving legitimate recognition and pleasure. However, the more you delight in yourself and the less you delight in the praise, the worse you are becoming. This goes beyond vanity, which is a less severe form of pride. The vain person wants praise too much and is always angling for it. Yet, this is a childlike fault and shows that you overly value what others think of you. A vain person is not content with one's own admiration. You hit rock bottom when you look down on others and don't care what they think of you. To quote C. S. Lewis, "We must try not to be vain, but we must never call in our pride to cure our vanity; better the frying pan than the fire."

Fewer men are more difficult to reach than the talented man. It is easier to bring the gospel to a rich man and find reception than to a talented man. Why? Because a talented man feels in his heart that he doesn't need God to accomplish the things he wants. Operating successfully in the world, the talented man moves at ease and accomplishes many of his goals, adapting to the system of the world and all its rules, and feeling that God is not necessary in his life. He utilizes worldly principles in serving his own needs. A person of faith operates and seeks to redeem mankind by changing hearts. One good is temporal, the other good is eternal. If there is not an injection of faith into the talented man's life, that man in time will become more proud than any other and will often suffer more pain until he submits to God's will.

Faith is a gift to man that can be received or rejected with free will. For those without faith, answers are sought for human problems with human means. Not seeing with God's eyes, there is a general drift away from Divine perspective. For the spiritual man, answers are sought according to God's perspective. This is the culture war in our midst, manifested each and every day. Faith is like a muscle; if not used, it will atrophy and become useless. For those with faith, utilizing Divine wisdom and strength, more light is shed and they see the world more as God wants them to see it. The unseen world makes more sense to the man with faith. No explanation is necessary to the man with faith concerning the supernatural because he knows in his heart that God is alive and at work in the world.

We need to be cognizant that piety is a desired virtue that places the proper perspective on delight in praise. How is it that so few people pray for and desire piety? Is it that pride of one's heart prevents us from seeing the merits of piety? Can we distinguish correctly between the value of earthly riches and its human welfare versus sanctification and its eternal reward? Jesus said, "But seek you first the kingdom of God and his justice: and all these things shall be added unto you.... For where your treasure is, there will your heart be also" (St. Luke 12: 31 and 34).

It is the pride of man legislating what stood for centuries as good and virtuous. It is the pride of a secular humanist society thinking it has a better way to define a family than what God has ordained. Each year we build lie on top of lie to the point where families feel betrayed by authority figures in their lives. The ultimate sin of pride is thinking one is smarter than God. As we push God out, we come up with new definitions of perversity. Many people have felt helpless as this has been going on in all areas of their lives. Families have watched the old ways disappear. We continue to capitulate to contemporary thinking and trends that have removed God from the equation.

Today, our nations, families and souls need a deluge of humility. St. John Chrysostom said, "Would you like to see God glorified by you? Then rejoice in your brother's progress and you will immediately give glory to God. Because his servant could conquer envy by rejoicing in the merits of others, God will be praised" (Homily in Latin 71, 5, pp. 60 & 448). Or look at the song of praise (the Magnificat) by Mary, Jesus' mother, who says, "He has shown might in his arm: he has scattered the proud in the conceit of their hearts. He has put down the mighty from their seat, and has exalted the humble. He has filled the hungry with good things; and the rich he has sent empty away" (St. Luke 1:51–53). Only when we are brought down, can Christ raise us up. For the record we all know the final outcome. It is no accident that Jesus said, "Because every one that exalts himself, shall be humbled; and he that humbles himself, shall be exalted" (St. Luke 14:11).

Seven Things the Lord Hates

Proverbs 6:16–19 speaks emphatically with little doubt on where the Lord stands with pride. "Six things there are, which the Lord hates, and the seventh his soul detests: Haughty eyes, a lying tongue, hands that shed innocent blood, a heart that devises wicked plots, feet that are swift to run into mischief, a deceitful witness that utters lies, and him that sows discord among brethren." Notice the first point is haughty eyes—pride. Only when God breaks a man to where that man is willing and capable of saying, "Your will, not mine be done," can that man be used in the work of the kingdom of God. Jesus was able to pray the high-priestly prayer of St. John 17 because His will was submitted to the Father. He was willing to go to the Cross because of obedience to the will of the Father. Only in submission to the will of the Father were higher spiritual goals realized.

Similar circumstances of a man's will being broken surround Moses. Once in the court of Pharaoh as an educated, privileged and cultured man, Moses was sent into the desert for many years to change his focus. It took a desert experience to transform Moses, whom the Bible says was "the meekest on earth." "Meek" is another word for "humble," the opposite of "proud." People are much like a wild bronco horse until their will submits to a heavenly agenda. Until broken, they cannot be saddled or ridden. Once broken they can be used. Once broken they are still strong horses, but now capable of more things—more useful things. Moses, St. Paul, St. Peter and others still maintained their physical and intellectual gifts; they just decided to use them for a higher good when touched by Heaven. It takes a passion to cure a passion. It is the reason Saint Paul can one day be killing followers of Jesus, and soon after be His ardent disciple. It is the lukewarm and indifferent whom the Lord has trouble reaching. Would St. Paul have given so much to the world if Gamaliel had not tutored him? St. Paul's gifts become the property of Heaven rather than his own after acknowledging the presence of the living God on the road to Damascus. He ceased to be a nationalistic Hebrew, but became an apostle—a follower of Jesus who didn't see nationality in men, but men with souls.

One should shudder with fear for the United States of America with flags, placards, and signs on houses and cars everywhere saying "United We Stand," "These Colors Don't Bleed" and "Power of Pride," but with no repentance of our sins. Former New York City Mayor Ed Koch said only three days after the destruction of the Twin Towers, "We will build them bigger, stronger, taller." This is the hubris spoken of that is destructive. Graces simply will not come no matter how much we wave our flag. In no way is the material presented in this book a knock on U. S. sovereignty or its political system of government as envisioned by the framers of the Constitution. What it precisely does say is that if we continue down our godless path, we will have no future, no matter how many flags are unfurled. The Lord is not interested in seeing our passport at Heaven's gates; what He is intent on seeing is if we are obedient to what He asks us. The trash heap of recorded history is filled with the pride of nations. Obadiah 1:3–4 states, "The pride of your heart has lifted you up, who dwells in the clefts of the rocks, and sets up your throne on high: who says in your heart: Who shall bring me down to the ground? Though you be exalted as an eagle, and though you set your nest among the stars: from there will I bring you down, says the Lord."

National pride, cultural pursuits, and patriotism are all ingredients of proud nations in a positive sense, i.e. admiration. However, when there is an excess of the Yankee Doodle Dandy, the perspective is lost by that nation of who it is before the throne of God, Who grants favors on the people—His people. Cultural and national pride are healthy in the proper dose; a mixture of extreme pride and no repentance is explosive. This excessive pursuit or obsession by an individual, a people, and a nation represents a multi-threaded issue repeated throughout history that ultimately decides why we either prosper or perish. Americans think we are different, but we are not. This can be rationalized a thousand different ways, but history shows if a people worships something other than God alone, for He is a jealous God, it will move in incremental steps to worship Baal—any god—and slowly but surely to worship Asherah. Is the Lord impressed with our fiber-optic trans-Pacific cables, radio frequency communications, space travel, and a million other things? The answer is no, because first and foremost He came to change hearts. If He were interested in regal splendor, history may not have had Him born in a cow pen, a refugee in Egypt, and itinerant preacher for three years. It is for this reason that He never addressed politics the way the Jewish leaders of His day wanted. Our pride will be our undoing because we are consumed as a society with the secular and the physical. As the Lord said to Obadiah, "From there will I bring you down."

Submitting the Will

The name of God is holier and sweeter than any other name, and He is a God Who in His immeasurable love created mankind. With the Incarnation, man's lips were cleansed and able to rise to the kingdom of

God on earth. The kingdom of God is in hearts, in families, among citizens and nations. When asked, the believer is called to suffer and work and sacrifice for the Kingdom in the promise of eternal life. The earth is a mirror reflecting the life of Heaven in each individual. Centuries of tears and blood, of errors, persecutions, of darkness relieved by flashes of light radiating from the mystical light of the Church, have preceded where the kingdom will be restored to earth. The fidelity of God to those who are faithful is like a boat that can never be sunk: tossed around by the wind and surf on occasion, but "the gates of hell shall not prevail against it" (St. Matthew 16:18). That is God's promise.

The submission of one's will to the will of another person can be accomplished only when one reaches perfect love for that creature. The submission of one's will to God is achieved only when one acquires possession of the theological virtues to a heroic degree. In Heaven, where everything is faultless, God's will is done. The task of the believer is to create heaven on earth on an individual basis, thus creating harmony in the domestic church—the home. When peace is achieved, there is peace and justice in the society. The Lord is a loving God, and when living the commands asked for, you can "Ask, and it shall be given you: seek, and you shall find: knock, and it shall be opened to you" (St. Matthew 7:7).

Wherever there is a manifestation of life, God is present. When a man of God speaks to Him, when a holy sculptor sculpts, a holy poet breathes, a mother nurses her young, a farmer toils in the field, an animal moves, God is there as the author of it all. He comes for His own, in the rumble of the earthquake, or the peel of thunder, in the light of stars, in the flood tide and ebb tide, in the flight of the eagle—our mind is too finite to grasp the work of the Creator. All He has asked is for us to love Him.

Man is flesh, thus perishable due to his mortal body, but something in him is immortal. This is the consequence of the soul which is alive and present even in the pagans whose souls are famished longing for the true God whom they inherently know but choose to ignore. All civilizations experience some form of pagan worship, whether it be one of Roman pagan deities of worthless value or America in its obsession for human deification.

Yet, even the ignorant pagan whose simple statement, "I do not believe in God," presupposes another faith—in oneself, or perhaps in one's proud mind, but one always believes in something. It is like thinking. If you say "I do not want to think" or "I do not believe in God," by those two simple sentences you prove that you are thinking, and you do not want to believe in Him Whom you know to exist. With regards to man, to express the concept correctly one would say, "Man like an animal is born through the union of male and female." But the soul, which distinguishes the animal-man from the animal-brute, comes from God. The soul separates man from all other creatures. At the moment of conception in the womb, the Lord is stamping His signature of His likeness on that soul; otherwise, it would be an animal.

The soul's design is to know only God and His divine will exclusively. Through the misuse of free will, the soul's fall from Grace, that is Original Sin, introduced a competing alternative of wrong versus right with the devil being given authority to test all mankind. Consequently, the soul is subjected to three phases. The first is its creation, which is common to all men. The second is a new creation, which is a state of just people who by the Grace of God choose to elevate their souls to more completeness, joining their good works to the perfection of God's work. The third phase is the subjection of the flesh and ego that reaches a stage more in conformity to the will of God for a person's life. This is the life of a saint as they reach a state of perfection along the lines of the Gospel.

After the fall of Adam and Eve, God's mystical mercy offered a second chance for all mankind to experience. Few, if any, passages in Scripture better illustrate the thinking of the awesome grandeur and mercy of God than Job 38, 39 and 40. Job was tested in a way few men could handle. The Lord gave Satan an opening to test Job, as Satan argued the only reason Job was faithful was because he had been given wealth. Satan said that Job would curse God if his wealth were taken away. As Job was tested, he lost his cattle and sheep on a thousand hills, his children were stripped from him, and he was reduced to a body of boils. At the urging of his wife, who has no name in the story (Job's wife), Job is on the verge of cursing God. There is no language in all of Scripture where God talks to a man like this about the mysteries of the world.

Chapter 38: Then the Lord answered Job out of a whirlwind, and said: Who is this that wraps up sentences in unskillful words? Gird up your loins like a man: I will ask you, and you answer me. Where were you when I laid up the foundations of the earth? Tell me if you have understanding. Who has laid the measures thereof, if you know? Or who has stretched the line upon it? Upon what are its bases grounded? Or who laid the corner stone thereof, when the morning stars praised me together, and all the sons of God made a joyful melody? Who shut up the sea with doors, when it broke forth as issuing out of the womb: when I made a cloud the garment thereof, and wrapped it in a mist as in swaddling bands? I set my bounds around it, and made it bars and doors: And I said: Hitherto you shall come, and shall go no further, and here you shall break your swelling waves. Did you since your birth command the morning, and show the dawning of the day its place? And did you hold the extremities of the earth shaking them, and have you shaken the ungodly out of it?... Have you entered into the depths of the sea, and walked in the lowest parts of the deep? Have the gates of death been opened to you, and have you seen the darksome doors? Have you considered the breadth of the earth? Tell me, if you know all things? Where is the way where light dwells, and where is the place of darkness... Have you entered into the storehouses of the snow, or have you beheld the treasures of the hail: Which I have prepared for the time of the enemy, against the day of battle and war? By what way is the light spread, and heat divided upon the earth? Who gave a course to violent showers, or a way for noisy thunder... Who is the father of rain or who begot the drops of dew? Out of whose womb came the ice; and the frost from heaven who has gendered it?... Shall you be able to join together the shining stars the Pleiades, or can you stop the turning about of Arcturus? Can you bring forth the day star in its time, and make the evening star to rise upon the children of the earth? Do you know the order of heaven, and can you set down the reason thereof on the earth? Can you lift up your voice to the clouds, that an abundance of waters may cover you? Can you send lightnings, and will they go, and will they return and say to you: Here we are? Who has put wisdom in the heart of man? Or who gave the cock understanding? Who can declare the order of the heavens, or who can make the harmony of heaven to sleep? When was the dust poured on the earth, and the clods fastened together? Will you take the prey for the lioness, and satisfy the appetite of her whelps, when they couch in the dens and lie in wait in holes? Who provides food for the raven, when her young ones cry to God, wandering about, because they have no meat?

Chapter 39: ...Will you give strength to the horse, or clothe his neck with neighing?... He breaks up the earth with his hoof, he prances boldly, he goes forward to meet armed men.... Does the hawk wax feathered by your wisdom, spreading her wings to the south? Will the eagle mount up at your command, and make her nest in high places? She abides among the rocks, and dwells among cragged flints, and stony hills, where there is no access.

From there she looks for the prey, and her eyes behold afar off.... And the Lord went on, and said to Job: Shall he that contends with God be so easily silenced? Surely he that reproves God, ought to answer him. Then Job answered the Lord, and said: One thing I have spoken, which I wish I had not said: and another, to which I will add no more.

Chapter 40: And the Lord answering Job out of the whirlwind, said: Gird up your loins like a man: I will ask you, and do you tell me. Will you make void my judgment: and condemn me, that you may be justified? And have you an arm like God, and can you thunder with a voice like him? Clothe thyself with beauty, and set thyself up on high and be glorious, and put on goodly garments. Scatter the proud in your indignation, and behold every arrogant man, and humble him. Look on all that are proud, and confound them, and crush the wicked in their place. Hide them in the dust together, and plunge their faces into the pit. Then I will confess that your right hand is able to save you....

Who can speak and have anything important to say? Where is the eloquence of Churchill, the rampage of the marching machine of Napoleon, where are Pol Pot, Stalin, Lenin, Marx, Alexander Graham Bell, Mao Tse-tung, Hitler, George Washington, Thomas Jefferson, Hamilton, Benjamin Franklin, Socrates, Pericles, Caesar, Alexander the Great, Roosevelt, Louis XIV, Columbus, and on and on? In the end all are bit players on a world stage reserved only for the Creator. No person before or after will play the role of God Who alone can say, "Where were you when I laid up the foundations of the earth?... Who shut up the sea with doors?... Did you since your birth command the morning, and show the dawning of the day its place" (Job 38:4, 8, 12)? For over one hundred and twenty verses, Yahweh "beholds every high thing, he is king over all the children of pride" (Job 41:25). The mysteries of life and the universe are asked of Job, and he does not have a single answer. "Where were you?" "Have you entered into the storehouses of the snow" (Job 38:41)? Question after question and no answers. None. The proud are reduced to the moronic in the presence of Grandeur. No man can dialogue or answer Divinity. The secrets of the universe are secret to the proud, but the humble know their origin, "that no flesh should glory in His sight" (1 Corinthians 1:29).

Faith: The Glue of Civilizations

Faith is the glue that holds it all together. Although the rich do not think they need faith because of their creature comforts, in the end they succumb as all others. To the poor, faith is often all they have to grasp onto. Faith has been the elixir of all mothers wanting to instill a morality, starting with melodies and stories in the crib. "It has conferred meaning and dignity upon the lowliest existence, and through its sacraments has made for stability by transforming human covenants into solemn relationships with God. It has kept the poor (said Napoleon) from murdering the rich. For since the natural inequality of men dooms many of us to poverty or defeat, some supernatural hope may be the sole alternative to despair. Destroy that hope, and class war is intensified. Heaven and utopia are buckets in a well: when one goes down the other goes up; when religion declines communism grows."[3] Democracy only works when the people decide to abide by a higher moral law. It is for this reason communism of Russia, China and everywhere this doctrine was promulgated and enforced, was under suppression and the barrel of a gun. Because Christianity was of another world, all men were subject to her laws. Kings had moral responsibilities higher than any written with the ink of a temporal power. The divine right of kings from King David on down was subject to sack cloth and ashes under the watchful eye of a clergyman. The Order of Melchisedech, to which Abraham paid tithes, moved to the Levites of Israel and on to the successors of Peter.

Puritanism and Paganism in History

"Puritanism and paganism—the repression and the expression of the senses and desires—alternate in mutual reaction in history. Generally religion and puritanism prevail when the laws are feeble and morals must bear the burden of maintaining social order; skepticism and paganism (other factors being equal) progress as the rising power of law and government permits the decline of the church, the family, and morality without basically endangering the stability of the state. In our time the strength of the state has united with diabolical forces to relax faith and morals, and to allow paganism to resume its natural sway. Probably our excesses will bring another reaction; moral disorder may generate a religious revival; atheists may again (as in France after the debacle of 1870) send their children to Catholic schools to give them the discipline of religious belief. Hear the appeal of the agnostic Renan in 1866:

Let us enjoy the liberty of the sons of God, but let us take care lest we become accomplices in the diminution of virtue which would menace society if Christianity were to grow weak. What should we do without it?... If rationalism wishes to govern the world without regard to the religious needs of the soul, the experience of the French Revolution is there to teach us the consequences of such a blunder.[4]

"Does history warrant Renan's conclusion that religion is necessary to morality—that a natural ethic is too weak to withstand the savagery that lurks under civilization and emerges in our dreams, crimes, and wars? Joseph de Maistre answered: 'I do not know what the heart of a rascal may be; I know what is in the heart of an honest man; it is horrible.'[5] There is no significant example in history, before our time, of a society successfully maintaining moral life without the aid of religion. France, the United States, and some other nations have divorced their governments from all churches, but they have had the help of religion in keeping social order."[6]

The above quote about the heart of a rascal and an honest man is similar to the quote in Scripture which says that in the heart of man dwells no good thing. All men are enslaved to Original Sin and can only rise above a life of animal instinct by the grace of God, faith, and the mastery of the will. A theme throughout the Scripture passages cited in this book is how civilizations rise and fall. In their rise and fall emerges a warlike nature. "War is the ultimate form of competition and natural selection in the human species. Peace is an unstable equilibrium, which can be preserved only by acknowledged supremacy or equal power. The causes of war are the same as the causes of competition among individuals: acquisitiveness, pugnacity, and pride; the desire for food, land, materials, fuels, mastery. The state has our instincts without our restraints."[7] "Even a philosopher, if he knows history, will admit that a long peace may fatally weaken the martial muscles of a nation. In the present inadequacy of international law and sentiment a nation must be ready at any moment to defend itself; and when its essential instincts are involved it must be allowed to use any means it considers necessary to its survival."[8] As a nation becomes belligerent towards another, defense is necessary as it is weak nations that are invaded, conquered, and occupied. Are the cracks in American walls becoming more apparent to rogue nations?

The Enemy inside the Gates

Recall the curse of foreign ownership of business cited earlier from Deuteronomy. An example of democracy in excess is what the Chinese government was recently able to accomplish by purchasing Global Crossing from bankruptcy. One should note with concern the January 28, 2002, announcement that Hutchinson-Whampoa Limited and Singapore Technologies Pte, Ltd., plan to invest $750 Million in Global Crossing for a majority stake in the company. This is on the heels of Global Crossing recent Chapter 11 bankruptcy filing and restructuring efforts. The concern ought to be the strategic capability that a modern, worldwide fiber optic network with international and intra-national cross-connect Points of Presence (PoP) presents to the People's Republic of China (P. R. C.). Hutchinson-Whampoa, a corporation that already has the exclusive managing rights to the Panama Canal, which is a choke point for trade in the Americas, and that has been shown to be directed in part by the Army of the People's Republic of China, now has global telecommunications access to major international cities and their surrounding secondary and tertiary local markets. This includes not only all the major commercial and financial/banking centers but most of the major western government capitals. For example, according to Global Crossing's web site, its infrastructure includes over 26 international network landing points or interconnects between countries including but not limited to six cities in the U. S. (Los Angeles, New York, Seattle, Washington, D. C., Miami and San Diego), and five European cities (Amsterdam, Brussels, London, Copenhagen, Dublin) as well as numerous international interconnects in Southeast Asia (including Peking), Central and South America and the Caribbean. Connected to these international exchanges are over 140 additional PoP's worldwide with interconnection agreements within the local countries. These PoP's include, but are not limited to Boston, Chicago, San Francisco, Houston, Tokyo, Seoul, Manila, Frankfort, Milan, Paris, Madrid and Stockholm. Global Crossing claims that it serves the world's largest corporations, providing a full range of managed data and voice products and services with the world's first integrated Internet Protocol-based network reaching over 200 major cities worldwide. Nowhere is it mentioned that the acquisition is under scrutiny of the U. S. Government for national security reasons. Layer on top of this telephony network the Chinese Academy of Sciences' pursuit on behalf of the military of a strategic software programming competencies that includes building software program viruses which could be launched over its global network and selectively injected into western civilization's government, telecommunications and commercial/financial systems via its interconnect agreements with those countries. In the event of a confrontation with China, this could present a potentially devastating strategic blow to the U. S. and any other western nation that would be fighting the P. R. C.

Will the demise of the U. S. be immediate? Probably not, as it could take some time to bring down a superpower like the U. S., because if we fall, a lot of nations will go with us due to the interdependence of the world economy. The Scriptures quoted in this book show that the Lord can use a boy with a slingshot or plagues of weather to "raise up" or "bring down" a nation. Is the case of Global Crossing and China a particular threat like the Trojan Horse inside the gates? Is it corrupt politics inviting disaster? Terry McAuliffe, head of the Democratic National Committee, parlayed a $100,000 investment into $18 million, as a result of his efforts to smooth the way for China's involvement. Global Crossing gives the Chinese access to what could be considered our central nervous system in the U. S. with its network capability. With China in control of this, the damage they could do to U. S. communications and our military's command and control network is unbelievable. They can hack into U. S. corporations to wage industrial sabotage. In fact, in April 2002, the CIA released a previously classified report stating that U. S. intelligence analysts had become increasingly convinced that communist authorities in Peking were actively planning to damage and disrupt U. S. computer systems through the use of internet hacking and computer viruses. The report warned that this is, indeed, China's goal.[9]

The sad truth is that the corrupt U. S. government leadership, in cooperation with the military-industrial complex, has provided the P. R. C. with intellectual property far more strategic than Global Crossing's telecom network. This includes turning a blind eye on industrial espionage and the licensing of technologies regarding our W-88 missile during the first Bush presidency and our latest generation of Multiple Independent Re-entry Vehicle (MIRV) ballistic missiles under the Clinton Administration. To say America has fallen asleep is an understatement. When a country is disobedient, its downfall can be from any direction. In the near and long terms, China, like Russia, will be a threat to the United States.

What Is a Nation?

"Civilization is defined as 'social order promoting cultural creation.' It is political order secured through custom, morals, and law, and economic order secured through a continuity of production and exchange; it is cultural creation through freedom and facilities for the origination, expression, testing, and fruition of ideas, letters, manners, and arts. It is an intricate and precarious web of human relationships, laboriously built and readily destroyed."[10]

No matter the knowledge and expectations of the reader, all would agree that civilizations preceding ours had a beginning and an end. Greece, Rome and others show this as they progress in time, and as they near the end, a moral code is no longer capable of being enforced. In times of threat to a nation, the single biggest contributor to its ongoing growth and peaceful existence is the raising up of good leaders. There are many examples of this in Scripture, and it is God's grace to send prophets to warn the people and bring a person of such stature who can turn around the present course of events. One such example is the shepherd boy, David, facing a Philistine. It was clearly Yahweh who saved Israel. A boy with a slingshot is no match for a giant warrior. It is people of virtue who alter history. Although all men have feet of clay, it was men like Churchill who saved England. Charlemagne's courage made Europe Christian, and the Holy Roman Empire was proclaimed in the year 800. People who make daring decisions against public sentiments do simply what is right and let the consequences follow. Challenges are met with equal or greater force than evil. Illustrating Jesus' words, "You are the salt of the earth" (St. Matthew 5:13), it has been the believer in a higher moral code that has saved nations from falling. The rise and fall of nations is directly proportionate to the action of its leaders. Would the American Civil War have turned out differently if Abraham Lincoln had stayed a country lawyer? The United States of America should shudder at its pride in thinking that its salvation is based upon political social agendas, and reliance on public education policies. America will be good when it seeks the mind of God in obedience to the commandments. We have drifted very far from the vision of what made America great. We are so educated in secular formulas we have become simply a dumb nation spiritually. We are scripturally illiterate as a society. Our spirituality has become a state religion as most fall into conformity with political correctness.

Woe to the person who calls sin for what it is. Woe especially if it is a teacher in a public classroom who disciplines and is not sensitive to a student's rights. We have today acronyms such as HDT, ADD, ADHT, and a psychological alphabet of clinical terms. There are times for drugs, but the spread of drugs is largely due to a lack of discipline in the home and thus the nation. Common sense is no longer commonly found. The U. S. and the West are now trapped as they move from one ideology to the next—on all fronts. Since we have abandoned the Ten Commandments, a *potpourri* of philosophies prey on the nation. As we restlessly succumb to pampering youth with $40,000 SUV's, tens of thousands in personal debt, exorbitant credit, and families mortgaged to the hilt on liberal terms, there is an anxiety in people and families. The more we have, the more we are unhappy. Never in history has anyone ever lived like an American sitting in the hot tub drinking wine in an air-conditioned home, draining 26 percent of the world's resources.

A small remnant fights to stay in fidelity to the faith. That group swims against a strong current daily to maintain those views and lifestyle. With abundance comes a selfishness to have more. The problem with more in an imaginative soul is that more is never enough. Governments, like people, are no different. In selfishness, governments issue decrees that in time squelch fortitude and hope even in the faithful remnant because of fear of governmental reprisals. Big government crushes those it was meant to serve. In time, laws designed to rule the masses conquer the spirit of the nation and kill private initiative.

Is the United States in decline? The answer is unequivocally yes. Will we perish from the earth quickly? It is equally likely that America will die from within due to moral decay as it will from outside. Who knows, perhaps a combination of the two will bring chaos and defeat to our nation. It appears that unless things change dramatically for the better and soon, we are destined to play a less dominant role in the future. Perhaps another power will be our master in spirit, or overcome us with foreign troops; possibly the demise of our economy combined with a series of severe natural disasters will cause a national calamity making us irrelevant to the rest of the world. America's destiny depends on the leadership of our elected officials, the Church hierarchy, and the faithfulness of believers. It should also be kept in mind that a nation deserves the leaders it elects. Polls determine votes in the Congress. Due to the excesses of our democratic republic, it likely would take fascism and more strident and binding laws to govern the U. S. in the future. Unfortunately, power tends to corrupt those it touches. America has grown fat and content and does not maintain a proper and sensible militancy for its faith. Anything in excess ironically soon becomes its opposite. Our freedoms misapplied with irresponsibility have made us soft and unwilling to sacrifice for what is noble and good. Alexis de Tocqueville once said that when he searched for what then made America great, he found it in her churches. As St. John Bosco said, "The power of evil men exists and lives on the cowardice of the timid and the good." So, if America is living with little to no faith, what can it expect in the future?

The Culture of Death

Men either choose to be governed by God, or condemn themselves to be ruled by tyrants.

Is there possibly one great area that makes judgment inevitable? If so, it would be the murder of the innocent unborn. Before dismissing this subject as hopeless and annoying, consider the following bet and related questions: Are you prepared to bet your eternal soul that God does not care whether man intervenes in His creation and murders an unborn child? If God does care, would He not hold every indifferent soul on earth accountable as those who promote, enforce and execute abortions? Is not the infinite loss of eternal happiness worth an ounce of time and effort—call it insurance if you wish—to discern God's will in this matter?

The legal reasoning and arguments about abortion are over. No one is swayed by a legal opinion over whether the unborn child is a glob of tissue or a real person made in the image and likeness of God at the moment of conception. "Before I formed you in the bowels of your mother, I knew you..." (Jeremiah 1:5). Despite the apathy of many regarding this subject, there is no one on the fence anymore on this issue. You are either for or against abortion—no one is intellectually or emotionally neutral. The camps are stridently divided. If a child was twelve years old in 1973 when *Roe v. Wade* was signed into law, which legalized abortion on demand in the U. S., he or she would now be over forty-one years old. Beginning with that generation, children have been raised while being thoroughly indoctrinated with promiscuous ideas and behavior devoid of Christian ideals and virtues—all the while living with the terrible knowledge that they, too, might have been legally aborted had their parents considered them unwanted or inconvenient. Such a fundamental insecurity on the part of so many young people cannot help but have a profoundly negative influence on society's morals and values. For that whole generation, abortion has been the way (or more properly, the most common end to life) of life in the U. S. Until mankind understands that God is the author of life, and that babies are gifts, there will always be division between spiritual and natural man. The responsibility, the primary role, of husband and wife is to turn their children back to the Lord as men and women of God. Faith and reason make good citizens in any country.

The exercise of personal freedom has become paramount for people, especially young adults, who know no moral boundaries. Thus, sexual promiscuity legitimizes as good the sins of impurity. The consciences of even little children see nothing wrong with the profane, in which a relationship before marriage is perceived as licit and good. The complete justification and the exaltation of impure acts against nature are promulgated in laws that even put homosexual cohabitation on a par with marriage. Movies, television, and Hollywood throw the homosexual agenda at us daily so as to make this thinking mainstream and "politically correct." The rainbow of tolerance for homosexuals, and the fact that the public outcry is largely over, would indicate that the diabolical agenda has established a place of normalcy and acceptance in society.

The very taproot of this disease is contraception. The pill allowed generations of people to abandon the responsibility of thinking of what the marital act is before the eyes of the Creator. The contraceptive mentality opened the door for multiple partners with no responsibility to the sacrament of marriage, which recognizes marriage as a covenant with God. The unitive and procreative act is the literal signature of the covenant where the personality of God can be seen on a human level. The transmission of life is God's thumbprint on humanity. In Satan's finest hour, he has gone right into the sanctuary of grace and ripped out God's creation. Evil has created a widespread swath where from the time of infancy the media has programmed our youth that this type of behavior is acceptable. Young people reason that if something is legal it must be all right. Many of the ranking clergymen of today bought the lie of contraception years ago, and the fruits are the blank faces staring back at them from the pews. That same group is having to deal with the fruit of that belief in scandals today, partly because contraception has drastically cut the size of families from which good priests would have come. Undesirable candidates were thus admitted into clerical ranks, their permissive ways of thinking have caught up with them.

Once the innocence of the individual is violated by a perverse interpretation of God's law, the sexes know no bounds. The latency period of youth has been ruthlessly stripped away, and sex becomes more distorted and perverted. With schools and parents dispensing birth control pills to children, it was inevitable that abortion would follow. Euthanasia was the next stop on the train once countries like the Netherlands legalized it, followed by liberal laws in others. The

ABC Evening News reported on April 1, 2002, that euthanasia was fully legalized in the Netherlands parliament, although it had been tolerated for decades before that. Doctors kill an estimated 20,000 people directly or indirectly each year (estimates are approximately 4,000–5,000 through lethal injection). It is not surprising that 50 to 60 percent of people polled in a recent study in the Netherlands were afraid that their lives would be ended against their own will. Ninety-five percent of those living in nursing homes believe they will die of euthanasia without their permission.

The moral slide and encroachment of euthanasic thinking has increased on U. S. shores. On April 17, 2002, a federal judge ruled that the Bush Administration lacked authority to overturn a voter-backed Oregon law permitting physician-assisted suicide. Attorney General John Ashcroft was accused of usurping states rights. *The Brave New World* of Huxley is more commonplace universally than is publicly acknowledged. Following the bread trail of logic, cloning is the next step, followed by designer babies and still more wicked doings of man. For those who do not see the progression of evil, there is a numbness, if not cold-heartedness, to long-standing spiritual truths that will outlive all of us.

The tendency of the believer is to give up. If anything, however, now is the time to fight. It's easy to be saint when a bike can be left on the front lawn unattended. Years ago, car keys could be left in the ignition in suburban communities. Doors didn't need to be locked. Kids could stay out past dark and parents would have no fear. Now they are rare parents who will even let their young children walk a short distance to school. The fear is greatly justified. How many times have you heard from older people, "I'm glad I'm not bringing up my children today. The country where I was brought up is gone." The system of order, the civility of the neighborhood, and the safe refuge of the church have all disappeared. Father O'Malley of *The Bells of Saint Mary's* and *Going My Way* was very typical of the American clergyman. In 1947, 70,000 *men* marched in the Holy Name Parade in Boston. It ended up in Fenway Park for Benediction. Men crowded the stands, the infield and adjoining streets in a public display of faith. Where did all this go? What happened? Everyone knows there is something dreadfully wrong, but no one can seem to put his finger on it. Many older people refuse to believe that the Church and schools are in such a state of decay. People were taught from the time of their birth that the Church was supposed to be safe. The reason few can believe what is going on is that it was carried out according to the diabolical plan of Antonio Gramsci: Infiltrate from within, say anything necessary, and destroy. The destruction of order over a deliberate period of time was planned, it didn't just happen.

The person of faith must begin to connect these dots to create a new image to discover the truth. The issue of abortion with its carnage is just another example of the suffering and pain around us. The system failed many people because it went through a frontal attack bent on enslaving America to socialism. Inch by inch, everything is a cinch. The kneelers are removed from churches, statues and other images of the saints are taken away, and then the tabernacle is off in another room. Abortion is simply a symptom of a nation without faith. The assault on life was virtually unthinkable years ago. Even for leading feminists like Susan B. Anthony it was not an issue to be challenged. Our culture of death has evolved incrementally.

Thousands of religious left the Catholic Church in the mid-1960's, and the Roman collar was replaced with a Nehru jacket and a ponytail. In 1977, Communion in the hand was heavily pushed on the laity. One summer people were told it wasn't permissible, and next people were told by their pastors to do it. Why the change? In 1994, altar girls were pushed in the Catholic Church in America, yet there was no approval from Rome. One pastor said no to something, and yes to another. In a parish a mile away people heard the exact opposite. Confusion was everywhere—and it has become worse. The battles rage in seminaries and rectories across America. The result is that the believer in the pew doesn't know which way to go on a myriad of issues. Orthodox priests with traditional views and liberal bishops over them have had the worst of it. For example, when priests have spoken out against voting for pro-choice candidates, they have often found themselves reassigned to remote parishes. So, on a litany of issues, priests have ceased to speak out, especially in the face of vocal parishioners who refused to obey Church positions on moral issues. Keeping their mouths shut became the "safe" way for many priests, especially when their bishops would not back them up, and might very well even castigate them for speaking the truth. Truth became silent. The culture of death thus had fertile soil in which to germinate and flourish.

The issue of abortion, like it or not, will not go away because it is the gravest moral issue of our day. What the Dred Scott decision symbolized to slavery is what Roe v. Wade decision symbolizes to abortion: The institution of a national sin. America in its early formative years was reluctant if not hostile to the abolition of slavery. Every U. S. president since George Washington knew that eventually slavery must be faced head on at some point. Courageous people, abolitionists, confronted the obvious flaw in our national character and like pro-life groups today, fought aggressively for change, and offered help to the enslaved while warning of the consequences if this evil was not corrected. All presidents prior to Abraham Lincoln ducked and successfully evaded the issue. A man who signed his name simply "A. Lincoln" met the political and moral challenge which divided a nation.

Our concerns should by no means be limited to the question of abortion and judicial activism, yet the abortion license is at the very core of the disordering of our liberty. In 1992, the Supreme Court, in its decision of Planned Parenthood vs. Casey, expanded the legal ground for the abortion license from an implied right of privacy to an explicit liberty right under the 14th Amendment. This sweeping redefinition of liberty ignores the right to define one's own concept of existence, and the meaning of the universe and of the mystery of human life. This decision reinforces the new tolerance belief that there are no absolute truths, with liberty being defined as nothing more than what is chosen by the autonomous, unencumbered self. Because they believe in no absolute truths, people go along with a person like Senator Ted Kennedy when he says, "I personally oppose abortion, but I respect the right to choose." Such a warped viewpoint only becomes possible and widely supported in a country that no longer accepts the basis of absolute truths.

At the 1992 Democratic National Convention in New York City, Pennsylvania Governor Robert Casey, Sr., was invited to give a speech. Pennsylvania ranks fifth in the Electoral College with 23 votes. As the convention platform went pro-homosexual and lesbian, Governor Casey was disinvited because he was a pro-life Democrat. In his place, an openly lesbian San Francisco County Supervisor was asked to give the platform speech. The message is clear: A candidate can't go anywhere in the Democratic Party and be pro-life.[1] Many times the Republican Party has been little better; while it officially claims to be pro-life, it frequently ignores or downgrades the concerns and priorities of the pro-life movement. America has had a vacuum of leadership on the hierarchical level. The role of the Church is to govern and determine the direction of culture, not the other way around. Where bad laws exist, if necessary, public non-violent disobedience needs to be organized and executed en masse as our modern day version of "sack cloth and ashes."

God will not be ignored or blasphemed. Given the commandment that "You shall not kill," we must assume that this most fundamental flaw of our national character is a 'litmus test'—not before a court of law but before the eyes of God. Whether many agree or not, we as

Christians are obliged to pursue democratic deliberations and decisions that protect the most defenseless group of our society. This is a Supreme and Natural law of God rather than an intellectual argument of man. We are morally, ethically and legally bound to correct this abomination before God, or else His Justice will strike exactly as it has done so many times in history. Such effort must be peaceful and constitutional, yet relentless.

Humanae Vitae and the Legacy of the Pill

It is a sad situation which exists in the world, let alone America, that Christians, especially many clerical and lay Catholics, are ignorant, indifferent or critical of the late Pope Paul VI's instructional and prophetic *Humanae Vitae* (Of Human Life). The Magisterium of the Roman Catholic Church knew full well that growing public acceptance of the philosophies of modernity and secularism would ultimately lure mankind to the delusion that it is acceptable, "even for the gravest reasons, to do evil that good may come of it," or as Pope Paul VI communicated in his encyclical on the regulation of birth, "in other words, to intend directly something which of its very nature contradicts the moral order, and which must therefore be judged unworthy of man, even though the intention is to protect or promote the welfare of an individual, of a family or of society in general."

He prophetically warned mankind in July of 1968 that the consequences of artificial methods of birth control "...could open wide the way for marital infidelity and a general lowering of moral standards. Not much experience is needed to be fully aware of human weakness and to understand that human beings—and especially the young, who are so exposed to temptation—need incentives to keep the moral law, and it is an evil thing to make it easy for them to break that law. Another effect that gives cause for alarm is that a man who grows accustomed to the use of contraceptive methods may forget the reverence due to a woman, and, disregarding her physical and emotional equilibrium, reduce her to being a mere instrument for the satisfaction of his own desires, no longer considering her as his partner whom he should surround with care and affection."

How prophetic indeed! Planned Parenthood, the pharmaceutical industry, doctors, and lawyers with a willing American public, collectively surrendered—as Pope Paul VI warned—"into the willing hands of public authorities the power to intervene in the most personal and intimate responsibility of husband and wife."

Outlined below is a brief history of some of the important events and milestones related to the growing public acceptance and government intervention for the use of oral contraceptive pills:

- In 1951, Margaret Sanger, founder of the International Planned Parenthood Federation (I. P. P. F.), convinced Katharine McCormick, the multi-millionaire daughter-in-law of Cyrus McCormick, inventor of the mechanical reaper, to finance Dr. Gregory Pincus, a research scientist of minor notoriety to the total sum of over $2 million to invent an oral contraceptive pill.[2]

- By 1956, Dr. Pincus began field tests of norethynodrel birth control pills in Brookline, Massachusetts, Haiti and Puerto Rico.[3]

- By 1961, 500,000 American Women were taking the pill. In 1962 the U. S. Federal Drug Administration ("FDA") approved the contraceptive drug, norethindrone.[4]

- The number of American women using the pill doubled year after year to four million by 1964.[5]

- In 1965, the U. S. Supreme Court struck down a Connecticut law that prohibited the use of contraceptives (*Griswold v. Connecticut, 381 U. S. 479, 1965*). This case was cited by the consenting opinion of the U. S. Supreme Court in the *Roe v. Wade* case, declaring that "personal, marital, familial, and sexual privacy said to be protected by the Bill of Rights or its penumbras..."[*Consenting Opinion (V), Roe, Et Al. v. Wade, District Attorney of Dallas County, 410 U. S. 113 (1965)]*

- By 1969, 7.5 million American women were taking the pill.

- By 1973, ten million American women were taking the pill.[6]

- By the mid-1980's, given concerns of serious side effects or longer term ailments and the successful commercial introduction of alternative pessary, for example vaginal suppositories, the diaphragm and the Inter-Uterine Device, the number of American women taking the pill declined to 8.4 million.

- In 1992, Pharmacia and Upjohn introduced an injection alternative, Depo-Provera. According to James Trussell, director of the office of population research at Princeton University, government statistics show that 7.9 percent of women between the ages of fifteen and nineteen use Depo-Provera and 3.9 percent of women between the ages of 24 and 29.

- As of the year 2001, approximately 10.7 million American women were using the pill. It is considered the most popular method of non-surgical contraception.

- According to pharmaceutical industry data, the U. S. market for Oral Contraceptives for the twelve-month period ending September 2000 is about $2.25 Billion. This compares to $1.92 Billion in 1999 or a 16.4 percent year over year growth.[7]

- Just prior to the 2002 Winter Olympic games, news articles appeared documenting how some female athletes prepare for important sport events months in advance by getting pregnant, typically by their coach, and aborting the unborn baby two to three months into the term. This practice avoids the use of illegal drugs, stimulating the woman's body to produce additional hormones that could improve her performance.

At today's medical schools rarely does a graduating class of medical doctors take the Hippocratic Oath. It is obvious that doctors, particularly Christian doctors, have ignored the advice to stay resolute in their faith and "endeavor to fulfill the demands of their Christian vocation before any merely human interest." Can it be that their impoverished moral upbringing and corrupted beliefs make them uncomfortable with the following words?

"I will give no deadly medicine to any one if asked, nor suggest any such counsel; and in like manner I will not give to a woman a pessary to produce abortion. With purity and with holiness I will pass my life and practice my Art.... While I continue to keep this Oath unviolated may it be granted to me to enjoy life and the practice of the Art, respected by all men, in all times. But should I trespass and violate this Oath, may the reverse be my lot."

The youth today have seen the medical profession not only abandon ethics and morality, but completely abandon faith as well. One could also question fortitude of the clergy who have chosen to remain silent. Is it a wonder that the youth today lack role models and direction? In the Old Testament, Yahweh held the Levites accountable when society experienced a downward spiral. It is the job of the clergy to speak the truth and lead the politicians and the people. Politics is of the temporal order, the Gospel is not.

The effects of the introduction of the birth control pill are far more devastating than even that of tobacco. Like tobacco companies, proponents of the pill, including Planned Parenthood and the pharmaceutical industry, ignore or hide damaging evidence from public scrutiny for fear of the consequences. Tobacco companies laced cigarettes with ammonia and other chemicals to induce a soothing feeling in the brain and make addiction more likely. They also knew that cigarettes caused cancer. Not only does the birth control pill cause cancer and infertility, it is the single largest contributing factor to the destruction of the family and the nation.

With America's acceptance of the pill the fear of pregnancy dramatically declined and a Pandora's Box opened American society to all forms of sexual perversion and fornication. Not surprisingly, marital infidelity and cohabitation became commonplace, while divorces tripled. *Penthouse*, *Playboy* and *Hustler* magazines came into vogue. The invention of the VCR tape, the internet and the broad commercial success of cable services, accelerated the introduction of graphic pornography into the family home. The Supreme Court of the United States approves of contraception and abortion, the latter being the final protector of selfish promiscuity—at the cost of the murder of tens of millions of innocent children. Meanwhile, traditional family life breaks down. One-parent families or cohabiting adults, including same sex partners, view the traditional family life as antiquated or insufficient. Groups like the United Nations have introduced language in official documents and treaties to redefine what constitutes a family. The tragic result is the unparalleled collapse of the American family, which can only be viewed as detrimental to the long-term survival of our nation.

America blasphemes God as irrelevant by ignoring His advice and counsel as given by the Church. We do not appreciate what lies in store for us when we arrive at what the Church defines as "The Last Four Things,"—that is Death, Judgment, Heaven, Hell. Recall the words from Holy Scripture, "They are a nation without counsel, and without wisdom. O that they would be wise and would understand, and would provide for their last end" (Deuteronomy, 32:28–29).

Volumes could be written on *Humanae Vitae* in what is possibly the most prophetic Church document of the 20th Century as it pertains to the direction of a nation if it violates natural and spiritual law. People can intellectualize all they want about the effects of violating the sacredness of life and procreation, but it is at root man "living by his glands" and an animal nature wishing to justify a contraceptive nature. Once America institutionalized contraception, abortion naturally followed. Once abortion became the law of the land in 1973, euthanasia gradually but inevitably worked its way into the national psyche. It is a natural progression. Once euthanasia became more generally accepted, the thinking moved on to cloning. One follows the other; whether it takes five years or a generation, one surely follows the other. The process of accepting lies and destructive thinking has been a long-term one.

A good analogy of this long-term thinking process is the Chinese bamboo shoot. When a bamboo seed is planted, it stays in the ground for four years and only breaks the surface in the fifth year. In the fifth year, the bamboo shoot can grow up to 80 feet! Our ideologies and godless ways have germinated for more than a generation. The youth today reflect the abandonment of truth by those who were supposed to hand it down to their children. This is what *Humanae Vitae* warned about. It should be noted that all major faiths of the world steadfastly and consistently warned about the inherent evil of contraception up until the Lambeth Conference of Anglican Bishops in 1930, which abandoned previous thinking on the inherent evils of birth control. The Protestant churches relaxed the standard and Planned Parenthood decided the only way to break the grip of the Roman Catholic view of contraception was to attack the Catholic hierarchy. People may disagree with the Church teaching, but "the fruit" is in the classroom, the home, the church, the Metro page of every newspaper in America on a daily basis. The very root of our rot in American culture is that we left spiritual truths and embraced other gods (Baal), which have led us to Asherah (the goddess of fertility and flesh). There are 2,500 teenage pregnancies every day in the U. S. alone, which translates to 900,000 a year. Three million teens a year pick up sexually transmitted diseases. Hopeful, at least, is that almost 90 percent of those who have been sexually active say they regret that choice.[8]

The Pill Creates Baal Worship, the Root of Our Problems

It would be difficult to have anything in history affect the morals of the world more than the birth control pill. What tobacco has done to the body over thirty years, the birth control pill has done in a far worse way to civilization. The pill became an instrument that breaks the very fabric of a person's life—thus destroying him. It created a "culture of death" in our midst, where the contraceptive mentality blossomed into the abortion mentality. The abortion mentality presently leads our nation into an intellectual dialogue for euthanasia—killing. The euthanasia movement mid-wived the reemergence of the subject of eugenics, which has promoted the use of cloning for short-term therapeutic needs and for the strategic propagation of a boutique class of super-humans and derivative lower-class sub-humans; when Frankenstein's monster emerges from the lab, it will be half man and half beast. If scientific research is not open to life as a gift of God, "it will increasingly generate great monsters until there is total destruction," warned Archbishop Javier Lozano Barragán, president of the Pontifical Council for Health Care Workers, when he addressed the general assembly of the Pontifical Academy for Life.[9] And what bodes for the rest of us in the interim? Recall earlier in this book the Ten Commandments of the New Age. Mankind needs to be reduced in population to 500 million people, or over a 90 percent reduction. What better way than war, famine, pestilence and death? The Culture of Death is in full bloom!

The root of our collective guilt regarding contraception and abortion began with a movement in the 1950's coincidental with the nation's prosperity after World War II. The sufferings of war and the experience of immigration brought with them a desire to better oneself materially. Along with a chicken in every pot, and a new car in the suburbs, came a push for more education. We had won a war on two fronts, we had no equal, and we were a military superpower. Parents, increasingly worshipping rationalism and materialism, realigned priorities within the family—neglecting to give priority to the necessity of sharing the faith with their children. Instead of vocations and pious living, a graduate degree in law, science, or medicine became the measure for success and happiness. Confession and the sacraments were gently pushed aside as Freud and other kooks convinced classrooms of attentive young adults that man's well-being is a product of one's environment and social status and sexual satiety. Prayer was considered old-fashioned and irrelevant and was pushed out of mainstream thinking.

Planned Parenthood began to promote the agenda that it was a woman's right to have an abortion. Using the falling away from the faith as an inroad, it was decided to gather support from the disgruntled faithful. Who would be an easier target than the Catholic hierarchy? Many thought the hierarchy was out of touch, so the agenda became one of separating the sheep ideologically from the shepherds. The strategy was to lead people to think that since the priests and religious are not married, they really don't care about the laity, or understand their concerns, or know anything about married life. The lie took root. The lie again became the perfumed pig, with Planned Parenthood playing the leading role. The people fell away in droves as trust in the clergy waned. The abandonment of faith then destroyed the family unit—the rock of all civilization. Planned Parenthood has followed the exact same strategy country by country with great effect. Even countries with a strong Catholic faith, like Ireland, the Philippines, and Poland, have fallen like dominoes. The faithful have been at a loss in knowing how to combat it because they never understood the strategy of the enemy until the damage was done.

Is there a connection among the secular attitudes in seminaries, homes, and schools and the wholesale abandonment of faith? Is there a falling away from the Faith, or an apostasy, as a result? Is there a connection between prayer being taken out of the classroom in 1962 by the Supreme Court and the Court's *Roe v. Wade* decision eleven years later? Is a permissive culture the result? Could we have moved into a natural debate over federal funding of euthanasia and cloning if one did not precede the other? It is never a single event that brings down a nation, but an ideology of godless thinking that takes root and spreads over decades or generations.

People in the West have been unable to see the connection. The great philanthropic foundations (tax-free, or in other words, funded indirectly by the taxpayers), which lean to the left concerning social policy, have been moving the world in this direction for a long time. The policy wonks on both sides of the legislative aisle continue to seek answers from a human perspective, rather than a divine perspective. "It is the Lord who raises up and brings down." *Humanae Vitae* spelled out in detail where the world would head if contraception was accepted. The result nearly forty years later is a family and church in crisis. If contraceptive devices had not been so readily available, would women have moved to multiple partners in light of a greater chance for pregnancy? The oldest profession, illicit unions of adultery, and perversions of every kind have been a staple of history; however, the numbers of people involved were dramatically less. Any sincere historian or social scientist would agree. The lust of the flesh and concupiscence has been present since Original Sin, but science has made it dramatically easier to violate the Ten Commandments.

Promiscuity in Anonymity: Urban Blight

"The Industrial Revolution changed the economic form and moral superstructure of European and American life. Men, women, and children left home and family, authority and unity, to work as individuals, individually paid, in factories built to house not men but machines. Every decade the machines multiplied and became more complex; economic maturity (the capacity to support a family) came later; children were no longer economic assets; marriage was delayed; premarital continence became more difficult to maintain. The city offered every discouragement to marriage, but it provided every stimulus and facility for sex. Women were 'emancipated'—i. e., industrialized—and contraceptives allowed them to separate intercourse from pregnancy. The authority of the father lost its economic base through the growing individualism of industry. Rebellious youths were no longer constrained by the surveillance of the village; they could hide their sins in the protective anonymity of the city crowd. The progress of science raised the authority of the test-tube over that of the Crosier; the mechanization of economic production spurred mechanistic materialistic philosophies; education spread religious doubts; and morality lost more and more of its supernatural supports. The old agricultural moral code began to die."[10]

This transition from the agricultural to the industrial age saw a transition of thinking like no other in history. The movement from the industrialized age to the technological has not been as profound because in the former shift the infrastructure of thinking, daily movements, and methods of thinking were entrenched over a period of nearly two hundred years. The present phase of globalization and technology is merely an outgrowth of the industrialized world. The urban industrialized society then bred the germ of both parents at work, which ultimately produced a generation of 'latch key' and abandoned children.

Is the U. S. A. today different in its decline from previous cultures and empires? The answers are no in the stage of similar steps of decline, but yes in the methods. The speed of our ascendancy and decline makes us a little different as well. Rome took several hundred years to decline and that was precipitated by the brute emperors like Caligula, Nero, and others. It was not until 476 A. D. that Rome fell to barbarians. The slide was slow and sure, but in the end Rome could not be held together. It was never possible for previous empires to tap into the internet and bring into their living rooms several hundred thousand pornography sites of every hue imaginable. In American families, only one in four have a mother and father with children living under the same roof. If present trends continue, America, too, will be relegated to the trash heap of civilizations. To date, there is no movement spiritually to reverse that trend. Will we be held responsible for parading our filth in front of God? When Ezechiel asked God why He judged Sodom, will the answers be the same: they "committed abominations before me: and I took them away as you have seen" (Ezechiel 16:50)?

Democracy in Excess Breeds Totalitarianism

Abraham Lincoln stated, "Our reliance is in the love of liberty which God has planted in us. Our defense is in the spirit which prized liberty as the heritage of all men, in all lands everywhere. Destroy this spirit and you have planted the seeds of despotism at your own doors. Familiarize yourselves with the chains of bondage and you prepare you own limbs to wear them. Accustomed to trample on the rights of others, you have lost the genius of your own independence and become the fit subjects of the first cunning tyrant who rises among you."[11]

In recent decades, our executive and legislative bodies have irresponsibly acquiesced or forfeited their constitutional authority and rights to a tribunal of hierarchical courts. The most visible example of this usurpation of power is abortion on demand. In the 1973 *Roe v. Wade* decision of the Supreme Court, suddenly a 'privacy' right to abortion was discovered abolishing the abortion laws of all fifty states in what many constitutional scholars have called an act of raw judicial power. Our concern must be for both the integrity of our constitutional order, which directs the enactment of laws through the representative political processes, and the fundamental truth that all human life is sacred, including that of the unborn—even though, in their case the Court decided to renege the Constitution's guarantee of equal protection and due process of law. Many of the people who brought *Roe v. Wade* to the Supreme Court were working at the time with the National Abortion Rights Action League (NARAL). Several of the chief participants, like Dr. Bernard Nathanson and Norma McCorvey (Jane Roe herself), have subsequently become committed Catholics and now admit that they fabricated crucial data and lied to the Court.

The institutionalizing of contraception and abortion will lead to the downfall of our Constitution within a generation or so. During an address to the Pontifical Academy for Life, Pope John Paul II warned that "if society does not rediscover the natural law, human rights will be relegated to the free will and interests of the most influential"; the Holy Father further stated that it "can also lead democratic regimes to a form of substantial totalitarianism."[12] A free society depends on voluntary compliance with the law. Christians comply because they believe in a God Who watches our every move, and holds us accountable, even when government does not. Those without a belief in God and absolute truth have no motivation whatsoever to comply voluntarily, and so an ever increasing body of law must be imposed by government through coercion on citizens in order to achieve order. In doing so, the government separates itself from morality and will in time become the chief lawbreaker. When the nation loses its moral life, the foundation of its culture will collapse.

This is why abortion is so heinous an act. A nation that murders the defenseless has no hope and no future. Violence brings death, and death destroys cultures. Once alienation from God is firmly entrenched in a society, no one sees anything wrong with any form of self-expression. As Jesus needed to be the bloody Sacrifice for the expiation of sins, Satan seeks a bloody sacrifice to defy and mock the authority of God. Alienation from God in the extreme seeks a bloody sacrifice. Alienation will end with a bloody sacrifice, and this is abortion. Abortion is the scapegoat, the bloody sacrifice, but in the end it is civilization itself that will die.

It is the challenge of the believer to be the light in the world. As C. S. Lewis said in *God in the Dock*, "We cannot remain silent and concede everything away." What is the answer? An official in the Southern Baptist Convention was asked what the future of America was. He responded, "If you put the U. S. against the Scriptures, we are in trouble. I think we are very close to the judgement of God. The problem with America is not the unbelieving world. It is the people of God. There are as many divorces inside the church as outside the church. There are as many abortions inside the church, as outside. When you compare what is going on inside and outside the church, there are no differences. How should we then live? Don't fuss at the world, it is acting out its nature. We have to be the salt and the light. We have to be an observable difference. The attention of God is upon his people. The future of America rests in our hands."[13]

Law of Innocent Blood

What about the scourge of abortion? What can this country expect in the way of punishment for its relentless insistence, since 1973, on the "legitimate" denial of life to the unborn? What does Scripture say about the taking of innocent life? As this nation has, throughout its history, gradually shed more of the protective armor of the laws of God, it has fallen further into the realm of injustice and perversity. Satan has as his chief purpose the destruction of humanity and its abode. An effective means is through large numbers of unnatural deaths. Unlimited warfare is a strong weapon at the enemy's hand, and he has successfully increased the violence, rapaciousness, ferocity and lack of restraint of wars. A Russia and China wedded to "unlimited war" could be instruments of Divine wrath. With the legalization of abortion and the nearly universal acceptance of birth control, Satan has taken life from the mother's womb, and removed its possibility from the very act of procreation. Through the rise of impurity and man's quest for pleasure, the physical act of love has been separated from its purpose, namely the begetting of new generations through a sharing in the divine action of creation; as lust has replaced love in the sexual act because the possibility or thought of children springing from this act has been quarantined or removed, so God has allowed man to follow his foolish path. Accordingly, God is holding man responsible and allowing him to suffer the consequences of his ways. If history is any indication, Heaven shall inflict a heavy punishment. From the earliest parts of Scripture, the shedding of innocent blood cries out. "And the Lord said to Cain: Where is your brother Abel? And he answered, I know not: am I my brother's keeper? And he said to him: What have you done? the voice of your brother's blood cries to me from the earth" (Genesis 4:9–10). Like Cain, those who shed innocent blood must pay a price as even the earth calls for vengeance.

The Lord holds especially accountable those responsible for the blood of innocents, such as the slaughter of the unborn, as is shown in Deuteronomy: "Then there shall be found in the land, which the Lord your God will give you, the corpse of a man slain, and it is not known who is guilty of the murder, your ancients and judges shall go out, and shall measure from the place where the body lies the distance of every city round about: and the ancients of that city which they shall perceive to be nearer than the rest, shall take a heifer of the herd, that has not drawn in the yoke, nor ploughed the ground, and they shall bring her into a rough and stony valley, that never was ploughed, nor sown: and there they shall strike off the head of the heifer: and the priests the sons of Levi shall come, whom the Lord your God has chosen to minister to him, and to bless in his name, and that by their word every matter should be decided, and whatsoever is clean or unclean should be judged. And the ancients of that city shall come to the person slain, and shall wash their hands over the heifer that was killed in the valley, and shall say: Our hands did not shed this blood, nor did our eyes see it. Be merciful to your people Israel, whom you has redeemed, O Lord, and lay not innocent blood to their charge, in the midst of your people Israel. And the guilt of blood shall be taken from them: and you shall be free from the innocent's blood, that was shed, when you shall have done what the Lord has commanded you" (Deuteronomy 21:1–9).

The birth control pill has led to ever-greater perversity seeping into the sexual act itself. The marital act must always have as its primary purpose, by divine design, a complete openness to the creation of new life, which is a co-operative act with the Creator, and thus should be a means of coming closer to God. Limiting or cutting off this co-operation with God results in the lessening or removal of love, which is then replaced by lust. This is a denial of God's presence in the act of procreation, and it leads to the glorification of man's physical passion.

Because of limitations on the possibility of procreation, and the resulting increase of impurity, man has more and more become a sexual addict. The sexual act, to satiate man's increasingly inordinate desires, now ranges, even with widespread though misplaced social acceptance, to seeking outlets within one's own gender. Homosexuality, now rampant and accepted by many, is the perverse offshoot of the splitting of the procreative act into sexual gratification on the one hand, and sterile human reproduction on the other, which is now showing itself ever more commonly in tragic practices such as test-tube conception, cloning, and even the mingling of the essence of man with the essence of beast to create monstrous hybrids. In the homosexual act, the very possibility of new life is completely denied—the ultimate goal of Satan—while man has taken upon himself, with the advent of scientific human reproduction and genetic determination, the role of deciding who (or should we say what?) will have life.

What does Scripture say about the consequences of man turning from God's way, of sowing injustice and wrong in people's minds, of denying the law of God that is found within him, of turning from the right worship of Him, and of countenancing such abomination? St. Paul's letter to the Romans is quite clear: "For I am not ashamed of the gospel. For it is the power of God unto salvation to every one that believes, to the Jew first, and to the Greek. For the justice of God is revealed therein, from faith unto faith, as it is written: The just man lives by faith. For the wrath of God is revealed from heaven against all ungodliness and injustice of those men that detain the truth of God in injustice: Because that which is known of God is manifest in them. For God has manifested it unto them. For the invisible things of him, from the creation of the world, are clearly seen, being understood by the things that are made; his eternal power also, and divinity: so that they are inexcusable. Because that, when they knew God, they have not glorified him as God, or given thanks; but became vain in their thoughts, and their foolish heart was darkened. For professing themselves to be wise, they became fools. And they changed the glory of the incorruptible God into the likeness of the image of a corruptible man, and of birds, and of fourfooted beasts, and of creeping things. Wherefore God gave them up to the desires of their heart, unto uncleanness, to dishonour their own bodies among themselves. Who changed the truth of God into a lie; and worshipped and served the creature rather than the Creator, who is blessed for ever.... For this cause God delivered them up to shameful affections. For their women have changed the natural use into that use which is against nature. And, in like manner, the men also, leaving the natural use of the women, have burned in their lusts one towards another, men with men working that which is filthy, and receiving in themselves the recompense which was due to their error. And as they liked not to have God in their knowledge, God delivered them up to a reprobate sense, to do those things which are not convenient; being filled with all iniquity, malice, fornication, avarice, wickedness, full of envy, murder, contention, deceit, malignity, whisperers, detractors, hateful to God, contumelious, proud, haughty, inventors of evil things, disobedient to parents, foolish, dissolute, without affection, without fidelity, without mercy. Who, having known the justice of God, did not understand that they who do such things, are worthy of death; and not only they that do them, but they also that consent to them that do them" (Romans 1:16–32).

A Gospel of Life

The issue of abortion has received widespread attention from the press over the years. It is the issue of our time. *Newsweek* devoted a cover story to the encyclical, *Evangelium Vitae* (The Gospel of Life, 1996), which religion editor Kenneth Woodward praised as "the clearest, most impassioned and most commanding encyclical" of the pontificate, one that would be John Paul's "signature statement" in history.[14] Paperback editions of the encyclical soon appeared in bookstores and supermarket checkout counters. Protestant and Jewish scholars were complimentary and moral theologians who had been

113

highly critical of *Veritatis Splendor* (The Splendor of Truth, 1993) found many things to praise in *Evangelium Vitae*.[15] The encyclical evidently spoke to a widespread concern that the use of abortion for "family planning" and campaigns in favor of euthanasia bespoke a general coarsening, even cheapening, of life that ought to be resisted somehow.[16] It would be claiming too much to suggest that John Paul's deeper analysis of the "culture of death" was seriously engaged by the public in the older democracies, but his defense of the dignity of life, even on such bitterly controverted public policy issues as abortion and euthanasia, struck a chord. Perhaps, he mused to guests, things had gotten bad enough that attention could now be paid.[17]

Evangelium Vitae had implications for the Church, too. If, as the encyclical strongly suggested, the "Gospel of Life" was, in fact, *the* Gospel—if the issues the encyclical addressed were not peripheral, but were at the core of Christian belief—then *Evangelium Vitae* would eventually reshape the ecumenical dialogue between Roman Catholicism and those liberal Protestant communities whose views on the moral issues involved were quite different. Post-Vatican II ecumenism had downplayed these divergences to concentrate on what were considered central theological issues, such as justification, ministry, sacraments, and authority. *Evangelium Vitae* suggested that such bracketing was inappropriate and that unity in the truth included unity in moral truth on issues of this gravity.[18]

In the early days of the Republic, Americans were proud of their strong sense of individual responsibility, but that did not lead them to build an immoral radical society. Pope John Paul II writes about America, "Individualism did not mean pagan or immoral. The early settlers built a community-based society, with a great openness and sensitivity to the needs of their neighbors...." Close to the New Jersey shore, he noted, "there rises a universally-known landmark which stands as an enduring witness to the American tradition of welcoming the stranger, and which tells us something important about the kind of nation America has aspired to be." The Statue of Liberty was a reminder that "the United States is called to be *a hospitable society, a welcoming culture.*" Today, he continued, it was the unborn child who was the "stranger" to be welcomed and brought into the circle of society's protection, along with the immigrant, the poor, the elderly, the handicapped—all those "others" he had defended at the U. N."[19]

Why Does That Monkey Glow in the Dark?

*Cloning brings conception and gestation into the
bright light of the laboratory, beneath which the
child-to-be can be fertilized, nourished, pruned,
weeded, watched, inspected, prodded, pinched,
cajoled, injected, tested, rated, graded, approved,
stamped, wrapped, sealed, and delivered.*
                          —Leon R. Kass, chairman of President
                          George W. Bush's Council on Bioethics

The Progress of Humanism: Cloning

What does the future portend for the human race as a species?
Kass's point is that once human life is special-ordered rather than
conceived, life will never be the same. No longer will each of us be a
person who is unique from all others who have ever lived. Instead our
genetic selves will be molded and chiseled in a petri dish to comply
with the social norms of the day. And if something goes wrong, the
new life will be thrown away like some defective widget or other
fungible product. Mankind will proclaim, "So long, diversity; hello
homogeneity." Perhaps even worse, widespread acceptance of cloning
would be a deathblow to the sanctity and equality of the life ethic—the
cornerstone of Western liberty. The premise of the sanctity of life ethic
is that each and every one of us is of equal, incalculable, moral worth.
Whatever our race, sex, ethnicity, stature, health, disability, age,
beauty, or cognitive capacity, we are all full moral equals within the
human community—there is no "them," only "us."[1]

With the advent of cloning, the commercial markets are investing
billions of dollars into laboratories of the neo-eugenicist (modern Dr.
Frankensteins), with the sincere determination of accumulating
substantial and enduring returns from a pagan and barbaric society.
This will be a society self-centered sufficiently enough to dispose of
any undesirable characteristic, ailment or feature in man and the rest of
God's 'imperfect' creation, while spending limitless sums of money to
play god by accelerating the evolution of creation to man's whims, with

a total disregard for God's law impressed on what remains of our community of uncloned hearts.

Modest success is being promoted by the cloning industry and the media to justify the enormous investment. For example, Copy Cat is the first cloned pet that has made headlines. The news was released February 14, 2002, (Valentine's Day) that scientists in Texas had created the first cloned cat, a calico named "CC," which took a controversial place in history as the first cloned domestic pet. Born December 22, 2001, by caesarian section in a laboratory, the cat was the sixth kind of mammal to be created from a single adult cell—after sheep, mice, cattle, goats, and pigs. The trend is continuing as mad scientists at a top-secret lab in Seoul, South Korea, were recently found to be inserting human cells into 15,000 freezer-stored bovine eggs to generate cloned human embryonic stem cells for transplant treatments. In Asia and elsewhere, researchers are turning to animal eggs of a variety of species because they are much easier and cheaper to obtain than human eggs.[2] Welcome Brave New World.

Modern-day Dr. Frankensteins race to reap enormous adulation and financial gain. In a recent book authored by Lori Andrews and Dorothy Nelkin titled, *Body Bazaar: The Market for Human Tissues in the Biotechnology Age*, the authors argue that the value of human body tissue in the biotechnology age—and the potential for profitable patents derived from it—encourages doctors and researchers to think about people differently: "...body parts are extracted like a mineral, harvested like a crop, or mined like a resource." One can just imagine hearing the following financial news every morning as you drive to work: "Today, the market in sow bellies is down, soybeans are stable, and human embryos are up." Recent developments in embryonic research have moved us one step closer to that scenario. This is no exaggeration. The Jones Institute for Reproductive Medicine in Virginia announced in July 2001 that they intentionally created human embryos from donor eggs and sperm with the sole purpose of conducting destructive research on nascent humans. The twelve egg donors were paid $1,500 to $2,000 each—about what the average egg donor receives. The sperm donors were paid about $50 each. So, that means the money earned from the destruction of human offspring can pay a month's house mortgage for a woman and dinner for two for a man.[3]

To further substantiate Andrew's and Nelkin's claims, just look at Advanced Cell Technology's ("ACT") business strategy. ACT is pursuing successfully an intellectual property rights strategy and has nearly all patents or patents pending on the methodologies for making these "embryo-like entities." ACT has essentially created human embryos whose parts they can sell so that other companies can develop therapies that will allegedly treat or heal all of our ailments.[4] Furthermore, those who invested large sums of money in cryonics over the past 30 years, placing their loved ones in a state of frozen animation at a temperature of minus 196° Celsius, are probably waiting with bated breadth to spend considerably more money to clone such bodies after the technology is proven and the bodies are thawed. One can only conclude that cloned embryos and their embryonic stem cells already are viewed in terms of their commodity value, which raises the ethical issue of commercializing our genetic offspring.

The deliberate creation and commercialization of such embryos amounts to enslavement, and as such they are created solely for use by other human beings. Without a quick and decisive effort to ban all such cloning, it appears inevitable that the U. S. Supreme Court will one day conclude that an embryo, like any unborn fetus, is not a child with rights and therefore subject to being treated as property by its owner. Our society would further unravel. Then it would be just a matter of time before the U. S. would behave like the People's Republic of China, where prisoners on death row (who are going to die anyway, according to proponents) have their life-sustaining organs removed just prior to, or as part of, their execution as a means of prolonging the lives of others. With abortion, cloning, and compulsory organ removal and transplant made legal, can euthanasia be far behind? Continuing along the line of this trend, we will see "organ farms" in the near future—and all of this will be legal.

And forget about the recent publicity of combining genetic material from a jelly fish into a cloned monkey causing the monkey to glow. That's kid's stuff! Already, advocates of cloning are suggesting that we clone an Elvis, Marilyn Monroe, George Washington, Abraham Lincoln and Albert Einstein from a lock of their hair or remnant from the grave. Some cloning advocates mockingly suggest that mankind can accelerate the Second Coming of Jesus Christ by cloning Him from blood samples contained in the Shroud of Turin (ironically claimed to be a fraud by a segment of the scientific community).

Oh, the possibilities! Yet, Jesus warns us, "...you are they who justify yourselves before men, but God knows your hearts. For that which is high to men is an abomination before God" (St. Luke 16:15).

Knowing No Bounds

Like society today, the Israelites of the Old Testament failed to live up to God's commandments. God commanded that the Israelites worship only Him. While believing in the God of Abraham, Isaac and Moses, God's Chosen People nonetheless also worshipped other gods. Even King Solomon eventually worshipped other 'gods,' including Astarthe, the goddess of the Sidonians, and Moloch, the idol of the Ammonites. Worshippers of Astarthe committed sins of the flesh. What greater sin of the flesh is there then to attempt to perpetuate a primitive form of immortality through reproductive and therapeutic cloning?

Let anyone who has eyes to see and ears to hear take note: Cloning is an abomination that will make us desolate. It explicitly ignores God's almighty and absolutely necessary role in the creation of a being made in His image and likeness. Cloning blasphemes God's will, directly attempting to intervene immorally in both the cause and prevention of fertility and illness. With unmitigated pride neo-eugenicists claim that man has the right to create rather than procreate. Like 19th Century secular humanists such as Jeremy Bentham and John Stuart Mill, their ultimate agenda is nothing less than to help lead in the evisceration of Judeo-Christian belief and practice and the institution of what they believe is a superior moral and spiritual social establishment, that is, the "Religion of Humanity." John Stuart Mill wrote to a comrade, Auguste Comte, in 1841, "I always saw...in the idea of Humanity the only one capable of replacing that of God. But there is still a long way from this speculation and belief to the manifest feeling I experience today—that it is fully valid and that the inevitable substitution is at hand." The neo-eugenicists and their human secularist supporters enthusiastically perceive the fulfillment of Mill's vision as being imminent, should society allow man to create man. Cloning necessitates that man look neither to God for His blessing to procreate, nor secondarily to the traditional father and mother as the only source of the combined genetic code which constitutes the newly created life. It is the quintessential utilitarian enterprise. With society's acceptance and the commercial success of cloning, the moral foundation of what constitutes life becomes absolutely relative and therefore compromised, or to put it another way, some of us are better than others. In a utilitarian world the neo-eugenicists will lead mankind to "improve" humanity by breeding out the undesirable traits of those deemed less worthy. Where have we heard or seen that before? In this country alone, tens of thousands of people were involuntary sterilized. In Puerto Rico the practice is quite common. In Western Europe, a eugenics belief system combined with social Darwinism and anti-Semitism to produce the Nazis and the subsequent Holocaust. The Netherlands is a leader of eugenic thought in Europe. It is arguably one of the world's most spiritually bankrupt nations. Cloning is a by-product of spiritual bankruptcy.

If biblical history is any indication, all this can lead to is severe chastisement. This is the story of the Bible. Unrepentant sin leads to the purification of peoples and nations. Open any book in Scripture and it is there. Recall the reprimanding words of warning of the Lord to Moses, "Thus shall you say to the children of Israel: If any man of the children Israel, or of the strangers that dwell in Israel, give of his seed to the idol Moloch, dying let him die.... And if the people of the land neglecting, and as it were little regarding my commandment, let alone the man that has given of his seed to Moloch, and will not kill him: I will set my face against that man, and his kindred, and will cut off both him and all that consented with him, to commit fornication with Moloch, out of the midst of their people" (Leviticus 20:2,4–5). Moloch is a particularly noteworthy Ammonite god from the Old Testament. Moloch's sacrificial victims were human, particularly young children. Moloch's image was a hollow brazen figure, with the head of an ox, and outstretched human arms (without a ban on cloning it appears inevitable that scientists will combine attributes and possibly features of animals with humans). The image was heated red-hot by a fire from within, and the innocent victims were placed in its arms to be slowly burned, while to prevent the parents from hearing the dying cries, the sacrificing priests would beat drums loudly. Our society's modern day sacrifice to Moloch is comprised of the killing of an innocent human being, whether fetus or embryo, whose cry no one can hear, all for mankind's utilitarian benefit. One can only conclude that as individuals and as a nation, we explicitly choose to ignore God's will and His words to Jeremiah, "Before I formed you in the bowels of your mother, I knew you: and before you came forth out of the womb, I sanctified you..." (Jeremiah 1:5).

When America embraced relative truths, sin in all of its forms became manifest. Outside of the moral order there are no boundaries, and man does whatever seems expedient—or profitable. America has come to the point of embracing a civil religion where liberty and personal freedoms express themselves in the forms of social and economic justice. The highest value of this civil religion is not obedience to God, but additional personal liberties—or rather, license. Each year, the expression of this boundless freedom that ignores God's law becomes more bold. We now see state-sponsored cloning in its infancy. In time, this abomination will only grow worse.

Time to Take a Stand

Life is all about choice. Whether in our personal lives or by our pluralistic society or its republican form of government, Americans, including leaders from all segments of our society, regularly face difficult choices. President Lincoln confronted slavery against the popular opinion of much of the country. President Lyndon Johnson confronted segregation and discrimination head-on, including the enactment and enforcement of our civil rights laws. President Reagan chose to attack world communism square in the face, radically redirecting government expenditures and converting public opinion using what was initially viewed by many as outdated imagery, even referring to the former Soviet Union by the pejorative term, "the evil empire."

Americans must realize that our current conundrum regarding cloning is simply the next "Fabian" step, that is, a gradual progression pursued by secular humanists. Cloning is a logical next step following society's acceptance of promiscuous sexual behavior, birth control and abortion. Americans must insist on an immediate and total government ban of the scientific pursuit of reproductive and therapeutic cloning. As Leon Kass asserts, *"Anyone truly serious about preventing human reproductive cloning must seek to stop the process from the beginning, at the stage where the human somatic cell nucleus is introduced into the egg."*

Due to the very nature of science, cloning and the imagination of man will see no end to the possibilities. Cloning is in its infancy and horror stories are already emerging. Recently, two deaf lesbian mental health therapists wanted a deaf child. To increase that likelihood, they chose a deaf sperm donor, and in true designer fashion, son Sauvin was born deaf. In this case, the designer baby was born with a defect as the "mothers" wished.[5] Is any of this really different than the medical experiments of the Nazis under the barbarism of the Third Reich? What America and the world do not yet understand is that when you do it to one person, you condemn the nation.

Our political and religious leaders must engage openly and honestly in a debate to help attain a public mandate to codify cogent laws based on Judeo-Christian ethics that would protect human life from conception to its last breath. Ultimately, such laws require more than vigorous enforcement. Our country needs to re-educate itself thoroughly on our faith and what God expects from us. This would be a relatively massive education and propaganda effort that may require years, possibly a generation's worth, to bear good fruit. The reason the Church is in scandal after scandal and such a state of decline is because on the important issues it has remained silent. Many in the Church have lacked the courage to speak out.

But have no fear that the biotech industry and the media are silent about the subject of cloning. They continually promote the fact that other nations are ignoring morals and principles while pursuing aggressively the commercialization of cloning techniques. Countries like Germany, England, France, Japan, and others will walk in and take the profit from biotech industries if we don't. There is supposedly too much money to be made and lost, which is precisely why we will proceed. It will boil down to big profits. This is the nature of the competitive global business structure today. The U. S. will not allow another country to profit with billions at stake. Observing no absolutes in life, the reasoning is, "Why not?" Cloning is inevitable in the U. S. because America believes it must not have a strategic gap versus the rest of the world. This calls to mind the sudden emotional commentary of the bombastic General Buck Turgidson (played by George C. Scott) in the movie, *Doctor Strangelove*. Upon listening to the advice of Doctor Strangelove regarding the strategic importance of caves and mines as the places where people would have to live and repopulate for years while waiting for radiation levels to recede after the use of a "Doomsday" machine, Turgidson stridently declared, "Mr. President, we must not allow a mine shaft gap!"

Theodore Roosevelt, the 26th President of the United States, a soldier, author and 1906 Nobel Prize Winner, with grave intuition gave the following ominous warning: "Progress has brought us both unbounded opportunities and unbridled difficulties. Thus, the measure of our civilization will not be that we have done much, but what we have done with that much. I believe that the next half-century will determine if we will advance the cause of Christian civilization or revert to the horrors of brutal paganism. The thought of modern industry in the hands of Christian charity is a dream worth dreaming. The thought of industry in the hands of paganism is a nightmare beyond imagining. The choice between the two is upon us."[6]

Americans would be wise to apply to the subject of cloning the following lesson taught by Jesus Christ: "He that sows the good seed is the Son of man. And the field is the world. And the good seed are the children of the kingdom. And the cockle are the children of the wicked one. And the enemy that sowed them, is the devil" (St. Matthew 13:37–38).

Endangered Species

But he that shall scandalize one of these little ones that believe in me, it would be better for him that a millstone should be hanged about his neck, and that he should be drowned in the depth of the sea.
—St. Matthew 18:6

Nowhere have we seen the destruction of Western Civilization more than in the family, and at no time have we seen so many youth living with such lack of purpose, vision, and a sense of hope for the future. The corruption of the American child is occurring faster and more furiously than at any time in history. Children are being exposed to more immorality, impurity, and vile concepts at younger and younger ages. Many children are defenseless due to their near abandonment by working parents. Children are being brought up in a world totally devoid of good spirituality. The net result is that what these children do, think, and say reflects virtually no sense of right or wrong. They live amoral lives in a spiritual wasteland.

The following is an edited collection of revealing statistical evidence, conclusions and commentary regarding the historical collapse of the American family into immorality as researched by Patrick Fagan, the William H. G. FitzGerald Fellow in Family and Cultural Issues, and his colleague, Robert Rector, Senior Research Fellow in Domestic Policy Studies, at The Heritage Foundation in Washington, D. C.

Impact of Broken Families on Children

These studies show that income disparity in America is affected mostly by the stability of a child's home environment—primarily, whether that child has married parents or is part of a broken family. Consider:

- ❖ In 1950, twelve out of every 100 children born entered a broken family; by 1992, 58 out of every 100 children born entered a broken family.

- ❖ Children living with a single mother are six times more likely to live in poverty than are children whose parents are married.
- ❖ Of families with children in the lowest quintile of earnings, single parents head 73 percent; in the top quintile, married couples head 95 percent.
- ❖ In 1994, over 12.5 million children lived in single-parent families that earned less than $15,000 per year; only three million such children lived with families who had annual incomes greater than $30,000.
- ❖ Three-quarters of all women applying for welfare benefits do so because of a disrupted marriage or live-in relationship. Those who leave the welfare system when they get married are the least likely to return.
- ❖ Cohabitation doubles the rate of divorce. Cohabitation with someone other than one's future spouse quadruples the rate of divorce.
- ❖ Divorce reduces the income of families with children by an average of 42 percent. Almost 50 percent of these families experience poverty.
- ❖ Married couples in their mid-fifties amass four times the wealth of divorced individuals ($132,000 versus $33,600).
- ❖ Children in stepfamilies and single-parent families are almost three times more likely to drop out of school than are children in intact families.[1]

In light of all of this fracturing of families, what type of family structure do most American children have? From newborn American children to 18-year-olds:

- ❖ 47 percent live with parents in their first marriage—"the intact family";
- ❖ 19 percent live in stepfamilies (the vast majority of these the result of a divorce);
- ❖ 6 percent live with adults who cohabit;
- ❖ 6 percent live with always-single parents (who bore the child out of wedlock and did not marry later);
- ❖ 16 percent live with divorced or separated parents; and
- ❖ 6 percent live with widowed parents.

Impact of Divorce on Children: Numerous social science studies and related literature on the effects of divorce on children clearly agree that the effects of divorce are pervasive; for instance:

❖ In the areas of government and citizenship, divorce is followed by increases in the rates of juvenile crime, abuse and neglect, and addiction.

❖ In education, divorce is followed by diminished learning capacities and less high school and college degree attainment. Children from divorced homes, for example, perform more poorly in reading, spelling, and math, and repeat a grade more frequently than do children from two-parent intact families.

❖ In the marketplace, divorce precedes reductions in household income and the lifetime accumulation of wealth by family members. For families that were not poor before a divorce, income can drop by as much as 40 percent. Almost 50 percent of the parents with children that are going through a divorce move into poverty after the divorce. Children raised in intact families have higher earnings as adults than do children from other family structures.

❖ In the realm of spiritual development, divorce is followed by a drop in both worship and recourse to prayer. Therefore religious worship, which has been linked to better health, longer marriages, and better family life, drops after the parents divorce.

❖ Divorce weakens the health of children and shortens their life spans. It increases the likelihood of child abuse and the rate of behavioral, emotional, and psychiatric problems, and suicide.

❖ Divorce increases the likelihood of permanently weakening the child's relationship with his or her parents and peers. Divorce often leads to destructive ways of handling conflict, a diminished competency in relationships, the early loss of virginity, and a diminished sense of masculinity or femininity. Divorce likely leads children to greater acceptance of and frequency of cohabitation, higher expectations of divorce in the future and rates of divorce as an adult and a lesser desire to have children.[2]

These effects on the family life of the children are disturbing because they compound the downward spiral of social decay in many communities and cities. Though any one particular child may overcome these weaknesses—because of the great love and dedication of one parent or stepparent, or thanks to the special help of a teacher or the friendship of someone in the community—as a group the children of divorce bear the burden of these weakening effects. The layering of one generation of broken family life on top of another results in:

* Higher numbers of children leaving home earlier, as well as higher levels of cohabitation for these children; and keeping the cycle expanding;
* Higher rates of divorce for the children of divorced parents.

These dramatic changes gives us a clear picture of the turmoil America's children are experiencing. However, the statistics also tell a startling story about what has been going on between men and women in American society. The vast majority (60 percent) of American men and women who have brought children into the world cannot stand each other well enough to raise their children to adulthood. Such a massive level of alienation and rejection between fathers and mothers has massive consequences for society through the effects on the children involved (six out of every ten children). The deepest concern is that a stable and peaceful nation cannot last on this diet of rejection and alienation. Like a cancer, this culture of rejection and alienation will at some time undo the glue that binds America together.

The Impact of Abortion on Families: The growing cancer of children entering broken families since 1950 looks even worse when we add the very high numbers of children who are aborted each year by their mothers. This number has begun to decline recently, but the statistics are still shocking: *Of every 100 children conceived each year, one-third will be killed in their mother's womb, one-third will be born out of wedlock, and of those born to married parents one-half will see their parents divorce before they reach the age of eighteen.* With the continued promotion and growing acceptance of the culture of rejection and alienation that dominates America's family life, our country is increasingly becoming a scary place to be born. Abortion is one of the most contentious issues in the United States today, but what is constantly avoided in the abortion debate is the relationship between abortion and sexual intercourse outside of marriage. Studies show, the overwhelming number of abortions—82 percent—occur to women who are not married. Only eighteen percent of abortions are attributed to women who are married. According to national sample data collected by the Alan Guttmacher Institute, since abortion became a protected "right," this proportion has generally not changed. The inescapable conclusion is that abortion acts as the ultimate "protector" of extra-marital sexual relations.

Impact of Out-of-Wedlock Births: With the breakdown of families and associated morals, out-of-wedlock births have risen over the last half-century from four percent to 33 percent. One glimmer of hope is that this proportion has remained steady at 33 percent for the last few years. Research shows that out-of-wedlock births increase the national incidence of

- ❖ lowered health for newborns and an increased chance of dying;
- ❖ retarded cognitive, especially verbal, development of young children;
- ❖ lowered educational achievement;
- ❖ lowered job attainment as young adults;
- ❖ increased behavior problems;
- ❖ lowered impulse control (aggression and sexual behavior) ; and
- ❖ increased anti-social development. Together all these effects help change their communities from being a support to being a danger to the development of families and their children, and increases the crime rate in their community.

The combined effect of divorce and out-of-wedlock childbearing means that more than half of America's children will spend all or part of their childhood living in a single-parent, divorced, or remarried family. The Federal Reserve Board's 1995 Survey of Consumer Finance shows that only 42 percent of children ages fourteen to18 live in a "first marriage" family, generally an intact two-parent married family with both biological parents. Some 21 percent of teenage children live with a single parent who is divorced or separated, while 22 percent live in a two-parent household with one stepparent.

Age of First Intercourse: The earlier a girl has her first sexual encounter, the more sexual partners she is likely to have, the more susceptible she is to contract a sexually transmitted disease, and the more likely she is to become a single mother. The numbers of American girls having intercourse for the first time by age fifteen rose sharply between 1975 and 1988; the rate, which began to drop in 1995, is still startlingly high—over twenty percent.

- ❖ In 1970, 4.6 percent of American girls had lost their virginity by age 15;
- ❖ By 1975, the number had increased to 9.8 percent;
- ❖ By 1980, 16.7 percent of girls had their first intercourse by age 15;
- ❖ By 1988, the number peaked at just over 25 percent; and
- ❖ By 1995, the number had dropped slightly to just over 22 percent.[3]

Influence of Peers and Worship: According to a study of sixteen-year-old children by a team of Midwestern researchers, peers have quite an impact on teenage virginity. The findings of this study are rather dramatic. For teenagers who do not worship at all and whose friends are sexually active, 96 percent of such teenagers are likely to be sexually active. For teenagers who worship weekly and whose friends are not sexually active, 97 percent of these teenagers are likely to be virgins. Clearly, friends and worship are powerful influences on sexual experiences.[4]

Relationship with the Father: The effect of peer influences can be altered quite a bit by how close a female teenager feels to her parents, especially her father. A girl who has a close relationship with her father is more likely to maintain her virginity for a longer period of time. If she believes he cares about her, she is likely to remain a virgin far longer than one who believes her father does not care about her. With the absence of fathers in the home so prevalent today, the implications of this fact for society are enormous.[5]

Parents Who Worship: Whether or not a teenager's parents worship matters. When neither parent worships, the rate of virginity of children is small. When a mother worships but the father does not, the rate is higher. When fathers worship but the mother does not, the rate of virginity is somewhat higher still. When both mother and father worship, children show the greatest capacity to maintain their virginity. A series of federal national long-term studies indicates coincidentally that religious worship by men in their twenties has quite an impact on their capacity to sustain their own virginity.

The Most Sexually Content Adults: These findings fit very well with the findings of the most comprehensive survey on sexuality in America, presented in *The Social Organization of Sexuality*: Those who have the most enjoyable sexual relations as adults are married adults who worship God every week and have had only one sexual partner—their spouse. This is a very different profile from the one put forth by the purveyors of the sexual revolution over the past three decades.[6]

This ends the Heritage Foundation data.[7]

Census Data Findings

In the year 2000, the 1998 census data became available. Here are the findings:

- Households headed by unmarried partners grew 72 percent in the last decade.
- Households headed by single mothers or fathers increased 25 percent and 62 percent respectively.
- Nuclear families dropped below 25 percent of households in the U. S.
- 33 percent of all babies were born to unmarried woman compared to 3.8 percent in 1940.
- Other studies show cohabitation increased 1000 percent from 1960 to 1998.
- Households headed by same sex couples are soaring.
- More unmarried women in their twenties and thirties are choosing to raise children alone.
- The divorce rate is as high among born-again Christians as among the general population for the first time, according to Dr. James Dobson of *Focus on the Family*.

What It Means

The data leaves little doubt that the culture has abandoned the sacrament of marriage and that the family is unraveling. Parents have not passed on the faith, children have not seen a good example in the home, and they have no role models. The fact is that for most youth today, God is irrelevant, a complete non-factor. Many children today have several mothers and fathers, and can have six sets of grandparents. At the Parents Teachers Organization (PTO) meeting, when the teacher asks a father to identify himself, two or three people may stand. The impact of the breakdown of the family on society cannot be understated. Everything in society is directly affected by broken families, and the kids are the walking wounded playing out their fear and confusion in many ways.

The devastating impact of family disintegration on children is indisputable. A special U. S. commission consisting of authorities on child development was convened in the 1990's to examine the general health of adolescents. The report from this commission, called *Code Blue*, concluded, "Never before has one generation of American teenagers been less healthy, less cared for, or less prepared for life." The data gets worse each year. This is occurring in one of the most affluent and privileged nations in the history of the world. It is a direct result of marital disintegration and related forces at work against the family.[8] If you are not alarmed by the data, you should be. Seventy percent of all African-American babies and nineteen percent of all white in the U. S. are born out of wedlock. Only 34 percent of all children in America will live with both biological parents through the age of eighteen. It gets more alarming, because 62 percent of mothers with children under the age of three are employed. In 1975, the number was half that. Fully 72 percent of mothers with children under eighteen hold jobs. That means there is no one home to nurture and raise these children.[9] Is it any wonder that America is a mess? The above data is stunning in its social implication for the next generation.

The prison population is where we see the most revealing data. Prisons are filled primarily by men who were abandoned or rejected by their fathers. Motivational speaker and writer, Zig Ziglar, quoted his friend, Bill Glass, a dedicated evangelist who counseled incarcerated men every weekend for 25 years. Glass said that of the thousands of prisoners he had met, not *one* of them genuinely loved his father. Ninety-five percent of men on death row hated their fathers.[10] With this being the state of the family, what does the future hold?

Pollster George Barna reveals that if a child hasn't been introduced to Jesus by the time he or she is fourteen, there is a four percent chance of becoming a Christian by the ages of fourteen through eighteen, and a six percent chance in the remainder of life. The family is critical to the propagation of the faith. The health of the domestic church (the family) is critical to the health of civilization.

For those who do not think a healthy home is important to school performance, observe the following data. In an editorial on the ineffectiveness of government fixes for schools dated January 6, 2002, columnist George Will writes, "The crucial predictor of a school's performance is the quality of the children's families." The presence of two parents in the home is "supremely important," he goes on. Quoting a study by Paul Barton, "America's Smallest School: The Family," he points out that "North Dakota ranked first in math scores and second in the percentage of children in two-parent families. The District of Columbia ranked next to last in math scores and last in the family composition scale." The rest of the state rankings fall in line with this factor. Further, "In 1999 almost half (48.4 percent) of all children born to women ages twenty to 24…were born out of wedlock…. Between birth and their 19th birthdays, American children spend nine percent of their time in school, 91 percent elsewhere. The fate of American education is being shaped not by legislative acts but by the fact that, increasingly, 'elsewhere' is not in an intact family."[11]

If anyone does not think a stable home is important in the development of youth, consider the case of Taliban John Walker, also known as "Jihad Johnny." When he was seventeen years old, John Walker's mother became a convert to Buddhism, and his father separated from his mother and moved in with a man to pursue a homosexual relationship. Meanwhile, young John was reading the autobiography of Malcolm X. When his father, Frank Lindh, deserted his family in 1997, John Walker Lindh began to move to the strongest male figure he could find—Mohammed. Taking the cause a step further, the hurt and confused young man moved to Pakistan to study the ways of the Koran. The rest is history.[12]

Hidden Scars—Divorce

Divorce levels in Anglo-Saxon nations have been high for many years. A Rutgers University study published last June noted that 40–45 percent of marriages in the United States will end in divorce, if current trends continue.

The divorce mentality is beginning to grip other countries too, including ones of long-standing Catholic traditions. In Italy, divorces tripled during the period 1980 to 1999, according to an October 20, 2001, report in the newspaper *La Repubblica*. In Spain, where divorce was legalized twenty years ago, one out of every three marriages ends in divorce, the Madrid paper *ABC* reported on December 17, 2001.

A number of recent studies have clearly established the high costs of the breakdown of marriages. In 2000, Judith Wallerstein published "The Unexpected Legacy of Divorce: A 25 Year Landmark Study," which found children who grew up in divorced families were less likely to marry, more likely to divorce, and more likely to have children out of wedlock and to use drugs.

Wallerstein based her conclusions on in-depth interviews with 100 children in a Northern California community who were followed by researchers for 25 years. She observed that the adult children of divorce tend to expect their relationships to fail and they struggle with the fear of loss, conflict, betrayal and loneliness.

Another work on divorce also published in 2000 was *The Great Divorce Controversy* by Edward S. Williams. Part of the book is dedicated to compiling information from studies on the consequences of divorce. Williams notes that in the 1960's and 1970's pro-divorce academics produced a number of reports alleging that divorce could have beneficial consequences for some children. Further research has proven that optimism to be false.

In 1994, for example, an investigation among 152 families in Exeter, England, showed that even in high-conflict (but intact) families, fewer children were unhappy compared with those in broken homes.

Children, in fact, were prepared to put up with family conflict, and preferred their parents to remain together.

Williams cited another study of 5,000 cases of child abuse in England from 1977 to 1990. Children who live with a mother and father substitute are almost nine times more likely to be abused than children living with both their married parents in a traditional family.

As for the adults, the book quotes from a California study that showed how a third of parents were severely depressed after divorce. Depression was particularly common among women, affecting almost 50 percent. Even ten or fifteen years after the event, the hurt and humiliation of divorce continued to occupy a central position in the emotions of many adults.

Further material on the ill effects of divorce are contained in Jennifer Roback Morse's 2001 book *Love and Economics: Why the Laissez-Faire Family Doesn't Work*. Reviewing a number of recent studies, the book observes that children of single-parent families are more likely to drop out of school, have babies out of wedlock, or abuse alcohol and drugs.

Morse also noted that children in single-parent environments have between 50 percent and 80 percent higher scores for anti-social behavior, peer conflict and social withdrawal. They are also more likely to suffer from anxiety, depression and hyperactivity. Moreover, these ill effects are not primarily due to the economic hardships after a divorce. Income differences, observes the book, account for only a portion of the problems.

The book also deals with the argument of those who defend divorce by alleging it is better for all involved to put an end to unhappy marriages. While it is true that some children benefit from the ending of high-conflict marriages, such situations represent a small proportion of divorces. Physical abuse is simply not a factor among the vast majority of married women. In fact, unmarried, cohabiting women are more likely to be abused than are wives.

In Australia, evidence on the costs of divorce are contained in Barry Maley's book *Family and Marriage in Australia*, recently published by the Center for Independent Studies. In a December 8, 2001, article for The Age newspaper of Melbourne, Maley wrote, "In the past generation, Australian family life and marriage have undergone a revolution that has left wounds in the lives of thousands of adults and children."

Forty years ago, observed Maley, 90 percent of children grew up in married families, living with their natural parents. That figure is now down to 68 percent. In this same time span, violent juvenile crime increased fourfold, suicide rates for young male adults quadrupled, and taxes rose sharply to pay for the large numbers of single mothers on government welfare.

Maley argued: "The consequences of divorce for children may mean, on average, a period of emotional disturbance, separation anxiety, unhappiness, often-difficult life adjustments, lower school and career performance, and, for many, difficulties with relationships in adulthood."[13]

Pope John Paul II restated the traditional position of the Catholic Church regarding divorce on January 28, 2002, when he met with lawyers and judges of the Roman Rota, the Court of Appeals for the Holy See that is responsible for, among other things, pronouncing sentences of marital nullity. The Holy Father said, "Agents of law in the civil area must avoid being personally involved in anything that might imply cooperation with divorce.... In exercising a liberal profession, lawyers can always decline to use their profession for an end that is contrary to justice, such as divorce." The lawyer is not to use his talents to destroy families, but to help those "undergoing marital crises" to reconcile. "It might seem that divorce is so rooted in certain social environments, that it is no longer worthwhile to continue to combat it, by spreading a mentality, a social custom, and civil legislation in favor of indissolubility," the Pope said. "And yet, it is worthwhile! In fact, this good is part of the foundation of every society, as a necessary condition for the family's existence." A marriage is only to be declared null—invalid—when it "took place under duress or out of fear, by deceit, or by rejecting some of its essential elements."[14]

The Relentless Homosexual Agenda

The Pacific Justice Institute recently filed a lawsuit, on behalf of parents, against the Novato Unified School District in Novato, Calif., for authorizing pro-homosexual assemblies without any prior notice or parental consent. The suit alleges the parents' fundamental constitutional and civil rights to direct the upbringing of their children and the free exercise of religion were violated.

"This is the beginning of a litigation campaign to defend the rights of parents," declares Brad Dacus, president of the nonprofit legal defense organization specializing in the defense of religious freedom, parental rights and other civil liberties.

The presentations, entitled "Cootie Shots," exposed elementary school children as young as seven to skits containing homosexual and lesbian overtures. "Cootie Shots: Theatrical Inoculations Against Bigotry" is a collection of plays, songs and poems written by members of Fringe Benefits Theatre, a coalition of theater activists who, according to their web site, are "dedicated to building bridges between gay, lesbian, bisexual and transgender (GLBT) youth and their straight peers, teachers and parents." The United Teachers of Los Angeles and the Gay Lesbian Straight Education Network (GLSEN) of Los Angeles created a classroom activity guide to accompany "Cootie Shots" which GLSEN sells on its web site.

"Cootie Shots," according to its authors, seeks to "address acceptance and tolerance of homosexuals and lesbians in an age-appropriate manner" and "celebrate diversity by presenting role models from many different races, classes, genders, abilities, sexual orientations, religions, ages, shapes and sizes."

In an interview with TCG books, co-author Mark Rosenthal describes, "My biggest success came after a show I had just performed, when a small group of kids approached me. The spokeschild asked if I was gay, and when I said yes they shrieked and ran away, giggling. A few minutes later, they reappeared, and the spokeschild apologized. She said she was sorry if she had hurt my feelings. We had a conversation, where the children asked several times if I was really gay, several saying that they had never met a gay person. I told them it's quite possible they had, but he or she might have been afraid of their initial reaction. They reflected upon this, and seemed to be considering this possibility for the first time."[15]

The onslaught against traditional values continues everywhere. For example, the American Academy of Pediatrics has endorsed homosexual adoption, saying homosexual couples can provide the loving, stable, and emotionally healthy family life children need. Citing estimates suggesting that as many as nine million U. S. children have at last one homosexual parent, the Academy urged its 55,000 members to take an active role in supporting measures that allow homosexual adoption. Joseph Hagan, Jr., chairman of the committee, says, "there is no existing data to support the widely held belief that there are negative outcomes" for children raised by homosexual parents. The Academy said it is more crucial for pediatricians to get involved because homosexual households are becoming more prevalent.[16]

The result of a home not living as God intends has been a disaster in every aspect for American life. Destroyed lives are the result. The issue is obedience to what God has asked and intends for humanity. Unless there are wholesale changes, the future is going to be an unstable and uncertain place for all of America, and especially for its youth who will be subjected to increasing assaults by homosexuals.

Seeking Fellowship with the 'Shrink'

At New York's Columbia University, 2,600 students sought aid from the campus counseling center in 2001, a forty percent increase since the 1994–95 academic year. It is not just the Ivy League schools that have witnessed the rise in a perceived need for mental health assistance among its students, as is shown by the forty-eight percent-increase in demand for the same type of care over three years at the State University of New York at Purchase. Adding greatly to the onslaught of the mentally overwhelmed were the terrorist attacks of September 11. Besides the old problems of leaving home, fitting in, finding the right career, and other issues, there are concerns born of modern societal dysfunction, such as split families, eradication of whole classes of traditional careers, technological and informational bombardment, and "sexual-identity" decisions. Many students, contrary to earlier generations, now feel no stigma about seeking mental help. Indeed, many of these offspring of the psychotherapy generation that came of age in the sixties and seventies were brought up unloading many of their problems to psychiatrists. Contributing to the situation is the exposure to ridiculous pressures at much earlier ages, for example, preschool development programs that Baby-Boomer-and-beyond parents believe will give their children intelligence advantages later in life.

A couple of the common problems plaguing college-age students are anxiety and depression. One young lady at Columbia, described as "a quintessential overachiever," complains, "It's like a compulsion. I just have to do well." She has panicked to the point of loss of control during tests and has tried anti-anxiety medication. She considers herself to be "pretty high-strung," but says that she has learned how to recognize when she was putting too much pressure on herself.

A young man at Columbia, who feels tremendous pressure to follow in the footsteps of his father and uncle, who were Fortune 500 executives, has felt at times that "every conversation was a sham," has wondered how many true friendships he had made at college, and was disappointed that none of his dates had led to a long-term girlfriend. He took to holing himself up in his room for days, ordering in food and refusing to see anybody. Soon thereafter, he embarked on an ongoing series of therapy sessions, both on and off campus.

The more materialism, designer this and that, sexual license, and life without boundaries, the more that youths are sitting on couches. As the world disconnects from the purpose of life, the more this trend will increase.

Universities are responding to the overwhelming increase in reported mental problems with expensive and complete overhauls of mental health services. The Massachusetts Institute Technology, owner of the highest student-suicide rate in the country, showed a fifty percent increase in the use of its mental health facilities from 1995 to 2000, along with an increase of 69 percent in student psychiatric hospitalizations. Columbia just instituted a $100,000-a-year study tracking 200 freshmen to determine why certain students encounter mental problems and others do not. This is on top of the cost to employ the equivalent of twenty full-time psychiatrists, psychologists, and other mental health professionals. Even with all this, there is great concern that not enough time can be allotted to all that seek help.[17]

As Goes the Family, So Goes the Nation

The family, traditionally defined as the rock of civilizations, is an endangered species. Satan has attacked the family relentlessly and effectively to the point where normalcy is not even understood let alone sought. Americans have blindly followed their base instincts and desires of the flesh, creating a paganish lifestyle devoid of the grace necessary to obtain happiness and peace in their personal lives, family lives, and within their communities. America has invited 'foreign' cultural beliefs and perverted lifestyles into its everyday existence. Yet, dissatisfied temporally and spiritually with the outcome, Americans increasingly look towards what Saint Paul says are "doctrines that tickle the ears." including fornication and drug and alcohol abuse as a means to offset their personal responsibilities to their families and to God.

America has lost its sense of what is wrong. In Scripture the Lord calls it sin. The clergy of all denominations stopped talking about sin long ago. The judicial system simply calls it tolerance. The psychiatric community calls it irreconcilable differences, complexes, phobias, neurosis and all sorts of psychobabble. The result today is that no one is a sinner. A generation of youth is lost. Their loss is the direct consequence of the present adult population's corruption and abdication of spiritual and family responsibilities. What families need right now is a healthy dose of intolerance sprinkled with correction. "No!" is a complete sentence. Today's youth will eventually become our adult citizens and leaders. What does that suggest for our nation's future? Is America any different than previous civilizations that perished for precisely the same reasons?

10

The Great Idol

This is serious business: Sex and Violence and Rock 'n Roll!

This quote from a John Cougar Mellencamp song of the same title concisely summarizes what virtually every American family fails to appreciate: ***This is serious business!***

Let's take a look at an example of the influence of the entertainment industry on our children. On April 20, 1999, Eric Harris and Dylan Klebold launched an assault on Columbine High School in Littleton, Colorado, murdering thirteen and wounding 23 before turning the guns on themselves. Although it is impossible to know exactly what caused these teens to attack their own classmates and teachers, several factors were surely involved. One contributing factor was violent video games. Harris and Klebold enjoyed playing the bloody, shoot-'em-up video game Doom, a game licensed by the U. S. military to train soldiers to effectively kill. The Simon Wiesenthal Center, which tracks internet hate groups, found in its archives a copy of Harris' web site with a version of Doom that he had customized. In his version there are two shooters, each with extra weapons and unlimited ammunition, and the other people in the game can't fight back. For a class project, Harris and Klebold made a videotape that was similar to their customized version of Doom. In the video, Harris and Klebold dress in trench coats, carry guns, and kill school athletes. They acted out their videotaped performance in real life less than a year later. An investigator associated with the Wiesenthal Center said Harris and Klebold were "playing out their game in God mode."[1]

Every family member is deluged by a multi-billion dollar mega-group of companies through various forms of electronic (television, cinema, video games, internet services and music) and print media, which collectively is diabolically capable of effectively indoctrinating each and every citizen of America, changing attitudes, beliefs, interests, opinions and actions away from traditional Judeo-Christian ideals towards the new world order of paganism and barbarism under state oversight.

Television since the 1960's has had an incalculable effect on America's families. Never as today have immorality, impurity and obscenity been so continually propagandized, through the press and all the means of social communication. Above all, television has become the perverse instrument of a daily bombardment with obscene images, directed to corrupt the purity of the mind and the heart of all. The places of entertainment—in particular the movies and clubs—have become places of public profanation of one's human and Christian dignity. Television has molded the minds of the world's youth. The invention of the television has been Satan's finest hour. In the 1950's and 60's, America had uplifting television programs like *Leave It to Beaver*, *Make Room for Daddy*, *Father Knows Best*, and *The Wonderful World of Disney* on Sunday nights and other similar family shows. Forty years later, it is barely possible to find a show on television that is not steeped in the carnal, with "Viewer discretion advised."

The latest craze among the youth is the leader of the former 1970's heavy metal band, Black Sabbath. Ozzy Osbourne, also known as "the Prince of Darkness," was the one, for those not familiar, who bit off the head of a bat while in concert. Osbourne and his dysfunctional family placed twelve MTV cameras throughout their home so the world could view everything that went on in their Hollywood mansion. It is touted as the 'family of today' replacing the 'old'—*The Osbournes* pushing out *Ozzie and Harriet*. From start to finish, the MTV cable show is steeped not just in the profane, but in raw evil. Due to the profanity, more words are bleeped out than are heard. It is the most popular show in the twenty-year history of the MTV network. Advertisers are flocking to it because of its tremendous following among eighteen to thirty-four-year-olds; and it also has a much stronger appeal to those 35 and older than does the other MTV fare. Osbourne's popularity even provided him the opportunity to dine with President Bush at the May 4, 2002, White House Correspondents Dinner as the guest of the Fox News' Greta Van Sustern. [2] *The Osbournes* is only one of many indicators that American morality is in a complete free fall.

Americans need to realize that $32.3 billion in 1999 television broadcasting revenue, generating tens of thousands of commercials a year with their dominating and pervasive influence, is just the tip of the iceberg. According to an industry research firm, Veronis Suhler, 1999 revenue for cable television is estimated at $45.5 billion, the newspaper business at $27.5 billion, Hollywood at $31 billion and professional and educational publishing $14.8 billion. Yet, the fastest growing segment of entertainment, where billions of investment dollars are directed into mass market and infrastructure development, is overseen by dated and ineffectual industry and governmental regulations. This segment includes audio/video systems, games, computer systems, satellite receivers, portable digital communications devices, and telecommunications and cable-based internet services. When Bill Clinton was inaugurated President in 1992, there were 100 internet web sites in America. When George W. Bush was inaugurated eight years later, there were tens of millions in the world. That's how quickly things have changed. These emerging products and services only magnify the problem. They mass-commercialize innovative means to introduce two-way, highly repetitive participation between the user and the service or program. One characteristic of this new generation of entertainment is its promotion of personal self-gratification through ever-escalating sexually explicit content, aggressive behavioral motivation techniques and violent outcome-based objectives and results. With the ever larger market penetration of the use of the internet and the introduction of higher-speed connectivity, for example, cable and Digital Subscriber Line (DSL) modems, the entertainment industry is morphing increasingly towards such two-way communications that is alarmingly unrestricted. It offers XXX-rated and violent subscription services, programs and games that are predominately unfiltered or sufficiently self-regulated by Internet Service Providers, the retail establishment, manufacturers or the government. Interactive sexual content is on the verge of dominating pornography, thus offering another dimension of perversion. Further exacerbating this problem is the inability of existing technologies at home on the computer desktop to filter effectively the types of services and programs parents wish their children to use or to avoid. This is particularly true of the recent introduction of a new generation of file sharing programs such as Aimster that became available coincidentally when Napster was taken to court. The sophistication of the service provider is making it difficult to filter what reaches your eyes.

This is all the more reason why Americans must make certain that the entertainment and communications industries and their related hardware and software "appliance" partners serve the public interest. This goes beyond the Communications Act, the Federal Communications Commission, the Federal Trade Commission, and Federal and State government agencies. This is a call to every parent in America to take responsibility and initiative to proactively supervise what types of entertainment is appropriate for the health and well-being of their children and our society. Accessing much of the media today is like hooking a pipe in your home to a sewer and spraying it around the house.

What follows is a compelling representation of statistics and commentary from an array of renowned subject matter experts and professional organizations which should sufficiently pique one's awareness of, and alarm at, the pervasiveness and severity of the problem with the entertainment industry. Much of it centers on television, which by its nature and history is the foundation of the emerging entertainment paradigm that is a greater threat to our families than television alone. The television in America has elevated itself to the level of a shrine, with most movement in the home centered around it.

Illuminating Statistics:

❖ Children aged two to five average 25 hours per week watching television.[3]

❖ Children aged six to eleven average more than 22 hours per week watching television.[4]

❖ Children aged twelve to seventeen average 23 hours per week watching television.[5]

❖ 30 percent of middle-aged men (median age in the study was 39.5) watch television three or more hours per day, while another 61 percent watch television one to two hours per day.[6]

❖ "By the time most Americans are eighteen years old, they have spent more time in front of the television set than they have spent in school, and far more than they have spent talking with their teachers, their friends or even their parents."[7]

❖ "By first grade, most children have spent the equivalent of three school years in front of the television set."[8]

❖ The Kaiser Family Foundations found that the typical American child spends more than 38 hours a week as a "media consumer" in a home that averages three televisions, three tape players, three radios, two VCRs, two CD players, a video game player and a computer, plus newspapers, magazines and comic books.

❖ 62 percent of fourth graders say they spend more than three hours per day watching television.[9]

❖ By the time today's child reaches age 70, he or she will have spent from seven to ten years watching television.[10]

❖ The typical American child will witness 8,000 murders and 100,000 acts of televised violence in his lifetime.[11]

❖ By comparison, the association, TV-Free America, estimates the number of violent acts children see on television by the age of eighteen as 200,000.[12]

❖ Number of hours per day the television is on in the average U. S. home: six hours, 47 minutes[13]

❖ Number of violent acts children see on television by the age of 18: 200,000[14]

❖ Number of murders seen on television by the time an average child finishes elementary school: 8,000[15]

❖ Number of 30-second commercials seen in a year by an average child: 20,000[16]

❖ Number of minutes per week parents spend in meaningful conversation with their children: 38.5[17]

❖ Percentage of four-to-six year olds, who, when asked to choose between watching television and spending time with their fathers, preferred television: 54 percent[18]

❖ "By the time adolescents graduate from high school, they will have spent 15,000 hours watching television, compared with 12,000 hours spent in the classroom.... American media are thought to be the most sexually suggestive in the Western hemisphere. The average American adolescent will view nearly 14,000 sexual references per year, yet only 165 of these references deal with birth control, self-control, abstinence, or the risk of pregnancy or Sexually Transmitted Diseases (STD). In a recent content analysis, 56 percent of all programs on American television were found to contain sexual content. The so-called "family hour" of prime-time television (8:00–9:00 p. m.) contains on average more than eight sexual incidents, which is more than four times what it contained in 1976. Nearly one third of family hour shows contain sexual references..."[19]

❖ "The Kaiser Family Foundation's biennial "Sex on TV" report revealed that television's sexual content has grown from about half (56 percent) of all shows in the 1997–98 television season to two-thirds (68 percent) last season. Three of four (75 percent) prime-time network shows included sexual content in 1999–2000, up from two-thirds (67 percent) in 1997–98.[20]

❖ Internet usage reached record levels in October (2001) as 115 million Americans went online, according to measurements released by Nielsen/NetRatings.[21]

❖ By 1998, approximately 40 percent of all U. S. households owned a personal computer; roughly one third of these homes had access to the internet. Many scholars, technologists, and social critics believe that these changes and the internet, in particular, are transforming economic and social life.

❖ The Parents Music Resource Center states that American adolescents listen to approximately 10,500 hours of rock music between the periods of 7th to 12th grades.

❖ A recent survey by the Recording Industry Association of America found that many parents do not know what lyrics are contained in the popular music their children listen to.[22]

Impact of Television and the Cinema on Intellect, Academics, Psychology and Social Behavior.
❖ There is a direct correlation between the amount of time a child spends watching television and his or her scores on standardized achievement tests—the more television watched, the lower the scores.[23]

❖ "Every day, all across the United States, a parade of louts, losers and con-men whom most people would never allow in their homes enter anyway, through television."[24]

❖ "Unsupervised television is like letting your children play out on the street at any hour of the day or night with whomever they come across."[25]

❖ "The primary danger of the television screen lies not so much in the behavior it produces—although there is danger there—as in the behavior it prevents: the talks, the games, the family festivities and arguments..."[26]

❖ Crime is at least ten times as prevalent on television as in the real world.[27]

❖ Our fellow citizens cherish the institution of marriage and consider religion an important priority in life, but the entertainment industry promotes every form of sexual adventurism and regularly ridicules religious believers as crooks or crazies.[28]

❖ Dr. Jennings Bryant of the University of Alabama declares that "some of the most durable and important effects of watching television come in the form of subtle, incremental, cumulative changes in the way we view the world." These cumulative effects are particularly potent for adolescents who are going through a "turbulent time of life in which very insecure people struggle with their self-concepts and their values on a daily basis...when values appear to be quite frail and very malleable." Dr. Bryant, citing three studies, concludes that "heavy exposure to prime-time programming featuring sexual intimacy between unmarried people can clearly result in altered moral judgment."[29]

❖ Dr. Bradley S. Greenberg of Michigan State University reports that adolescents take in some 3,000 to 4,000 references to sexual activity in movies and television each year. If they happen to watch music video entertainment for one hour per day, e.g. MTV, the total goes 1,500 times more a year in video-sex experiences.[30]

Violence is a recurring and dominating attribute merchandized by the entertainment industry. Here are some select commentaries on the nature of such violence and its impact on our society:

❖ "Much of what they (children) see on television represents violence as an appropriate way to solve interpersonal problems, to avenge slights and insults, make up for injustice, and get what you want out of life."[31]

❖ In our private lives, most of us deplore violence and feel little sympathy for the criminals who perpetrate it; but movies, television and popular music [add video games to this list—author's note] all revel in graphic brutality, glorifying vicious and sadistic characters who treat killing as a joke.[32]

❖ Nearly all parents want to convey to their children the importance of self-discipline, hard work, and decent manners, but the entertainment media celebrate vulgar behavior, contempt for all authority, and obscene language—which is inserted even in "family fare" where it is least expected.[33]

❖ More than 3,000 studies over the past 30 years offer evidence that violent programming has a measurable effect on young minds.[34]

❖ In 1980, the most violent prime time show on television registered 22 acts of violence per hour. In 1992 the most violent prime time show, *Young Indiana Jones*, registered 60 acts of violence per hour.[35]

❖ In 1992, WGN's *Cookie's Cartoon Club*, Fox's *Tom and Jerry Kids*, and Nickelodeon's *Looney Tunes* averaged 100, 88 and 80 acts of violence per hour, respectively.[36]

❖ Half of North America's murders and rapes can be attributed directly or indirectly to television viewing.[37]

A recent national poll of children, conducted by Children Now, and an analysis of the television content they watch indicates that a majority of children say that men and boys on television are often portrayed as focused on the opposite sex; as one boy said, "His main goal is to get the girl." The same study concluded that:

❖ 90 percent of our nation's boys regularly or often watch televised sports programs, with their accompanying commercials. One of sports coverage's dominant messages is that the most aggressive athletes are rewarded. Typical of sports coverage and commentary is the continual depiction and replay of athletes taking big hits and engaging in reckless acts of speed and violent crashes.

❖ The overall top three role models for boys are Will Smith, Bart Simpson, and Tim Allen.

❖ In music videos male performers are nearly three times as likely as females to have a primary theme of social protest or bravado, while females are four times more likely to feature a primary theme of love/romance.

❖ Over one-quarter of the music videos include some degree of attention to female breasts, legs or torsos. Almost two-thirds of videos feature females as props, characters who are used by the central performer in the course of his/her actions or who appear as background. Such female props are likely to be semi-nude (25 percent) or to be dressed in revealing clothing.

One would have to be near the level of idiocy not to see the connections between the media and the rise of immoral behavior. Immorality is spreading like a filth being propagated through television and the media. A subtle and diabolical tactic of seduction and corruption has found its way into every family. The most defenseless victims are the youth.

Impact of Violent Video Games

An illuminating report published in the *Journal of Personality and Social Psychology* offers significant insights into the possible impact of video games on the thoughts and behavior of the users of such games.[38] The study starts with the assumption (based on previous studies and findings) that children and adults derive behavior characteristics in part from lessons learned from television and movies. Therefore, it follows that one could anticipate that violent video games would have similar, if not larger effects on aggressive behavior. With the introduction and market dominance of dramatically more violent games in the 1990's, such as "Mortal Kombat," present research data indicates that potentially harmful consequences of playing violent video games is a valid concern. The researchers identified three dangerous characteristics of violent video games that suggest such games are more dangerous than violent television programs and movies:

❖ Unlike a viewer of television or a movie, the video game player assumes the identity of the hero, and sometimes chooses a character whose persona the player then assumes. The player controls the action of this character and usually sees the video game world through that character's eyes. In other words, the main character is synonymous with the game player, potentially heightening the game's impact. Researchers find this impact appears to be residual in nature with the player exhibiting greater aggression afterwards than a viewer of violent television or movies.

❖ Research reveals that the aggressive behavior experienced from the video game usually increases later aggressive behavior. The active role of the video game player includes choosing to initiate thoughts and actions in an aggressive manner. Researchers believe that this choice in the thought and action components of video games may well lead to the construction of a more complete aggressive bahavioral pattern or "script" than would occur in the more passive role assumed in watching violent movies or television shows.

❖ A third reason to expect video games to have a bigger impact than television or movies involves the addictive nature that is developed from their strong learning experience. The reinforcement characteristics of violent video games may also enhance the learning and performance of aggressive scripts from the reward and punishment outcomes that the games enforce. Video games are believed to be the "perfect paradigm for the induction of 'addictive' behavior."[39] This appears to be confirmed by a study in 1998 which indicates that one in five adolescents can be classified as pathologically dependent on computer games.

Longer-term effects are still being assessed. Nevertheless, a player of violent video games learns and practices new aggression-related scripts that become more and more accessible for use when real-life conflict situations arise. Repeated exposure to such games does indeed lead to effective altering of the player's basic personality. The consequences of this learned aggressive behavior could manifest themselves in everyday social interactions. With the recent trend toward greater realism and more graphic violence and sexual overtones in video games, combined with the rising popularity of these games, parents should ban these games in their homes.

Postmortem

When the movie, *Gone with the Wind*, was released in 1939, there was a war in Hollywood among censors over the use of the word "damn." Endless debates revolved around Rhett Butler's line, "Frankly, my dear, I don't give a damn." Only sixty years later look where we are. How did we slide so far so fast? What are the roots?

Leave It to Beaver debuted in 1957 on American television. On one of the opening shows a bathroom was censored from being shown. In a generation we've come a very long way. When Aleksandr Solzhenitsyn was asked how the Russian Revolution of 1917 destroyed Russia in such a short time, his simple and profound answer was, "Men have forgotten God." Once that happened, the lie became the pillar of the state.

When the U. S. Supreme Court decision of 1962 disallowed prayer in the classroom, the die was cast that would doom the next generation. Why? Because the root of all civilizations' problems, and the reason they perish, is an alienation from God. When man is alienated from God, he is alienated from himself. Once alienated from himself, he becomes alienated from others. Once alienated from others, he destroys others. If the pattern continues, he will destroy himself. Alienation from God is the root of violence in the world.

America's values and morals are being eaten away in part by an entertainment industry that with its collaborative partners in products and services appear to be devoid of any real public concern other than the sustained profitability and return to their shareholders. In a *Wall Street Journal* opinion piece on December 10, 1993, Bill Bennett described the current state of America as "a degraded society.... Specifically, our problem is what the ancients called acedia...spiritual torpor, an absence of zeal for divine things.... Acedia arises from a heart steeped in the worldly and carnal, and from a low esteem of divine things." The consequence is "a coarseness, a callousness, a cynicism, a banality, and a vulgarity."

Americans, especially Christians, Jews and Moslems, need to re-educate themselves on what their scriptures and traditions demand of them. Americans need to reflect in their hearts on what the possible consequences are should they choose to ignore history and the Ten Commandments. It would be best to remove ourselves far from anything that can contaminate the purity of our hearts and the chastity of our lives. Do not watch profane shows. Do not waste time before the television set, which is the most powerful instrument in the hands of Satan for spreading everywhere the darkness of sin and of impurity. Television is the idol spoken of in the book of Revelation, built to be adored by all the nations of the earth, and to which the Evil One gives shape and movement so that it might become, in his hands, a terrible means of seduction and perversion.

Throughout history, mankind has wondered what the idol might be. People of every faith have thought it to be a leader of a denomination they believed to be evil or in apostasy. Television is the idol that relentlessly seduces and perverts the will of Heaven.

11

Come See, Grandpa

The Lord spoke to Moses, saying: Speak to all the congregation of the children of Israel, and you shall say to them: Be you holy, because I the Lord your God am holy.

—Leviticus 19:1–2

Regardless of the debate between First Amendment and censorship advocates over pornography and its various derivative manifestations, a growing community of parents, psychologists, sociologists and religious leaders are increasingly concerned over the ease of access to, and the impact of, pornographic material from the television/cable networks and internet service providers. Hollywood is big business run by morally bankrupt people. Hollywood continues to hide behind the clout of people like Jack Valenti, President of the Motion Picture Association of America (MPAA), based two blocks from the White House. As a lobbyist, MPAA is extremely effective in killing legislation that that would regulate movie content. This association is one of many to blame for exposing America to entertainment filth because of the money changing hands between Hollywood and Congress. It always boils down to money.

Hollywood and Capitol Hill are deeply committed to one another, especially as it pertains to campaign contributions. The traditional allure of sex promoted from the public cinema and television networks has blossomed aggressively and privately into our homes, becoming more visually and audibly explicit over cable programs and internet services. The impact on the family and society as a whole is viewed as significant and detrimental. Research studies indicate that pornography encourages behavior that could harm individuals and their families. Pornography promotes the appeal of adultery and prostitution with a corresponding unreal expectation that can initiate dangerous promiscuous behavior. Pornography, often viewed in secret, creates deception, and brings a great deal of impurity into the relationship of a married couple—a situation that can easily lead to divorce.

Ask any parent and they will agree that significant harm is caused by child pornography, which consists of photographs, videos, magazines, books and films that depict children engaged in sexual acts, all of which are illegal. The only ones who don't seem to get it are the academics who publish bogus studies in favor of Hollywood. Yet, young people are exposed to sexually explicit material on a daily basis through network television, movies, music and the internet. The sad reality is that a majority of sex education is taking place in the media. Worse still, the most dangerous aspect of the internet is its use by pedophiles. The National Center for Missing and Exploited Children found that one in five children age ten to seventeen that regularly uses the internet has received a sexual solicitation while online. One in four was unwillingly exposed to images of naked people or people having sex, often in 'spam' e-mails. What most parents do not know is that today's typical child molester befriends the child, often through internet chat rooms, and, after building "trust," exposes the child to pornography. This is done in an attempt to make the child think that this behavior is acceptable, and to lure him or her to participate. It is typical of a child molester to pose as youngsters on the internet to communicate with other children and, after gaining the confidence of the child, to attempt to arrange a meeting with the child in person. For children who are recruited successfully in this manner, the experience of exploitation and abuse ultimately becomes a lifelong struggle, leaving them with fear that their participation, or worse still rape or sodomy, will become public.

Presented below are various statistics and findings which present a clear picture of the nature of the problems that pornography in conjunction with the cable and internet industry presents to our families and society and the magnitude of their collective impact.

❖ Data collected by Adams Media Research, Forrester Research and Veronis Suhler Communications Industry Report indicates that the annual revenue from pornography for adult video, internet, pay-per-view, and magazines ranges from $2.6 to $3.9 billion.[1]

❖ "The pornography industry took in more than $8 billion dollars in 1999, more than all revenues generated by Rock-and-Roll and Country music, more than America spent on Broadway productions, theater, ballet, jazz and classical music combined."[2]

❖ In 1998, $1billion was spent in the U. S. online on "adult content," 69 percent of the total internet content sales.[3]

❖ Though a valuable information resource, the internet caused explosive growth for the pornography industry. Currently, there are over 300,000 pornographic web sites on the internet, according to David Burt of N2H2. (The reader will see other totals for these web sites in this book as different sources are quoted.)

❖ A comprehensive two-year study by a leading web intelligence and traffic measurement service revealed "sex" was the most popular term for which people searched. Of all the terms searched for online, 0.3289 percent—or roughly one of every 300 terms, were "sex." According to their online searching habits, people want "sex" more than they want "games," "music," "travel," "jokes," "cars," "jobs," "weather" and "health" combined. "Porn" (along with "porno" and "pornography") was the 4th most popular search term. "Nude" (and "nudes"), "xxx," "Playboy" and "erotic stories" (and "erotica") were also among the top twenty. The most popular celebrities searched for were Britney Spears, Pamela Anderson, Backstreet Boys, Jennifer Lopez and Eminem. Pokemon was the most popular specific toy or game searched. Playboy was the most popular media property.[4]

❖ "A nationwide survey of 1,031 adults conducted by Zogby International and Focus on the Family March 8–10, 2000, found that twenty percent of the respondents—which represents as many as 40 million adults—admitted visiting a sexually-oriented web site. Thirty-seven percent of males between the ages of eighteen and 24 admitted they had visited sex sites. Almost eighteen percent of those who identified themselves as Christians and eighteen percent of married men also admitted viewing these sites. According to the Nielsen Net ratings, 17.5 million surfers visited porn sites from their homes in January, a 40 percent increase compared with September of 1999."[5]

❖ Children spent 64.9 percent more time on pornography sites than they did on game sites in September 2000, and 27.5 percent of children age seventeen and under visited an adult web site, which represents three million unique underage visitors. Of these minors, 21.2 percent were fourteen or younger and 40.2 percent were female.[6]

❖ "A new study released this week by the Family Research Council, 'Dangerous Access, 2000 Edition: Uncovering Internet

Pornography in America's Libraries,' says that the American Library Association is ignoring a 'sea of evidence' that 'internet pornography and related sex crimes are a serious problem in America's libraries.' The study used the Freedom of Information Act to get library reports of internet traffic. With only 29 percent of libraries responding, researchers found 2,000 incidents of patrons, many of them children, accessing pornography in America's public libraries."[7]

❖ According to *Adult Video News*, "Ten years ago, 1,275 hardcore (video) titles hit the market, compared with 11,041 for 2000."[8]

❖ "A recent study by researchers at Stanford and Duquesne Universities claims at least 200,000 Americans are hopelessly addicted to e-porn."[9]

❖ "The National Council on Sexual Addiction Compulsivity estimated that six to eight percent of Americans are sex addicts, which is sixteen million to 21.5 million people."[10]

❖ "...Sixty-one percent of all high school seniors have had sexual intercourse, about half are currently sexually active, and 21 percent have had four or more partners. Although other developed countries have similar rates of early sexual intercourse, the United States has one of the highest teenage pregnancy rates in the world. In addition to pregnancy, early sexual intercourse carries the risk of contracting a sexually transmitted disease (STD), including Human Immunodeficiency Virus (HIV). Adolescents have the highest STD rates. Approximately one fourth of sexually active adolescents become infected with an STD each year, accounting for three million cases, and people under the age of 25 account for two thirds of all STD's in the United States."[11]

❖ "In fiscal year 1998, the FBI opened up roughly 700 cases dealing with online pedophilia, most of them for posting child pornography, and about a quarter dealing with online predators trying to get children under eighteen to meet with them. By 2000 that figure had quadrupled to 2,856 cases."[12]

❖ "Nearly 1.4 million Americans are stalked each year—four out of five are women—and stalkers are increasingly using the internet, e-mail and other electronic communication devices to frighten them and wreak havoc in their lives.... The Los Angeles District Attorney's office estimates that about twenty percent of its stalking cases involve electronic harassment, while the New York City Police Department says almost 40 percent of its computer investigations do."[13]

❖ Dr. Mary Anne Layden, director of education, University of Pennsylvania Health System, points out, "I have been treating sexual violence victims and perpetrators for thirteen years. I have not treated a single case of sexual violence that did not involve pornography." She draws here a direct connection between pornography and violence. This statistic alone is sufficient evidence of the impact of viewing pornography.[14]

A study of 1,001 adults and 304 children between the ages of ten and seventeen with home internet connections has revealed that children, under the right circumstances (such as manipulation by advertisers), will give out all kinds of sensitive information over the internet.[15]

❖ 39 percent of youngsters would disclose what they get for allowances, what their parents said about politics, and what the family did on weekends.

❖ 77 percent of parents worried their children would give out family information on the web. By comparison, 72 percent of parents worried their children would come across sexually explicit web sites and 62 per cent worried about internet violence.

❖ 84 percent of children say they would give out information with their parents' consent, but 72 percent admit they would give it out anyway even though they would be nervous about it.

Other Impacts of Internet Use

Recent research conducted by Carnegie Mellon University provides a surprisingly consistent picture of the consequences of using the internet. The research reinforces the belief that using the internet adversely affects social involvement and psychological well-being. The researchers concluded that greater use of the internet causes a decline in social involvement among internet users and their family and their broader social network. A corresponding increase in loneliness, a psychological state associated with social involvement, is typical of internet users. Greater use of the internet was also associated with increases in depression. The researchers noted that a paradox exists where the internet is a social technology used for communication with individuals and groups, but those relationships are typically weaker than relationships established in a conventional manner, therefore internet usage is associated with a decline in social involvement and the psychological well-being that goes with such social involvement.[16]

Erotica As Mainstream

On Super Bowl Sunday, February 3, 2002, the NBC reality television show, *Fear Factor*, ran an episode using *Playboy* Playmates designed to pull viewers from the Fox Super Bowl halftime show. Each year, ever-stronger sexual content is showing up across the American landscape—in every possible media. A thread in this book is that as a nation worships Baal, the worship of the god of fertility and flesh is the natural extension; history shows no exceptions. As our culture drifts further away from God, there will be no bottom in depravity unless the Lord intervenes. Writing for the *Christian Science Monitor*, Gloria Goodale, the arts and culture correspondent, gives an overview of America:

> At Christmas, a fifteen-year-old California girl received a "fun gift" from another teen: a makeup bag, part of a new teen line from the hardcore pornography publisher, Hustler, complete with an embroidered logo and a tag touting the magazine.
>
> In November, ABC aired a "Victoria's Secret Fashion Show" so explicit the network decided it should blur out areas of models' bodies.
>
> Pornographic images, erotic paraphernalia, and raunchy sexual talk are reaching a near-saturation point in the daily lives of Americans, through television, movies, magazines, and the internet, say a growing chorus of expert voices. And the target market is an increasingly younger audience.
>
> The prevalence and commercialization of extreme sexual behaviors and attitudes is hard for youngsters still figuring out male-female relationships, says media expert John Forde, who hosts a PBS television show that examines television advertising. How can they put a violent sex toy in perspective when they are still worrying about their first kiss? he asks.

"Erotica has gone completely mainstream," says Jane Buckingham, president of Youth Intelligence, a New York–based think tank that tracks youth trends.

From the sex toys used by star Jim Carrey in his recent film, *Me, Myself & Irene*, to clothing catalogs so graphic that Abercrombie & Fitch stores must ask for adult ID's to sell them, the environment for youths has become sexualized in ways that used to be considered extreme, Ms. Buckingham says.

She points to what she calls "porn chic" as the easiest evidence: lewd sexual phrases and imagery on jewelry and clothing; print and television ad campaigns that suggest rape or group sex; and explicit sexual references to pornography in teen films such as *Scary Movie* and *Not Just Another Teen Movie*.

The influx of this imagery has increased dramatically over the past decade, she adds, and includes using younger models. "Now that pornography has become acceptable, anything goes."

Accompanying this is a trend toward more and more explicit sexual environments in film and television. In a recently released biennial report, the Kaiser Family Foundation found that two out of every three television shows include sexual content, up from one-half of shows just two years ago. The many examples cited include characters on ABC's cancelled *Two Guys and a Girl* using the *Kama Sutra*, an ancient Eastern sex manual.

A study released by the Parents Television Council found that the number of "raunchy" sexual references on cable television shows has more than doubled in the past two years. These occur more than twice as often as on network television shows.

Several factors have contributed to erotica working its way into mainstream American media, says legal expert Bruce Taylor, president and chief counsel for the National Law Center for Children and Families:

- The number of state or federal prosecutions for violations of obscenity laws over the past decade stopped almost completely when the Community Decency Act of 1996 was struck down as unconstitutional.

- The rise of the internet as an easy way to deliver explicitly sexual material to a wide, undifferentiated market.

- The expansion of the entertainment marketplace from a few networks to a vast world of satellite, cable, video, and pay-per-view options.

It all boils down to money, says Mr. Forde, host of the PBS show, "Mental Engineering," which ran its own counter-programming on Super Bowl Sunday, 2002.

Immediately following the game, Forde's show analyzed the underlying messages of the Super Bowl ads. The goal of advertisers "is to win, and if they pass the social cost of pornography onto others, that's of no concern to them, because they are concerned solely with profit," he says.

"The feminine is commercialized and commodified," he says. "This undermines the spiritual dimension of being a human being."

One network, NBC, has been frank and unapologetic about its need to compete with the more explicit world of cable television. It recently decided to be the only big broadcast network to air ads for hard liquor. As for the choice to put Playmates in prime time, Jeff Zucker, president of NBC Entertainment, responds, "It's been a difficult year; we're just having fun."

Over the years, American courts have grappled with the issue of pornography versus First Amendment freedoms. Former federal prosecutor Bruce Taylor says the absence of prosecutions has sped the spread of erotica.

"Over time, if you don't prosecute a store or a web site, families and kids grow up not seeing any cases, and they think, 'This must be OK, because if it was illegal, the police would be busting them,'" Mr. Taylor says. "That attitude has affected prosecutors, who are afraid to go to jury trial, and the industry is growing less afraid of being busted."

The result, he says, is the increasing availability of hardcore material, including rape, bestiality, child porn, and sado-masochism themes. This acceptance of material that used to be considered extreme affects the entire culture, he says.

In a recent episode of television's number one–rated show, NBC's *Friends*, the entire cast becomes obsessed with watching a pornography channel.

Hollywood has even the good guys in its shows looking at porn and using sex toys," he says. It's "the movies that are targeting the largest consumers of films, which is teens…and it can't help but affect them."

"This is what I call the heroin effect of porn," says Taylor, who handled more pornography cases during his twenty-year tenure than any other federal prosecutor.

"This rape and incest porn that's being consumed, kids being introduced to group sex, none of us know the effect for certain," he says. But he points to an FBI profile of serial murderers and sex offenders conducted over a period of twenty years. Nearly all of them, he says, were addicted to adult and child pornography.

"Pornography is awful for guys: It affects their attitudes toward sex. It makes them sexually insensitive and jerks toward women, at least. At most, when it becomes an addiction, it becomes an element of psychosis."[17]

"Come see, Grandpa"

On February 7, 2002, the PBS show, *Frontline,* ran an episode on how pornography is being accepted in mainstream America. Where once it was called "smut" and reserved for sections of the city near the bus or train station, it is now being piped into or being made available to tens of millions of American homes. It is an industry made up of the largest law, accounting, and advertising firms in America, who represent blue chip clients. It is so pervasive that a company like General Motors wholly owns Direct TV, a distributor of hardcore pornography going into 40 million homes. G. M. has moved off its old advertising jingle that said "Baseball, hot dogs, apple pie and Chevrolet" are good for America. A. T. & T.—Ma Bell, the staple of American telecommunications for generations—has joined forces with Comcast Cable and will have entrée into over 70 million homes with its own hardcore cable service, Hot Network. Nothing shows up on corporate balance sheets indicating they are in this business. A. T. & T. shows its revenue in the billions from pornography simply as "Broadband Services." When religious leaders like Cardinal Keeler of Baltimore met A. T. & T. chief executive officer, Michael Armstrong, Armstrong simply stated that there was too much money in it to pass it up. Where once porn had operated in the shadow world, it is now out in the open as a multi-billion-dollar business annually.

The figures are staggering. Sophisticated MBA's; Ivy Leaguers heading studios; firms making 80 films a year; editing studios being used three shifts, 24 hours a day, seven days a week; distributors in over 30 countries; internet porn doubling in the last five years; one store in Hollywood selling 10,000 videos a month and building three more stores of over 4,000 square feet each; the L. A. Convention

Center now hosting the annual porn convention with audiences three times bigger each year, where anyone can roam in a modern-day Sodom and Gomorrah for a $15 entrance fee; Larry Flynt of Flynt Publications worth an estimated $400 million; 200,000 commercial porn sites on the internet (this figure varies depending on the source); porn studios now family-owned with a 70-year-old mother as receptionist and bookkeeper; films that cost $25,000 to make, grossing over $10 million; hotel chains like Hilton, Marriott, and Westin accepting free televisions and cabling from porn providers if porn is allowed in the rooms—the statistics go on and on.

Several forces are at work according to *Frontline*. One we all know is the convergence of the internet and technology, but the other major reason is less obvious and has allowed the genie out of the bottle. Under Attorney General Janet Reno, the Clinton Administration stopped prosecutions by what had been called the Obscenity Task Force in the Department of Justice. It was now blue sky and green lights, a tidal wave of converging factors allowing production and distribution. Pornography lawyers openly admit that they flourished during the Clinton Administration. They knew that there would be no enforcement if Clinton were in the White House and they publicly stated that on *Frontline*. As usual, Larry Flynt sees the porno rage as no big deal. He says, "Television today is where our magazine was in 1974." The internet has now greatly expanded what the VCR and porn videos started. The internet porn providers continue their innovation to get youth to their sites. To lure the next generation of addicts, they now snare children by posing as toy stores. While looking for Ken and Barbie dolls, youths are transferred over to hard core porn sites. Children as young as five are viewing porn.[18]

On April 16, 2002, the pornographers got another green light from the U. S. Supreme Court, which struck down a federal ban on "virtual" child pornography. At issue was the 1996 law aimed at cracking down on computer-generated child pornography by "prescribing prison terms for those who possess or distribute images of minors engaged in sexually explicit conduct." Eighteen states had laws on the books prohibiting such material, but the new ruling negates all attempts by the states to control internet pornography. U. S. Attorney General John Ashcroft stated, "This ruling will make it immeasurably harder to prosecute pornographers and is a big setback to the Justice Department."[19]

With satellites, cable, the internet and the most powerful combustible on earth—money, lots of it—there is no end to pornography in sight because elected leaders lack the moral courage to stop it. Is America who it says it is? Is America what it thinks it is? Will Yahweh need to apologize to Sodom and Gomorrah? Now in the works is a cable channel geared strictly to homosexuals.

Several years ago a grandfather called this author and told a story about his ten-year-old grandson. His son and daughter-in-law had been divorced for many years and the children were left at home alone after school every day. They had become addicted to the internet. When visiting his grandfather one summer, the ten year old had found his favorite hardcore pornography site and was so excited he yelled, "Come see, Grandpa." Welcome to the next generation.

Impact of Music

Much has been said over several generations about the impact of music, particularly jazz, blues and rock 'n roll on the children of America. It would take a monumental effort to compile and summarize in an intelligent fashion all the history on the debate of this subject. As an alternative, let's read what U. S. Senator Joseph Lieberman stated on November 6, 1997, to the Government Affairs Committee, Subcommittee on Oversight regarding "The Social Impact of Music Violence." Senator Lieberman (D-Connecticut) gives a profound and enlightening testimony to the current state of the music industry and its collaborative efforts with the rest of the entertainment service industry, the home entertainment systems providers, and organized crime.

Many of you know that Senator Lieberman championed the cause of morality in media even alongside people like Bill Bennett. How ironic and sad that after becoming a candidate for Vice-President on the 2000 Al Gore ticket, he conveniently forgot all that he knew and bowed down and kissed the rings of the very Hollywood moguls perpetuating the immoral agenda he had had previously publicly opposed. His true colors shone brightly, and all familiar with what was happening saw clearly: Hollywood and the entertainment industry can and do create public servants, and they can help create presidents. As Deep Throat of the Watergate era said, "Follow the money." Money talked so loudly that Senator Lieberman forgot what he had previously believed. Here is his 1997 testimony:

> At the risk of sounding like a broken record, I want to talk briefly today about our broken culture and the risk it presents to our children and our country.
>
> In taking stock of our social environment, it's hard not to notice a surreal, *Alice in Wonderland* quality. Our children are often better

159

armed than our police. We throw new bouquets of celebrity at the feet of luminaries like NBA's Dennis Rodman with each brazen elbow he throws at an opponent and/or cameraman. And we don't seem to blink when prominent corporate citizens sell music to our children that celebrates violence, including the murder of police, gang rape, and sexual perversity, including pedophilia.

Surreal though it seems, these cultural indicators have very real implications. They bespeak a breakdown in the old rules and limits that once governed our public lives and the way we raised our children. We are left with a vacuum, a values vacuum, in which our children learn that anything goes, and which I believe is at the heart of our society's worst problems.

This vacuum is troubling in its own right, it is all the more profoundly unsettling when we consider what is filling it these days. The new values transmitters in our society are increasingly the television producers, the movie moguls, the fashion advertisers, the gangsta rappers and shock rockers, and a host of other players within the electronic media-cultural complex. These trendsetters exert an extremely powerful hold on our culture and our children in particular, and they often exhibit little sense of responsibility for the harmful values they are purveying.

As a result, the market place is flooded with perverse television shows like Fox's "When Animals Attack," which degradingly treats real-life terror as a form of entertainment; with video games like "Postal," marketed by Panasonic, in which the player is cast as a deranged gunman trying to wipe out an entire town, and whose marketing brochure promises "chilling realism as victims actually beg for mercy, scream for their lives, and pile up on the streets;" and with the inexcusable ads of Calvin Klein, which told a generation that is warming up again to heroin that it is cool to look and be strung out.

The music lyrics we are focusing on here today are of a piece with these messages and in many cases just as reprehensible. Consider a song like "Slap-a-Hoe" by the group Dove Shack, distributed by Polygram, which touted the virtues of a machine that automatically smacks a wife or girlfriend into line; or the vile work of the death metal band Cannibal Corpse, distributed through a Sony subsidiary, which recorded one song describing the rape of a woman with a knife and another describing the act of masturbating with a dead woman's head.

These songs and others like them contain some of the most disgusting thoughts I've ever heard, but they are more than just offensive. When combined with all the murder and mayhem depicted by the whole gamut of media, they are helping to create a culture of violence that is increasingly enveloping our children, desensitizing them to consequences and ultimately cheapening the value of human life.

We will hear testimony today about what social science can tell us about the impact that violent and antisocial music has on its listeners. But we should also take a close look at the real life experiences in the world of gangsta rap, a segment of the music industry that has glorified murder and mayhem on CD's and then lived it on the streets. The story of Tupac Shakur is well known. He and many other rappers recorded rhymes that help make killing cool, and it was the same kind of gangsterism they celebrated that claimed Shakur's life and that of the Notorious B. I. G. and has landed several other rappers in jail. Before he was killed, Tupac Shakur himself said he went beyond "representing" violence—"I represented it too much. I was thug life."

This music, reinforced by television through MTV and other music channels that present the gangster life as the high life, has spawned its own subculture, setting standards for how to dress, how to treat women, and how to resolve conflict cleanly with a bullet.

We are just learning, though, about what appears to be a very real criminal connection within elements of the rap industry, links to racketeering, money laundering, gang violence and drug running. Death Row Records, which gave us Tupac and Snoop Doggy Dogg and which was in business with Time Warner and then Seagram, is now the subject of an extensive Federal investigation involving the FBI, the DEA and the IRS. Among other things, these authorities are examining Death Row's ties to Michael Harris, reputed to be one of Los Angeles' most notorious crack dealers. Harris, now serving a 28-year prison term, claims he provided more than $1 million, likely the proceeds of drug sales, in seed money to launch Death Row. The FBI reportedly is also looking into reported connections between Death Row and its President, Suge Knight, and organized crime families in New York and Chicago. Mr. Chairman, there is enough evidence here that I think we need to pursue this connection in a little more depth in this hearing. In the meantime, I want to applaud you for holding this hearing reviving a dialogue that Bill Bennett, DeLores Tucker and I sought to engage in over the past two years and which we desperately need to have. It's unfortunate that many in the industry have refused to acknowledge our concerns. Often we've heard that a record never killed anyone and we are casually dismissed as prudes or as censors. This has got to stop. The men and women who run Seagram, Time Warner, Sony, BMG, EMI and Polygram must stop hiding behind the First Amendment and confront the damage some—and I emphasize some—of their products are doing.

We are not talking about censorship, but about citizenship. We're not asking for any government action or bans. We're simply asking whether it is right for Sony, for example, to make money by selling children records by the likes of Cannibal Corpse and rapper M. C. Eiht, who brags in one obscenity-filled song of using a gun to play connect the dots on his victim's chest. We're asking why a great company like Seagram is continuing to associate itself with Marilyn Manson and the vile, hateful, and nihilistic music he records?

By raising these questions, engaging in this dialogue, and informing parents about the kinds of music their children may be listening to, I hope we can make some real progress in dealing with this problem that for many is becoming a crisis. I hope the corporate giants of the industry, after hearing our pleas for them to exercise the kind of corporate responsibility we expect from the great companies they lead, will consider adopting some basic standards for the music they choose to sponsor and draw some lines they won't cross. I hope Seagram in particular will start by dumping Marilyn Manson. In the meantime, I hope the Recording Industry Association of America (RIAA) will consider improving its one-size-fits-all labeling system to give parents the basic information they need to make informed judgments for their kids.

12

Throwing in the Towel:
Drugs and Alcohol

For the wages of sin is death.

—Romans 6:23

There are numerous web sites, books, periodicals, commentaries, movies and documentaries on the subjects of alcohol and drug abuse. Before grappling with the vast details relating to these subjects, let's take a broader, more strategic view of 'the forest' from a distance in context to the general landscape, that is, our temporal and spiritual well being, to postulate whether such abuse is viewed by American society as being acceptable. Has America thrown in the towel and said, "Drugs have conquered us"? Is America becoming a nation where the majority of people compulsively seeks only material well-being or happiness accompanied by a self-centered compulsion and addiction to leverage whatever means are available, including chemical intoxicants and topical treatments, to at least create an illusion of well-being and happiness or to amuse themselves? There is a lot of data to show just how pervasive alcohol consumption and the popping of pills have become.

Perhaps former Federal Drug Czar William Bennett framed the problem in just the right way when he addressed publicly the subject of dealing with America's drug addiction. "The drug problem," he said, "is fundamentally a moral problem—in the end a spiritual problem—it is seeking meaning in a place where no meaning can come...."

The year 2001 was the fourth straight year in which prescription drug spending rose more than seventeen percent. Sales of prescription medication at retail stores and through mail order companies totaled $175.2 billion in 2001, an increase of $27 billion over 2000.[1] To drown out the effects of its increasing moral depravity, America is becoming a pill-popping, addicted culture. Drug sales for many companies are going through the roof. It doesn't stop with prescription drugs. Today's fifteen-year-old daughters are fifteen times as likely to be using illegal drugs as their mothers were.[2]

163

Before we go further, this chapter does not represent an attack on the fundamental merits of current medicine and the potential cures which often help improve lives. Nor does it suggest that alcohol has no merit or benign pleasure. As the wise man said, "Everything in moderation but love." What should concern Americans is the mass immoral use of drugs and alcohol. Americans are consuming drugs and alcohol far beyond their intended need or basic merits, mostly to drown out lives with no vision or purpose. Drug abuse goes beyond hard core narcotics and marijuana. It includes prescriptions and over-the-counter (OTC) drugs which are misused, used unnecessarily or illegally used. Prescription and OTC medicines may be the answer to many illnesses and pains—the crippling effects of physical agony. They may keep allergies at bay, cholesterol and blood pressure controlled, and social phobias defeated. However, for a growing number of people, popping prescription or OTC pills are not only dangerous but potentially fatal. It is a shameful, closeted habit. With "incentives" from the pharmaceutical companies, many in the medical profession often push drugs. Exacerbating our national foolishness are the pharmaceutical and alcoholic beverage industries, who with the mass media are marketing questionable remedies, amusement, sexual gratification, and higher self-esteem through the use of drugs and alcohol. Of particular concern is the way these industries aggressively target our youth, young adults and minorities. Presented below are some examples which illustrate the magnitude of these industries' efforts:

❖ The U. S. pharmaceutical industry spent approximately $27.4 billion for research and development in 2000 with sales believed to have increased by 11.2 percent to $149.1 billion.

❖ Spending on direct to consumer (DTC) advertising alone increased from $55 Million in 1991 to more than $2.28 Billion in 2000, a more than 40-fold increase.[3]

❖ To put the above in perspective, OTC drug advertising in 1995 amounted to $1.8 Billion.[4]

❖ To augment the advertising campaign pharmaceutical manufacturers have increased substantially the marketing of drug samples, by greater than 45 percent from $4.9 Billion in 1996 to $7.2 Billion in 2000.[5]

❖ In 1996 the Distilled Spirits Council of the U. S. revised its Code of Good Practice to allow members to advertise liquor in the broadcast media. The ban was in place for radio since 1936 and for television since 1948. Since the ban was lifted, such advertising has climbed about 1,000 percent even though television networks are just beginning to place such ads.[6]

❖ Alcohol advertising on television and radio totaled more than $787 Million in 1998 alone. Most television ads appear during prime time, late in the evening or on weekend afternoons. On radio, alcohol advertising often airs on youth-oriented rock and roll or album-oriented rock formats that target eighteen-to-24-year olds. Beer advertisers spend millions of dollars on campus promotions, most in the context of sports.[7] For example, Budweiser secured five 30-second commercials for Super Bowl XXXVI at a total cost of $9.5 Million.

❖ Nearly 75 percent of the nation's major concert facilities have beer company sponsors. Beer companies also sponsor the printing of sports schedules and advertise in programs.[8]

❖ Alcohol companies spent $93 Million on billboard advertising in 1998 with a disproportionate emphasis on inner-city and low-income communities.[9]

❖ In September 1999, the Federal Trade Commission found that the alcohol industry's voluntary advertising standards provided excessive access to underage persons. Aside from violations of their own standards, ads regularly reach audiences comprised of 50 percent underage youth.[10]

❖ Minority-owned television and radio stations, magazines and newspapers have become heavily dependent on alcohol advertising. Minority advertising agencies hired by the alcohol companies promote sponsorships and advertisements at sports, music and cultural events frequented by minorities.[11]

The consequential fruits of promoting alcohol use are particularly notable among college students eighteen to twenty-five years-old. What sort of generation of would-be, future leaders of our nation are we creating? It seems that an epidemic of heavy drinking exists on our college campuses with the following 'bad fruit.'

❖ In 1970, for the U. S. population fourteen years or older, the per capita consumption of beer totaled over 25¼ gallons, for wine nearly 1.9 gallons and for liquor/spirits nearly 2½ gallons.[12]

❖ A survey of students in grades five through twelve shows that 56 percent of the students say that alcohol advertising encourages them to drink. Is it any surprise that the average age where children begin to drink alcohol is about thirteen and that their total consumption is about ten million drinks each day?[13]

❖ Studies show that junior high school students can name more beer brands than presidents and younger children can sing the jingles and mimic the characters in alcohol commercials. Many youth oriented magazines such as *Rolling Stone*, *Details* and *Spin* feature a significant number of alcohol ads.[14]

❖ Underage youth consume in excess of a billion beers each year. Every week, more than 100,000 elementary-school-age children get drunk. More than 80 percent of all high school seniors have tried alcohol. In 1998, 23 percent of eighth grade students and 39 percent of tenth grade students reported using alcohol in the past 30 days.[15]

❖ A recent survey of students at 130 colleges showed that 43 percent of those responding had engaged in binge drinking. Frequent binge drinkers, that is, those who binge three or more times within a two-week period, totaled more than 21 percent of those surveyed.[16]

❖ 90 percent of all reported campus rapes involve alcohol use by the victim or the perpetrator, and 95% of violent crime.

The bad fruits derived from aggressive DTC and prescription drug marketing include:

❖ According to the *USA Today* article, "Today's youth don't see drugs' danger," illegal drug use among twelve-to-seventeen-year-olds has more than doubled since 1992.[17]

❖ Four million Americans over the age of twelve are using over-the-counter and prescription medicine for "non-medical" reasons.[18]

❖ Over three billion retail prescriptions were dispensed in 1999, amounting to sales of over $120 billion and averaging four million prescriptions written in a day. In 1998, refill prescriptions accounted for 1.1 billion of the total 2.5 billion prescriptions dispensed.

❖ Spending on prescription drugs accounts for more than eight percent of total national health expenditures and is forecasted to grow to 12.6 percent of the total by the year 2008.[19]

Hiding the Pain

We seek to manipulate our self-esteem or pride, foolishly creating the debilitating and addicting illusion or dream that offsets that which we perceive as inadequate, painful or shameful. In so doing we fail to learn the lesson which Jesus Christ so painfully taught. Recall, in St. Matthew Chapter 16, verses 21 to 23, where Jesus was being rebuked by Peter because he conveyed the plan that He must go to Jerusalem to suffer, die and be resurrected on the third day. Following Peter's rebuke that "this should not be unto you...." Jesus sternly replied, "Go behind me Satan, you are a scandal unto me: because you savor not the things that are of God, but the things that are of men."

When a society or nation turns its back from God's divine will, trusting instead gods associated with our need for self-esteem or ego, it is inevitable that we shall fall from God's grace and ultimately suffer His wrath as a means of His justice. When a nation lacks a vision of where it is going, its people say, "Why not indulge?" When people lack purpose in life, there is no end to the amusement they find to satisfy the flesh. The Scriptures are replete with historical examples of God's Chosen People failing to trust in His will regardless of whatever circumstance or outcome is present or forthcoming. The results are very predictable. "Their vines are of the vineyard of Sodom, and of the suburbs of Gomorrah: their grapes are grapes of gall, and their clusters most bitter. Their wine is the gall of dragons and the venom of asps, which is incurable.... And he shall say: Where are their gods, in whom they trusted?... See you that I alone am, and there is no other God besides me: I will kill and I will make to live: I will strike, and I will heal, and there is none that can deliver out of my hand" (Deuteronomy, 32:32–33, 37, 39).

Findings reported by the Drug Enforcement Agency (DEA) of the Federal Government based on fiscal year 2001 and prior year departmental surveys, studies and reports estimate that fourteen million

Americans were current users of illicit drugs. The fourteen million represents 6.3 percent of the population twelve years old and older. Regarding our nation's youth, Bill Clinton's Secretary of Health and Human Services, Donna Shalala, referred to a federal survey which showed that nearly eleven percent of the 22 million U. S. teenagers are using drugs—mostly marijuana, but also cocaine and LSD and other hallucinogens.[20] Examining the details behind this number reveals disturbing trends of drug abuse among America's youth. Related drug abuse statistics regarding middle age Americans offers alarmingly prophetic consequences of early age acceptance and abuse of drugs. In 2000, 7.1 percent of youths aged twelve to seventeen, who indicated that their "parents would strongly disapprove if they tried marijuana once or twice," had used an illicit drug in the past month. Also, 31.2 percent of youth in the other groups reported use of an illicit drug in the past month.

The Drug of Choice

Another plague on America's youth is the synthetic drug Ecstasy, which has been used increasingly among college students and young adults in recent years, with relatively high levels of use by America's 8th, 10th, and 12th graders, according to the 1996 study of the National Institute for Drug Abuse, "Monitoring the Future." Nearly five percent of 10th and 12th graders and about two percent of 8th graders said they had used Methylenedioxymethamphetamine or MDMA (a. k. a. "Ecstasy", "X," "E," and "Adam" to name a few) in the past years. The use of Ecstasy has been linked with a wide range of abnormalities such as impaired memory, chronic depression, anxiety, panic attacks, sleeplessness, "de-personalization," "de-realization," reduced cognitive ability, flashbacks, hallucinations, and paranoid delusions. Persons taking large quantities of Ecstasy in a binge pattern of use were especially at risk. Heavy users might develop depression and anxiety in the future. Any user potentially becomes a veritable neurological time bomb. According to research, "E" changes the chemical makeup of the brain. Previously outgoing people who use it become severely depressed and need psychiatric help. E literally eats away portions of the brain.[21]

The Drug Abuse Warning Network (DAWN) is a national probability survey of hospital emergency rooms (ER) designed to capture data on ER episodes that are induced or related to the use of an illegal drug or the non-medical use of a legal drug. It is important to remember that DAWN data show only one dimension of the total consequences of drug abuse, specifically the impact of drug abuse that manifests itself in visits to hospital ER's, and that DAWN does not measure the prevalence of drug abuse. However, based on DAWN's July 2001 national survey, there are good reasons to believe that trends and patterns in the data parallel those of the abusing population at large.

❖ Adjusting for population, young adults age eighteen to 25 had the highest rate of ER drug episodes: 426 episodes per 100,000. The next highest rate was reported for individuals age 26 to 34 (411); the rate for individuals age twelve to seventeen was 272 and the overall rate was 243.

❖ From 1999 to 2000, drug-related ER episodes increased twenty percent for patients age twelve to seventeen (from 52,783 to 63,448) and thirteen percent for patients age eighteen to 25 (from 109,580 to 123,438), but remained stable for older age groups.

❖ Patients age 35 and older accounted for the majority (55 percent) of heroin ER incidents in 2000. Between 1999 and 2000, heroin mentions among this age group increased eleven percent, while mentions involving patients age eighteen to 25 increased 22 percent, from 15,132 to 18,400.

Parents, Children, and Drugs

The Partnership for a Drug Free America monitors drug-related behavior and attitudes among children, teens and parents. It is the largest ongoing research on drug-related attitudes in the U. S., and the only ongoing drug survey that collects data on children as young as eight and nine. For this 13th installment (November 27, 2000, report), 7,290 teens completed self-administered, anonymous questionnaires. According to the study, 23.6 million teens are in grades seven through twelve in America today. Notwithstanding an apparent trend in declining use for a number of the drugs monitored, the magnitude of the problem remains significant and worrisome regarding the future of a large segment of American youth.

❖ Marijuana is by far the most widely used illegal drug among teens.

❖ 9.4 million teens (40 percent) have tried marijuana, down from 44 percent in 1997.

* 2.4 million teens (ten percent) have tried cocaine/crack, up from nine percent last year, and up significantly since 1993.

* 2.4 million teens (ten percent) have tried Ecstasy, up from seven percent, and doubled since 1995.

Where parents actively engage in constructive dialogue with their children about the dangers of drugs, Partnership's teen surveys appear to indicate a positive impact on a teen's attitude about drugs with a corresponding leveling off or decline in the use of drugs. Specifically:

* More than half (57 percent) of all parents now say they spoke with their children about drugs at least four times in the past year;

* 73 percent of parents spoke about how drugs can "mess up their child's mind," up significantly from 61 percent in 1998; and

* 68 percent of parents spoke about how drugs can "adversely affect a child's education," up significantly from 58 percent in 1998.

Parents: Clueless in America, or Just Too Busy to Pay Attention?

Despite their more active role, parents' confidence in their ability to safeguard their children is apparently waning and paradoxically America's parents still underestimate their children's exposure to illegal drugs. It is as if resignation has set in and the attitude "drugs are here to stay, and there is nothing we can do about it" is becoming more generally accepted by parents. The problem seems to be so overwhelming for parents that they have thrown in the towel.

* 75 percent of parents now think "most people will try marijuana sometimes," up significantly from 65 percent in 1995.

* 30 percent of parents believe there's "nothing I can really do to help the drug problem."

* 37 percent of parents of teens say that their teen has been offered drugs, but 54 percent of teens say they have been offered drugs.

Perhaps Lee Brown, former drug policy director and now professor of sociology at Houston's Rice University, has an insightful view regarding the inability of parents collectively to address drug and alcohol abuse in their own families. Brown offered the following as an explanation:

❖ Baby boomers who used drugs themselves won't criticize their children for doing what they did themselves.

❖ Drug use has been glamorized in the entertainment and communication industries.

❖ The mainstream media aren't paying as much attention to the problem as they used to and many corporations have slacked off their efforts to combat drug use in the workplace.

The War on Drugs

Sadly, as if to highlight Lee Brown's explanation, America had then-President Bill Clinton on MTV reply, "Yes!" If given another opportunity, he would "inhale" when he "tried marijuana." It should come as no surprise then to anyone, certainly not the media, to find that drug use among teenagers skyrocketed during the Clinton Administration. This is from a nation's president who supported his Surgeon General, Jocelyn Elders, who advocated the legalization of marijuana. Her son was arrested for selling it. What is even more provocative are the recurring allegations that when Clinton was the governor of Arkansas, billions of dollars worth of illegal drugs were allegedly flown into Mena, Arkansas, and distributed throughout the nation. When one considers the moral depravity of Bill Clinton's character, the films made about the "Mena Connection" are more than credible.

To counter this threat to our nation, what demonstrable effect has the "War on Drugs" achieved in the past decades? One should note that the DEA fiscal year budget from 1973 to 2000 increased from $750 million to nearly $1.6 billion, respectively, or on a year over year cumulative growth rate of 11.875 percent per annum. The total number of DEA employees has increased over the same period from 2,898 to 9,132 (4.3 percent year over year growth). To augment the campaign against drug abuse, state and local officers trained by the DEA from 1991 to 2000 increased from 23,794 to 226,304 (28.44 percent year over year growth). That's big growth in any organization.

According to the National Law Memorial Fund, the number of federal, state and local law enforcement officer deaths in the U. S. from 1986 through 1999 equaled 4,972. America's growing resignation regarding drug and alcohol abuse is attributable to spiritual and moral decline that accelerated rapidly in the early 1960's. Possibly a whole "biblical" generation could be categorized as spiritually corrupt, relying on modern day sorcery to address our perceived deficiencies. Keep in mind that the word "sorcerer" in the Greek language is *pharmakeus*—user of drugs, from which we get the word "pharmacy." In a world where "zero sum gain" is constantly taught and practiced and where material success is universally promoted as the measure of a variety of secular and utilitarian values, including but not limited to education, skin-deep beauty, sexual gratification, greed, health, pride, politics and power, perhaps our souls are sufficiently corrupt to perceive drugs and alcohol abuse merely as part of an immutable process, for which we refuse to bear responsibility or control. It appears that our society's use of drugs and alcohol artificially recovers what was lost or never achieved, temporarily numbing the pain of guilt or dissatisfaction which consumes our souls and creates a false illusion of hope.

What is the Lord's answer to a nation which foolishly pursues illusionary pleasure? "But they have gone after the perverseness of their own heart, and after Baalim, which their fathers taught them. Therefore thus says the Lord of hosts the God of Israel: Behold I will feed this people with wormwood, and give them water of gall to drink" (Jeremiah 9:14–15).

What is wormwood? According to biblical scholars, wormwood is used in a figurative fashion in the Old Testament. Wormwood symbolizes bitter calamity and sorrow, where unrighteous judges are said to "turn judgment to wormwood." It also applies to a bitter herb or drink. The Orientals represented sorrows, cruelties and calamities of any kind with plants of a poisonous or bitter nature. In our modern age, illegal drug use is a bitter pill to swallow and alcoholic abuse a poisonous drink. And what becomes of the victims of such abuse who are unable to gain freedom from this type of enslavement? Do they not ultimately fall prey to physical and psychological sickness, prostitution, criminal violence, thievery and death? Recall Scripture that says, "Neither did they penance from their murders, nor from their sorceries, nor from their fornication, nor from their thefts" (Revelation 9:21). Wherever there is reference to sorcery in scriptures, the use of drugs is implied. The "vine of Sodom" and the "grapes of gall" are considered by many biblical scholars as a reference to the use of the drug opium—how things have remained unchanged in the course of thousands of years.

Teacher's Little Helper

Out of the bowels of the medical profession's identification of attention deficit/hyperactivity disorder (ADHD) a 'promising' drug was introduced to our children called Ritalin. It is designed as a mild stimulant to help, especially children, improve concentration and behavior, particularly in school. The manufacturer, Novartis Pharmaceuticals, claims Ritalin is a safe and effective treatment for millions suffering from ADHD. The drug is prescribed to approximately 2.5 million children for ADHD, according to Ciba-Geigy. The National Institutes of Mental Health (NIMH) estimates that as many as six million American children suffer from ADHD. That's between three percent and five percent of the population. The federal government categorizes ADHD as a disability under the American Disabilities Act. Therefore, the Social Security Administration is paying families up to $500 per month for every child using Ritalin. Welfare families are running to the school administrators, teachers, and guidance counselors to get their children diagnosed as having ADHD in order to collect this additional income. The drug companies have created this market and legislation to bring in bigger profits, and over time it has become a cottage industry for welfare families.

To paraphrase a Rolling Stones tune of the 1960's, "Mother's Little Helper," about housewives' addiction to valium, etc., Ritalin established itself quite popularly as "Teacher's Little Helper." Thanks to the psychiatric industry's endorsement of the disorder called ADHD and pharmaceutical industry's promotion, Ritalin use became the darling of the National Education Association. According to the United Nations and DEA, Ciba-Geigy alone has contributed almost $1 million to Children and Adults with Attention Deficit Disorder (CHADD) between 1991 and 1994. Like direct-to-customer marketing methods, the DEA is currently investigating the relationship between Ritalin and its generic alternative, methylphenidate, or MPH, manufacturers and non-profit ADHD based organizations. "A lot of people don't know Ritalin is like cocaine," DEA diversion control head Gene Haislip said. "That doesn't mean don't use it.... It can be very dangerous and must be treated with respect. Obviously, it was not under surveillance." He called the relationship between Ciba-Geigy and CHADD an "unhealthy co-mingling of medical and commercial interests."[22]

Ritalin has become the vogue drug of choice for the young, upwardly-mobile parents who want their kids to be better students. After all, "The children are not responsible for themselves because they have a disorder." Using it has become the politically correct thing to do, and convenient for parents who spend only a few hours with their children every day because they work. It made parent-teacher conferences less heated, to say the least. Now Johnny and Mary are going to college, and guess what?

❖ According to the University of Michigan's annual "Monitoring the Future" studies, from 1988 to 1999 the percentage of high school seniors who reported using Ritalin without a prescription went from 0.3 percent to 2.4 percent. In fact, data in its 1994 report indicated that at that time, there were more U. S. high-school seniors who abused Ritalin than there were seniors who were legally prescribed the drug.

❖ A 1998 Indiana University study of 44,232 students found that 6.8 percent of ninth graders surveyed reported using Ritalin illicitly at least once.

❖ The Drug Enforcement Agency's "Drugs of Concern" bulletin lists Ritalin alongside cocaine, LSD and Ecstasy. Testifying before a House Subcommittee in May 2000, DEA Deputy Director Terrance Woodworth said that the extent to which adolescents are abusing methylphenidate is unknown, but that anecdotal evidence suggests that its incidence seems to have increased with the availability of the drug. In his statement to the committee, Woodworth said that "continued increases in the medical prescription of these drugs without the appropriate safeguards...can only lead to increased stimulant abuse among U. S. children."

Ritalin is now on the street with nicknames such as "Vitamin R", "R-Ball" and "Smart Drug." Kids are popping, snorting, even dissolving and injecting Ritalin, putting it in the same drug class as cocaine. But it's not for kicks alone—college students have extended illegitimately the use of Ritalin to boost alertness, especially for an important exam to get better grades. "People find this drug enticing because they can get their academic work done quicker or do more in a shorter period of time," said Dr. Eric Heiligenstein, of the University of Wisconsin. "So for students who have put off work or are not very strong academically, we find some are using it to kind of counteract or remedy their problems."[23]

Beyond the college environment, new reports show an alarming trend to extend the illegal use of Ritalin among younger teens for appetite suppression/weight reduction, wakefulness, increased attentiveness, increased focus and euphoria, and even adults who want to improve their work productivity or maintain a faster-paced lifestyle. Initial studies indicate illegal use in our nation's high schools last year of Ritalin/MPH from three percent to as high as seven percent. At the same time, a DEA study of Wisconsin, South Carolina, and Indiana found that about 30 percent to 50 percent of teens in drug-treatment centers said they had used methylphenidate to get high, although not as their primary drug of abuse. It is inexpensive to purchase from friends or dealers—between $.50 and $1 per pill. Not surprisingly, according to the DEA, Ritalin/MPH is now among the top controlled prescription drugs reported stolen in the United States and is listed by the federal department as among a dozen or so 'drugs of concern.' It seems that Ritalin could become a catalyst for renewed popularity in cocaine. "Cocaine is shorter acting, so it has more of a punch: People tend to prefer cocaine when they're sophisticated," says Dr. Peter Breggin, a leading critic of the use of Ritalin, "but before they get to that stage, they'll use Ritalin."[24] With the abuse obviously comes risk. This includes psychosis, higher blood pressure (and possibly a stroke), irregular heart beat, and possibly cardiac arrhythmia and sudden death.

Prozac: Big Money

As one of the first selective serotonin re-uptake inhibitors (SSRI), Prozac (generically referred to as Fluoxetine) was considered a medical breakthrough in the treatment of depression. As is typically the case for a new product, the subject matter experts (psychiatrists/psychologists), manufacturers, marketers and the media extolled the new anti-depressant drug as a marvel, if not miracle, of human endeavor. Underlying the design and marketing of SSRI products like Prozac is the theory, though never proven, that depression is as biological in origin as a lack of insulin is for diabetes. Therefore, depression is in effect nothing more than a brain serotonin deficiency. Intense marketing propelled the drug onto the front burner for the general public. In 1991, an advisory committee of the FDA cleared Prozac, with the noted exception that labels be added which provide yet-to-be-substantiated advice that the drug could cause "suicidal ideation" and "violent behaviors." To the public, Prozac became the "happiness pill" popularized by Peter Kramer's book *Listening to Prozac* (1993), which spent 21 weeks on the *New York Times* bestseller list. Peter Kramer claims that the drug transformed the personality of some of his patients, making them feel "better than normal" and even proposed that if Prozac were introduced into the general population's water supply, everyone who drank it would be happier. The commercial success of Prozac became phenomenal. With the hiring of a new chief executive officer in 1993, a 'stagnant' drug manufacturer, Eli Lily, viewed by industry analysts as anxious to renew significant and profitable revenue growth, aggressively marketed Prozac worldwide, garnering over $2.5 billion in sales revenue to date with claims that over 31 million patients worldwide are prescribed Prozac. Analysts predict that the market for SSRI could reach $4.8 billion of the total $8.6 billion anti-depressant drug market by the year 2009 with Eli Lilly getting $2.4 billion in that year. Money like that gives drug companies plenty of incentive to push their agenda, and that much money can buy plenty of lobbyists to push their agenda in Congress.[25]

Yet, disturbing evidence began to appear in the early 1990's which initiated a controversy regarding the approval and use of Prozac. One example was the book, *Talking Back to Prozac* (1994), by Dr. Peter Breggin. Breggin's criticisms of Lilly are devastating. He researched clinical trials of the drug before it was marketed and concluded that they were inadequate because:

- ❖ They were too short (four to six weeks);

- ❖ They did not include children, the elderly or the suicidal;

- ❖ Many patients dropped out following adverse reactions;

- ❖ Patients were given sedatives to reduce Prozac's stimulating effect;

- ❖ Fewer than one in three trials showed Prozac to be effective; even these suggested that it was no more effective than previous antidepressants.

Breggin further writes, "The FDA supports the drug industry and its needs at the expense of the public and the consumer," adding that an early in-house FDA report, ignored by the organization's top decision-makers, described Prozac as a stimulant that could, in a few cases, over-stimulate the central nervous system and worsen depression.[26] Further adding fuel to the fire of controversy, in 1994 David Healy (then consultant to Eli Lilly) published an article entitled "The Fluoxetine and Suicide Controversy, a Review of the Evidence," in which he opines that antidepressants, Prozac included, can indeed induce suicidal behavior in a minority of patients.[27]

Patients and their families, alarmed by the growing occurrences of violent behavior and attempted suicides of Prozac users, formed an organization called Prozac Survivors Support Group (PSSG) to warn the public and patients against the possible side-effects of Prozac. Litigation soon followed. The year 1994 saw a major milestone in Prozac's litigation history. As the first of some 160 cases filed, the Fentress Case (popularly known as the Wesbecker Case) was tried in Louisville, Kentucky.[28] Back in 1989, Jo Wesbecker had killed and wounded several of his coworkers, and thereafter committed suicide, a few weeks after starting a Prozac treatment. By a divided nine to three vote (the smallest possible margin), the jury denied the plaintiffs' claim against Lilly, but Judge John Potter's doubts about the proceedings led him to seek authorization for further hearings. A second notable case concerns William Forsyth, a retired businessman residing in Maui, Hawaii, who in 1993 stabbed his wife to death, then committed suicide, ten days after starting Prozac. His children are suing Lilly, claiming Prozac is to blame for their father's acts.[29] David Healy acted as an expert witness for the plaintiff in the trial.

It is now the professional opinion of many medical doctors that Prozac can induce psychotic episodes in a small percentage of patients (five percent to seven percent), especially those with borderline or manic personalities. In a small minority of these people, psychosis manifests itself by dangerous behaviors such as self-mutilation and suicidal/homicidal ideation and acts. Unfortunately, Eli Lilly, presumably to avoid any further litigation or perhaps to avoid substantiating any current claims, has refused to conduct (or publish the results of) double-blind research studies specifically developed to find out more about these possible side-effects.[30] By refusing to do so, Lilly's act of omission can only be viewed as immoral, definitively failing to meet normal standards in health care.

Concerns regarding violent behavior and suicidal tendencies of SSRI drug users are not limited to Prozac alone. Luvox, manufactured by Solvay, is said to cause mania during short-term clinically controlled trials in four percent of the children and youth tested. Mania is a psychosis which can produce bizarre, grandiose, highly elaborated destructive plans. What the public does not generally know is that Eric Harris, the "leader" in the Columbine High School tragedy, was taking Luvox for depression. This drug is typically given for the treatment of obsessive-compulsive disorders, yet doctors often give it for depression, since it is in the same SSRI class as Prozac.

America's Lust for Viagra

Thanks in part to a massive advertising campaign, including former Speaker of the U. S. Senate and former presidential candidate, Senator Bob Dole, urging men to pursue treatment for a condition often embarrassing to discuss, Viagra sales topped $1 billion in 1999. As of mid-year 2000, over 22 million prescriptions had been written. By April of 2002, over 100 million prescriptions had been filled, with over $1.5 billion per year in net sales for Pfiizer.[31] Judging by the rate of growth over the last two years, with double digit growth overseas, it would not be unreasonable to see over 500 million prescriptions filled by the end of the next several years. One could even estimate this number could even reach 700 million prescriptions because the drug is not new and has gained worldwide market acceptance. This doesn't even include the 25-plus competing products on the market, some with substantial sales of their own. Viagra, manufactured by Pfizer, Inc., offered the promise of being the first drug that could help men rediscover their lost sex lives. Pfizer is now offering a six pack of free pills to hook men on the drug. The drug is now mainstream. A television commercial shows a rugged racecar driver with a car sponsored by Viagra. Viagra was also a big sponsor of ads on opening night of the 2002 Winter Olympics in Salt Lake City. Analysts currently estimate that the condition, erectile dysfunction, affects an estimated 30 million American men over age forty. Now other pharmaceutical manufacturers are looking to cash in on the profitable and exploding erectile dysfunction treatment market. A new pill called Uprima, made by TAP Pharmaceuticals (a joint venture between Abbott Laboratories and Takeda Pharmaceuticals), though seen as having some undesirable side effects, is forecasted to grow to a $100-to-$300-million-per-year business. Uprima contains dopamine which, aside from its intended purpose, causes a sense of euphoria in the brain, which critics note could lead to stimulant abuse in order to achieve that feeling.

Researchers have found that hundreds of men with heart problems have died after using Viagra, yet medical doctors generally view the percentage at risk as substantially tiny and will continue to prescribe Viagra and Uprima, discounting sufficiently the concerns that cardiologists have regarding possible side effects. Regardless, knowledgeable doctors, such as Dr. Peter Kowey, a panel member and a cardiologist at Lankenau Hospital and Medical Research Center in Wynnewood, Pennsylvania, will favor a warning on Uprima "in bold letters that says if you take this drug you may pass out." He stated publicly, "The complications seen with this drug are frightening."[32]

Baal as a God of Flesh

The lust to eliminate unrequited sexual desire has opened new avenues of drug use and abuse. First, there is a growing trend of teenagers and college students abusing the drug Viagra, using it at rave parties in conjunction with alcohol or other club drugs. The drug is being sold illegally on college campuses for between $25 and $30 a pill. Viagra has also been associated with Ecstasy use as a way to combat male erectile dysfunction often caused by MDMA, the active ingredient in Ecstasy.

Second, the pharmaceutical companies have turned their attention to the other half of the equation. In fact, at least 40 percent of women in recent surveys in the United States and other countries report serious problems and lack of satisfaction in their sex lives. The root of these problems is hotly debated, but one thing is clear: 40 percent is a huge market. The pharmaceutical companies already have convinced the mass media, for example the *New York Times*, *Newsweek* and other national news sources, that a significant portion of women suffers from female sexual dysfunction, or FSD for short. Of course there is a dearth of professional research on the matter. The only apparent medical research article cited is in the September 1999 issue of *Urology*, which asserts that FSD is an epidemic and quotes doctors from Boston University Medical Center claiming, "Female sexual dysfunction is age-related, progressive, and highly prevalent, affecting 30 to 50 percent of women." The urologists define the problem as a "deficiency of sexual fantasies, thoughts and/or receptivity to sexual activity." They suggest physicians look into such complaints by taking a full medical history and checking this and that in a woman's private anatomy, then prescribing one or another hormone or drug. Since the disorder gets worse as women age, estrogen or testosterone might counteract the progression. Lucky for the drug companies, a whole series of treatments already designed for erectile dysfunction also makes the list of experimental options, including Viagra and testosterone.[33]

Dove-tailing from the drug abuse environments of the college and high-school campuses is a growing practice within the homosexual community concerning Viagra. According to local health officials, young homosexual men in San Francisco seeking a drug-assisted sexual high are taking Viagra without a prescription and in combination with other illegal drugs, particularly Ecstasy. A study found that homosexuals who visited a health clinic were almost five times as likely as heterosexuals to use the erectile dysfunction drug.

At a federally sponsored National HIV Prevention Conference in Atlanta, the results of a survey were released for 844 men who visited a clinic in San Francisco and were treated for sexually transmitted diseases from 2000 to 2001. The results indicate that 32 percent of homosexual men in the study reported using Viagra over the previous year, compared to only seven percent of the heterosexual men. Some of the men, including HIV-positive ones, are using Viagra under a doctor's supervision to counteract impotency problems. About three in every four of the men who used several drugs reported getting Viagra from friends. Viagra is used as a counteraction to any physical relaxation that may be caused by another drug. Unfortunately, combining Viagra with these other drugs presents potential complications including a loss of consciousness, severe drop in blood pressure, an extraordinarily painful erection, heart attack, stroke, and even death.[34]

Herpes: A Monumental Epidemic Reflecting America's Moral Crisis

With the growing moral decay of America, and its manifestation of combining promiscuous sex with drug and alcohol abuse, a rather devastating dividend is given to many of its victims—herpes. It is estimated that 50 to 80 percent of the American adult population has oral herpes. Twenty percent, or over 50 million people, are infected with genital herpes, and the majority of these cases may be unaware they even have it. Studies show that more than 500,000 Americans are diagnosed with genital herpes each year. There is no cure to date. Efforts to develop a vaccine by biotechnology companies are ongoing. Until an effective vaccine or cure for herpes infection is found, the prevailing approach to treatment continues to be suppressive antiviral therapy, predominantly using one of two drugs, Acyclovir and Valtrex. According to www.herpesrx.com:

❖ Percentage of adults that have herpes: one in four

❖ Estimated number of new cases of herpes a year: one million

❖ Percentage of infected persons who don't know they have herpes: Over 50 percent of those infected don't realize it because they don't have the classic outbreak pattern, and often dismiss it as an annoying itch or rash.

❖ More women have herpes than men.

❖ Incidence of herpes infection by age group: five to ten percent of teenagers, fifteen to twenty percent of those in their twenties, and 25–30 percent of those 30 years of age or older.

❖ Incidence of herpes has risen 30 percent since 1970.

How immoral are we? Over $8.4 billion is spent annually in the United States to treat the short- and long-term consequences of STD's. This is a highly conservative estimate because it includes only medical costs and does not consider lost productivity or the human costs of suffering. Roughly $4.5 billion is spent to treat HIV and AIDS, and another $1.6 billion is spent treating pre-cancerous cervical lesions and cancer of the cervix caused by human papilloma virus (HPV). Most of the $2 billion spent on bacterial STD's per year goes to treat the 1.5 million cases of pelvic inflammatory disease (PID), which has been linked to female infertility.[35] Gynecologists have long suspected that there is more than a casual connection between birth control pills and cervical cancer. Women infected with the common sexually transmitted papilloma virus have a higher risk of developing cervical cancer if they have taken birth control pills for more than five years.[36]

For those who don't think there are repercussions for sin and sexual promiscuity, look at the AIDS data. The number of people with HIV/AIDS through the end of 2001 was estimated to be 40 million. Due to the fact that this disease often lies dormant in the body for several years, researchers openly admit that the number of people infected could be double this amount—or 80 million people. In 2001, there were five million new HIV infections, and three million people died of AIDS. The future does not bode well for African and Asian countries that will lose so many young people to AIDS, while being crushed with the expenses of care and loss of their citizens.[37] Nowhere does the verse in Romans seem to be more accurately applied: "The wages of sin is death." After so many years of AIDS, Hollywood and all the beautiful people still wear the buttons and ribbons for the cure of AIDS, but it refuses to address the causes of the disease.

Regarding Life-Style Drugs or LSD, we could also add the following sad commentary: The Alan Guttmacher Institute has reported its analysis of the potential U. S. market, which states that there are nearly 60 million women of reproductive age, of whom 15.5 million would describe themselves as "worried about getting an STD." Using data from epidemiological studies, an estimated 12.6 million women would express interest in using a product designed to protect them from an STD, while 11.5 million women would be interested in such a product even if it were not 100 percent effective. An estimated 7.7 million women would be interested in such technology even if the product was not 100 percent effective and the cost was twice that of a condom (which was stated to be $1.00). To conservatively estimate market potential, this means that seven million women may be willing to pay $2.00/dose of product; with an estimated 100 sexual encounters per year, this brings the market total to roughly $1.4 billion in the U. S. alone.[38]

Lifestyle Drugs: The New "LSD" for a Narcissistic Nation

The pharmaceutical industry is presently reformulating its business and marketing strategies to reposition its research and development effort and an existing number of prescription and OTC products to generate greater revenue growth and profitability with a focus on improving the quality of life. One popular term for this product segment is Lifestyle Drugs, or ironically, LSD. This covers everything from foot fungus to acne, obesity, wrinkle removal, lips/eye/hair color changes, teeth whitening, scar removal, excessive sweating, growth hormones, and excessive hair removal to hair re-growth, fertility and sexual enjoyment. The industry has already reclassified a number of products to establish an estimated market size of $2.3 billion in revenue for 1999. *Med Ad News* apparently agrees stating, "Cosmetic problems, including excessive facial hair, wrinkles and nail fungus, create markets that are underserved or completely unserved."[39]

By comparison, analgesic sales, a major market segment, totaled $2.3 billion in 1999. According to some projections, if the industry exploited entirely all forms of quality of life needs to the point of vanity, the potential target-addressable market could grow to approximately $40 billion.[40] This includes targeting existing surgical procedures to address vanity needs, including chemical peel (acne), liposuction, vein surgery, hair transplant and botox injections (wrinkle removal), which generated $3.15 billion in revenue in 1999. Also targeted is the lucrative cosmetic market, which according to the Freedonia Group generated over $2.3 billion in revenue in 1999. With hair transplant, wigs/toupee and potions generating nearly $1.3 billion in revenue in 1997, the pharmaceutical industry also sees a great competitive alternative to address the needs of over 40 million people who have lost or are losing their hair. They view products like Viagra, Vaniqa (hair removal with a target segment of over 41 million people),

Rogaine, Proscar and Propecia as laying the groundwork for future LSD marketing endeavors. Motivated to make a buck, manufacturers view these LSD drugs as price insensitive, thus becoming profit drivers for de facto, price-controlled environments associated with medically necessary drug applications, for example Viagra (angina), Propecia (benign prostrate enlargement), Vaniqa (African Sleep Sickness).

Leveraging existing core competencies applied to the market introduction and broad commercial acceptance of the current inventory of products, especially DTC programs, the pharmaceutical industry is using what it calls Drug Therapy Value Propositions, or DTVP, to build a suitable "pharmacoeconomic" business case based on their version of the market mix or "7P's." This requires a comprehensive strategy that delivers compelling value propositions for patients, prescribers, payers, public, politicians, pharmaceutical executives and police/federal authorities. The emerging DTVP would move beyond medically necessary pharmaceuticals to lifestyle remedies focused, for example, on enhanced appearance or enhanced activity or activity enablement. The pharmaceutical industry is prepared to compete directly with the cosmetic industry which prides itself on overwhelming the American public with television, radio, internet and print media advertising, promoting fake tans, face lifts, silicone implants and even acid face packs. What can replace the rigid regimes, hours of exercise, mud baths and an array of herbal treatments that have become a daily routine of Hollywood babes, lily-skinned, nymph-like supermodels, pop stars, actresses and cosmopolitan career girls? It seems likely that the pharmaceutical industry will eventually apply the cosmetic industry practice of "puffery," which is a regulatory euphemism for exaggeration of claims. After all, the poor regulation of cosmetics seems to reflect a Puritan value that vain people deserve to be cheated.

Perhaps the publication, *The Nation*, summed it up best regarding the moral vacuum which paradoxically binds the vain American consumer to the drug industry, stating, "The drug industry's calculus in apportioning its resources is cold-blooded, but there's no disputing that one old, fat, bald, impotent, fungus-ridden, rich man counts for more than half a billion people who are vulnerable to malaria but too poor to buy the remedies they need."

The Cohorts of Heaven Battle

*Jesus therefore said to them:... Why do you not know
my speech? Because you cannot hear my word. You
are of your father, the devil, and the desires of your
father you will do. He was a murderer from the
beginning, and he abode not in the truth: because
truth is not in him. When he speaks a lie, he speaks
of his own: for he is a liar, and the father thereof.*
—St. John 8:42, 43–44

Four months after the terrorists hit the Twin Towers, Michael
Bloomberg was elected mayor in New York City. In the first two
weeks of his tenure as mayor, he was pushing for legislation making it
a requirement that all OB/GYN's have mandatory abortion training. In
addition, the attorney general of New York State, Elliott Spitzer,
wanted a law making it a hate crime for a pro-life person to picket an
abortion center. There is no doubt watching the press and politicians,
that they drew no connection between the bombing of the Twin Towers
and God allowing something to go through His permissive will to wake
up a sinful people. We have abandoned God, and most political
officials draw no connection. Today, the great majority looks through
the eyes of natural man. New York and America as a whole have
dramatically missed what it has all been about. Is this any different
than previous civilizations? The answer is a resounding "no," based
upon all civilizations preceding ours as well as the complete text of
Scripture. All data points to a merciful and loving God, but also a just
God. Will New York be judged further?

Chuck Colson of Prison Fellowship Ministries tells the following
story on Crosswalk News Channel:

We often hear that a person's private conduct is unrelated to
the performance of his or her public duties. This is especially true
if the private failings involve sexual matters. Advocates of this
point of view never tire of telling us about former presidents whose
marital infidelities didn't prevent them from political greatness.

This argument was made regularly during the debates over President Clinton's impeachment. The president's defenders told us that the Founders would have been dismayed at our making a man's private conduct the basis for judging his fitness for office. And especially is this so, they said, with sexual sin, which is something so personal you can be justified lying about it.

Well, a new book tells us that far from being dismayed, the Founders believed that private misbehavior would lead to a breach of public trust.

In his just released book, *On Two Wings*, philosopher/theologian Michael Novak makes a compelling case for the biblical origins of the American experiment. As he puts it, the way that the story of the American founding is told today cuts off "one of the two wings by which the American eagle flies." That cut-off wing is America's "compact" with the God of the Bible.

The Founders believed that there was a God who brings down the mighty and lifts up the poor. They relied upon this belief, and this belief is, as Novak writes, "an indispensable part of their story."

As you might expect, this belief shaped their understanding of morality and character, as well. They did not make the distinction between private and public conduct that we do. Novak tells the story of a prominent Boston doctor, Benjamin Church, Jr. Church's fellows Bostonians thought him to be a patriot and were subsequently shocked to learn that he had been selling his services to the British.

In a letter to James Warren, Samuel Adams offered an explanation that would be incomprehensible to many contemporary Americans: He linked the doctor's treason to his reputation as an adulterer.

Adams wrote, "He who is void of virtuous attachments in private life, is, or very soon will be, void of all Regard for his country." He added, "...there is seldom an instance of a man guilty of betraying his Country, who had not before lost the feeling of moral obligations in his private connections...." In other words, if a man or woman won't honor private obligations, why should we believe that he or she will honor his public ones? They won't.

If this seems hard to understand, the problem lies with us, not our Founders. Our culture has forgotten what the Founders knew and Novak's book asserts with ample evidence that the American experiment is a moral, not just a political, exercise. As such, it assumes certain things to be true about human nature and, as Novak tells us, about the authority of the God of the Bible. But these beliefs run contrary to today's American culture. And that's why the ordered liberty envisioned by the Founders has degenerated into a demand for personal autonomy that asks nothing of its citizens, not even their virtue.

As Novak brilliantly reminds us, private virtue, rooted in biblical faith, is essential for the American experiment to work as the Founders intended. And, it's vital that Christians understand this often-ignored "wing" on which our way of life depends. This is the wing that teaches us that, without virtue, there can be no greatness.[1]

Unfortunately we as Americans, deluded by relativism, seem all too willing to remove every virtue from our hearts, foolishly inviting the devil's vice as the replacement. As Novak contends, we have abrogated our compact with God. Like the chosen people, Americans now have multiple gods to worship. Whereas the seven theological and cardinal virtues are the fruits of living in the grace of God, Satan offers the capital vices (the "Seven Deadly Sins")to habitually live in the state of sin. When a person becomes a victim of any of the seven capital vices, he or she is gradually led away from the worship that is due to God alone. Each vice in essence has a false deity and blasphemes God. These vices are pride, envy, avarice, anger, gluttony, lust, and sloth. American families are consumed by these vices, and as a result all life has been sapped out of the home. Where the hearth was once a place of "fireside chats," today it is a place of discord and shouting matches. With a television in nearly every room, not only is there little conversation, but most often there isn't even a meal as a family. Like the Chosen People, as Americans serve multiple gods, we are likely to lose our 'Protective Hedge' which historically has kept America out of harm's way.

In the end, the Church will triumph. The forces of Hell and evil battle the forces of Heaven and goodness. There are no rules for Satan. Everyone and everything is in play. Many things on all fronts appear to be coming to a head. There is a confluence of events on the political, social, economic, and financial level that could tip the system over at any time. The world is poised for change. Nuclear war? A worldwide economic collapse ushering in new rules? Vast and uncontrollable epidemics or global natural disasters leading to a collapse of society? We are involved in a great battle, and if we do not entrust ourselves to the plan of Heaven, we will perish. Wicked spirits struggle against

God and against His royal dominion. Satan's plan is powerful, continuous, and universal; it's also devious and deadly. Satan succeeded in establishing his reign in the world and deludes himself that he is the sure victor. As the ultimate battle draws closer, it will be more fierce and terrible. The weapons used by the demons are those of evil, sin, hatred, impurity, pride and rebellion against God.

The weapons used by heavenly spirits are those of goodness, divine grace, love, purity, humility, and docile submission to the Will of God. It is comforting to know that when God is for you, who can be against you? Insurmountable odds will tilt in your favor. Disasters can be averted. It all starts with obedience to the laws of God. This is confirmed in Holy Scripture that says "obedience is better than sacrifices" (1 Samuel 15:22). We do many things we are not called to do. We are a society consumed with activity that is not asked for by Heaven.

For Heaven to get its way, even the laws of nature can be suspended. This is why a David can defeat a Goliath, Gideon with only three hundred men can defeat a large army, and through Moses' intercession, the Red Sea can part. In modern times, Jesuit and Franciscan priests and friars survived unscathed the atomic bombings of Hiroshima and Nagasaki, even though they were at ground zero. Barely a brick was left on a brick for as far as the eye could see, and death was all around them. When they were asked how they were not harmed, a Jesuit responded, "We're not quite sure, but in our house we were living the message of Fatima." The docile and the humble can win because the armor of battle for a believer is prayer, penance, and sacrifice. The armor of battle for a non-believer is hubris, high finance, military might, self-knowledge, and pride. The words of the proud and mighty are, "We will not have this man to reign over us" (St. Luke 19:14). Lamentably, how great today is the denial of God? How great is the number of those who wish nothing to do with Him?

These are the times where the cup of justice is full—nay, it is flowing over. The Lord will purify with the strong action of justice and of love. Painful and bloody hours are in preparation for America and the world. America, due to its perverse faith, nearly complete apostasy, and deep sin, will see things change in the near future. The drama is about to unfold as it did for civilizations of ages past. We may think differently, but if the past is prologue to the future, America may be finished as a dominant power. As we see from the Scriptures, God has His almighty ways to bend our will and the means are limitless.

The Road Less Travelled

No matter what the circumstances around us, Heaven watches over their consecrated souls. In the midst of turmoil and daily difficulties, the throne of Heaven is among us. There is no fear in followers of Christ Jesus when obeying the commandments, for they are safety, refuge, comfort, and security. The necessary material and spiritual goods will be provided. When a family dedicates itself to the Divine light of the Lord's presence, it will shine in purity and holiness. The state of grace will allow it to grow in a life of holiness through the exercise of all the Christian virtues. Because the sacrament of matrimony confers a particular grace for all to grow together as one unit, Heaven's task is to cement deeply the unity of the family, to bring husband and wife to an even deeper and spiritual communion, and to bring their love more perfectly together which will express itself in a pure and supernatural charity.

Then the Holy Spirit leads the family to a road of sanctity and joy, which must be built up and travelled where love will bring peace. Through these steps of dedication, and through the ways of the family, the summit of holiness can be reached. This perfection of love can make us all saints, where family unity can be more fruitful and strong. Heaven watches out for its own. The most precious gift to a family is its children. Jesus said, "But he that shall scandalize one of these little ones that believe in me, it were better for him that a millstone should be hanged about his neck, and that he should be drowned in the depth of the sea" (St. Matthew 18:6). Through the internet, media, and other exploitation, many will have a serious accounting. All of eternity has been traced out for children as Heaven takes them by the hand, as they become a part of Heaven's estate.

Peace seems to be written on the walls as you walk into the home of a family seeking the things of God. Disharmony is written with blood on the walls of a family's home where Heaven's ways are not acknowledged. The divine guidance of Heaven watches out in a special way for consecrated souls. The salvation process in a godly home is a unifying force as human collaboration and daily work intersect God's plan for the children. We have our part to do, and Heaven has its part. We must be willing to say "yes" to what is being asked of us. If the ego and self-will are accentuated beyond reason, God's best is never achieved. Within the Divine Will is a divine protection. The family will produce fruits that are useful for sustaining life for the further enrichment of the family. This is not to say there won't be some bumps in the road due to a chastising of our human foibles, but God promises His best for those doing His will and living in obedience to His commandments. Do we have any other acceptable choice?

Where the Lord is present, there is virtue. The light of His Divine Will orchestrates our activities and work. A family consecrated to the Sacred Heart of Jesus and the Immaculate Heart of Mary can take solace in the knowledge that Heaven is aware of our circumstances and ready to help us overcome any trial. If the tree is not pruned, it will not grow strong or produce fruit. The preoccupations of the family are many. In the midst of trials, purity of heart and intentions can be realized, and despite temporary setbacks, we can persevere and prevail.

Loss of Faith

Many point to the Scriptures saying that more serious times could be ahead of us. It would be foolish to predict when events may happen, but it seems on a macro level they are pointing to the fact we may be in for a season of change. To deny the reality of the facts would be similar to why the lawgivers and intelligentsia at the time of Jesus were unable to identify who stood before them. Are our times different from previous civilizations? What are the signs? First and foremost, never has the world had so much apostasy, which opens a floodgate of errors. With the teaching of errors on a generational basis, civilization loses its way. Desolation becomes its fruit. The teachings of the Gospel become anathema, as we see in our schools today. Then heresy is taught based on errors and on human reasoning. Arguably, this teaching of heresy is the greatest sign confirming the view of God's dissatisfaction with mankind.

When a society is corrupt, it can be manipulated by anyone, any doctrine, or anything. This is where the U. S. and the western world are now. Because there is no discernment into the reality of the Gospel, deluded leaders and false prophets are everywhere, bringing those of little faith with them. "Take heed that no man seduce you: For many will come in my name saying, I am Christ: and they will seduce many. And many false prophets shall rise, and shall seduce many" (St. Matthew 24:4–5,11).

David Wilkerson of Times Square Church in New York City used an appropriate term to describe these false prophets: "pillow prophets." In the late 1970's and early 1980's we saw them on television preaching the "bless me club" approach of Jesus without the Cross. The world is now filled with a mixture of the gospel lingo and pop psychology and a few teaspoons of "can I pray over your wallet?" It is all about marketing the illusion of avoiding pain and suffering.

Beginnings of Sorrows

Leading clergymen maintain a silence for fear of losing their status, prestige, job, the collection plate, and often, their general ease of living. In their status quo lifestyle, they lack the moral courage to proclaim the truth against threats of political correctness, or worse, an excessive tolerance. Good people, to blend in and go along, are being carried away by this wave of errors and evil. No segment of society seems to be spared from the encroachment of errors cutting off the living oxygen of truth. "But there were also false prophets among the people, even as there shall be among you lying teachers, who shall bring in sects of perdition, and deny the Lord who bought them: bringing upon themselves swift destruction. And many shall follow their riotousnesses, through whom the way of truth shall be evil spoken of. And through covetousness shall they with feigned words make merchandise of you. Whose judgment now of a long time lingers not, and their perdition slumbers not" (2 St. Peter 2:1–3).

Another sorrow is the outbreak of wars and fratricidal struggles. These wars have a choir of voices screaming death around it as earthquakes increase, floods, famines, and catastrophes of every kind ooze from the pores of hatred. Heresy and apostasy breed a lack of charity. "And you shall hear of wars and rumours of wars. See that you be not troubled. For these things must come to pass, but the end is not yet. For nation shall rise against nation, and kingdom against kingdom; and there shall be pestilences, and famines, and earthquakes in places: Now all these are the beginnings of sorrows. And because iniquity has abounded, the charity of many shall grow cold. But he that shall persevere to the end, he shall be saved" (St. Matthew 24:6–8, 12–13). Throughout the world, this is what blankets the network news. Each evening the news of conflicts cascades into our living rooms through various media outlets, and as the information becomes increasingly worse, the psychotherapists' coffers bulge revenue from with new patients as anxiety increases. The West has too many inputs destroying peace of soul. Just take a look in any large bookstore in America and see a hundred-plus feet of magazine racks over six feet high. America is burdened with 'overchoice,' which drowns out the voice of God.

Another sorrow is the destruction of the Church. As the gospel is preached in the whole world, Satan has become more active attempting to destroy those who oppose him. "Then shall they deliver you up to be afflicted, and shall put you to death: and you shall be hated by all nations for my name's sake. And then shall many be scandalized: and shall betray one another: and shall hate one another. And this gospel of the kingdom shall be preached in the whole world, for a testimony to all nations, and then shall the consummation come" (St. Matthew 24:9–10,14).

As conflict intensifies, it gets uglier. People actually set themselves against Christ and act as an antichrist perpetrating horrible sacrileges. Throughout history there have been people who have been antichrists with a small "a" like Lenin, Stalin, Hitler, Napoleon, Pol Pot, Mao Tse-tung and other tyrannical leaders. However, as there is a confluence of events on a financial, economic, social, and governmental level, the world will usher in a leader, or anoint one, who will provide a powerful delusion of a solution for a world in total chaos. Is mankind currently ushering in the age of the One-World Leader? It certainly is one possible scenario.

For anyone following the worldwide financial markets this is not a big stretch. It is a very fragile world economy. "Whose coming is according to the working of Satan, in all power, and signs, and lying wonders, and in all seduction of iniquity to them that perish; because they receive not the love of the truth, that they might be saved. Therefore God shall send them the operation of error, to believe lying..." (2 Thessalonians 2:9–10).

"When therefore you shall see the abomination of desolation, which was spoken of by Daniel the prophet, standing in the holy place: he that reads let him understand" (St. Matthew 24:15). Those who are moving with the agenda of Heaven can hear what the Holy Spirit is saying, but those who have shown no interest in a spiritual way of thinking will not even grasp the principles of Heaven's ways. "And from the time when the continual sacrifice shall be taken away, and the abomination unto desolation shall be set up, there shall be a thousand two hundred ninety days. Blessed is he that waits, and comes unto a thousand three hundred thirty-five days" (Daniel 12:11–12).

In the persecution of the Church by the man of perdition, the Mass will go underground just as in the days of the early Christians under persecution in Rome. As the New World Order continues to gain a place at the banquet table, the globalization of the world brings us a one-world government under a world body of supra-national government leadership.

Meanwhile, the skies continue to send forth phenomena we do not understand. As the star led the Magi to Bethlehem, so do celestial phenomena tell those in the Heart of Jesus where we are going. "And immediately after the tribulation of those days, the sun shall be darkened and the moon shall not give her light, and the stars shall fall from heaven, and the powers of heaven shall be moved: And then shall appear the sign of the Son of man in heaven: and then shall all tribes of the earth mourn: and they shall see the Son of man coming in the clouds of heaven with much power and majesty" (St. Matthew 24:29–30).

These are the issues and phenomena in our midst today. The proud in the day of Jesus did not know how to read or understand what the prophets said. It is no different today. As events increase in speed and severity, social disorder will increase. It will turn brother against brother, family against family, and confrere against confrere. Of this much we are sure: The events are accelerating and coming to us at breakneck speed.

Opposing Views of the World

When Jesus said He was giving "testimony to the truth" (St. John 18:37), this was the call to all who follow Him, whether it be an industrialist running a Fortune 500 company or the person tending the machines in the local laundromat. The compromising of truth is where things break down. The curse of the technological age driven by computers is that no one is accountable. No matter who we talk to over the internet, the phone, or in a phone tree on a message machine, no one seems to be accountable. Everyone speaks about doing their own job with an inability or unwillingness to take responsibility or make a decision. The infamous term, "they," continues to pop up no matter who we speak to. Yet Christ holds all believers individually accountable to a heavenly standard. It is why Purgatory exists as God's last act of ultimate Mercy. After our death, we come face to face with the reality of God, His divine will and our merits. It is our means of atonement for all the errors of commission and omission on earth. If we refuse to be held accountable on earth, God will insure our accountability after death. Purgation enables the soul to become divinely obedient, that is, saintly.

Believers know in their hearts "what is truth." It is written in the heart and soul of all men, whether we choose to acknowledge its presence or not. There will always be a primacy to spiritual values over temporal. There are profound differences in moral law and democratic pluralism. When a conscience is dull and not sensitive to Divine law, democratic bargaining has a greater role. To appease two or more sides of a political issue, the second best alternative is most often the view that becomes legislative law. The middle ground of "nothingness" or utopia's reality is often the legislative result because both sides negotiate from extremes and something in between is accepted to accommodate all. Hegel would be proud. This is why the political process frustrates nearly all who go near it. Many 'permanent' politicians in Congress have left over the last twenty years believing they no longer have a positive impact.

Jesus suffered death because systems of thinking are so opposed. It is for this reason the believer never feels totally comfortable with an earthly existence. The closer a person is to the Christ, the less attractive are the limited things of the world. However, man in his wholeness, in all the fullness and manifold riches of his spiritual and material existence, is the vehicle to bring the kingdom of God to earth. The Lord's Prayer does remind us, "...on earth as it is in Heaven."

Who Is Your Master?

Often there must be civil disobedience when it comes to the state's enactment of laws which defy divine or natural law. The preeminent social causes of our time are surely abortion, homosexuality, euthanasia, and cloning, which are most certainly crimes that no human law or authority can claim to legitimize. There is a grave and clear obligation to oppose them by conscientious objection, prayer and fasting. There must be at all times a necessity to challenge laws from legal situations created, according to the canons in democratic procedure. Under the divine law of the commandments of the gospel, no one can licitly take part in a political campaign favoring such immoral laws, nor vote for any such law, nor condone others who promote such laws. Notwithstanding the Protestant sects, when we see a majority of over sixty-plus million Catholics voting the same way as the unbelieving church, how can Americans, especially Roman Catholics, expect to pull our country out of the quagmire in which it finds itself? The so-called 'believing' and 'unbelieving' churches voting so similarly on serious crimes is the single best indicator that America is in trouble. The harm done is most often generational, and it may take generations to come back to a state of what is considered a Godly perspective. Today, on the major moral issues such as abortion, pornography, drugs, divorce, homosexuality, and cloning, the believer is significantly out-voted and appears to have only one remaining course of action, to plead with a humble and contrite heart for Divine Mercy, ever mindful that mercy may include justice.

A major impediment in our proud and haughty society is that, like ancient Israel, we think we have the answers to what ails us. When we reach the point of independence from God, we must often look for manmade or political solutions. Because we have lost touch with the spiritual dimension, we most often "do that what is right in our own eyes." The culture then drifts into a vast wasteland of laws that will contradict one another and become meaningless. At the center of the argument is man's search for meaning in laudatory thoughts and words, such as 'the right to freedom of thought, individual freedoms, and the right to manifest one's thinking individually or in the community,' in public, or in private. However, unless these thoughts are expressed in the proper and Godly interpretation of natural law, and a higher law than what is expedient for a society wishing to simply appease every whim of every citizen, the passage of those laws will over a generation crush those they're intended to help.

I have always sat in amazement and noticed the simplicity of the Ten Commandments. When followed, life seems to go much simpler. See them listed below.

1) I am the Lord your God; you shall not have strange gods before Me.
2) You shall not take the name of the Lord your God in vain.
3) You shall keep holy the Sabbath.
4) Honor your father and your mother.
5) You shall not kill.
6) You shall not commit adultery.
7) You shall not steal.
8) You shall not bear false witness against your neighbor.
9) You shall not covet your neighbor's wife.
10) You shall not covet your neighbor's goods.

The simplicity is amazing, as is their directness. The Ten Commandments have a total of only 75 words, yet court systems in the world have millions of people affiliated with issues of crime and punishment. God is order and simplicity. Pick any commandment and look at its sheer simplicity of words and notice the vast ramifications of breaking it. When the first one is broken, there is a gradual movement away from truth. The first three address man's vertical relationship to God, while the remaining seven speak of the horizontal dealings of man with man. When followed, our life seems to go more smoothly, but when ignored, problems emerge that can swallow us whole. When reckless and ungodly freedom of thought arises, along with the "right" to manifest views outside of the process of divine selection, then problems emerge.

Faith and Reason

The key point noted above is that America worked as a model for the world to emulate because the American experience was based upon a moral and biblical stance. This is why the world's emigrants sailed to U. S. shores. The framers of the U. S. Constitution were aware of Greek logic, Roman law, and the connection between God and laws for the public good. America took the best from those institutions and fashioned something that worked. Injustices in the economic order and in the spiritual order constitute the gravest threat to peace in the world, and a "humanistic criterion" based upon spiritual truths giving credibility to a Supreme Being or Creator is essential in evaluating social, economic, and political systems. The elimination of exploitation and free participation in economic and political life are the standards by which systems should be judged.[2]

Politics must first and foremost be about human beings and meeting all the needs of man, including the political, social, economic, financial, and spiritual. The reason for politics is the welfare of man temporally and spiritually, whether it be local, state, federal, or international, because legitimate politics always originates from God and is given to the exercise of man, for the benefit of man and the glory of God. If it does not adhere to these basic principles, there is no reason for it to exist. The utilitarian doctrine of man existing to serve the state, or the Motherland as the Soviets called it, is doomed to failure because the needs of the soul are unmet. Such systems are doomed to failure. Masonry knows this, which is why it is pitting communism against a 'flawed' Christianity. Regardless, God will simply not allow the will of a human to supersede His Divine Will. America may fail, as the Soviet experiment seemed to fail, because we are not meeting the needs of the soul either. Hegel, Marx, Feuerbach, and Schopenhauer were simply philosophers looking for a utopia that does not exist and will never exist.

Man's purpose is contained in the Incarnation and Resurrection of Jesus Christ. The search for meaning will never be found anywhere other than on the road to Calvary. This is why the wisdom of God is folly to the world. The systems of human thinking are typically on another plane of existence. One group is seeking the temporal and physical, the other group is seeking the spiritual and eternal. The methods of achieving these goals are very different, which is why there is so much friction in the world.

Unless we have a philosophy that reduces our thinking to man relating to a Supreme set of principles as they in turn relate to our fellow man, our lives will lack direction and meaning. Any real philosophy must have a vertical relationship to God and a horizontal relationship to man. All others are false and useless.

For a reason rooted most probably in Original Sin, man tries many doors before he is willing to go the final way and say, "I am nothing. I need something and someone. I will give Jesus a chance." To the extent we open that door, far or wide, to that degree we let in sunlight. So often there is an enormous amount of loneliness and pain before we are willing to let the light enter in.

George Weigel, writing in his biography of Pope John Paul II, *Witness to Hope*, speaks of the relationship between faith and reason, science, religion, philosophy and theology all pointing their way to God for those willing to listen and with an open heart.

> Philosophy ordered to transcendent truth is also crucial for religion, John Paul argues. Ancient Greek philosophy helped purge religion of superstition. The temptation to superstition is perennial, though, and sometimes takes the form of the claim that faith is not subject to rational analysis. In today's cultural climate, that has meant stressing faith as solely a matter of feeling and experience....[3] Believers are also thinkers: in believing, they think and in thinking, they believe. If faith does not think it is nothing."[4] On the edge of a 21st Century that seems destined to be heavily influenced by resurgent religious faith, this call to a reasonable faith looms large indeed. If faith and reason do not work together, a revival of religious conviction will not provide a secure foundation for human dignity. For that dignity is ultimately grounded, John Paul is convinced, in the human capacity to know the truth, adhere to it, and live it."
>
> To those "postmodern" theorists willing to allow religion a place at the table of intellectual life because religious truth is one possible truth among others, John Paul says, "No, thank you." Unless thinking is open to what *Fides et Ratio* (Faith and Reason) terms the "horizon of the ultimate," it will inevitably turn in on itself and be locked in the prison of solipsism [thinking of only oneself]. The marriage of ancient Greek philosophy and Christian theology in the early centuries of the first millennium taught a wiser lesson: human beings can know what is true, what is good, and what is beautiful, even if we can never know them completely. Recovering that sense of confidence, John Paul asserts, is essential to reconstituting a true humanism in the third millennium. The path to a wiser, nobler, more humane 21st Century runs through the

wisdom of the first centuries of encounter between Jerusalem and Athens (Faith and Reason).

The tragic separations of reason and faith, science and religion, philosophy and theology have been the fault of both philosophers and theologians, according to the Pope. When theologians demean reason and philosophers deny the possibility of revelations, both are diminished, humanity is impoverished, and the development of a true humanism is frustrated. "Faith and reason," John Paul writes, "are like two wings on which the human spirit rises to the contemplation of truth."[5] We can be sure, he suggests in *Fides et Ratio,* that we will need to fly with both wings in the millennium ahead. The quest for truth is an instinct built into us. And the grandeur of the human person, the Pope concludes, is that we can choose "to enter the truth, to make a home under the shade of Wisdom and dwell there."[6]

The First Vatican Council had taught in 1869–1870 that human beings could know the existence of God through reason, and Leo XIII's 1879 encyclical, *Aeterni Patris,* had proposed the philosophy and theology of Thomas Aquinas as the model for a synthesis of faith and reason. But much had happened in world civilization since the late 19th Century—not least, philosophy's drastically diminished confidence in its capacity to know the truth of things.

What the Pope describes as philosophy's "false modesty" had precluded its asking the large questions—Why is there something rather than nothing? What is good and what is evil? What is happiness and what is delusion? What awaits me after this life?[7] In addition to demeaning philosophy's true vocation, which was to be a servant of the truth, this "false modesty" had also opened the door to a culture dominated by various kinds of human hubris: an instrumental view of other human beings, a false faith in technology, the triumph of the will-to-power. The lethal effects of those forms of false pride pockmark the 20th Century."[8] It is long past time, John Paul suggests, for philosophy to recover that sense of awe and wonder that directs it to transcendent truth. The alternative is another century of tears.[9]

The Light of Hope

"Hope requires a secure foundation. This foundation is only found in Jesus Christ, in whose 'Death and Resurrection fully revealed God's love and His care for all creation.' That particular conviction led to a universal hope, for it was precisely because Christians believed that

God had become part of the history of humanity in Jesus Christ that 'Christian hope for the world and its future extends to every human person.' This is why Christian faith led not to intolerance, but to respectful dialogue with other religious traditions and to a sense of responsibility for all humanity."[10] This is precisely why the believer is not just a diplomat in a political sense. A person carrying Jesus Christ in his heart is a witness to hope, capable of transforming any given situation. This is why a believer can light up and transform a room by merely walking in. This transparent light is the very essence of life. It is to be fully alive and fully human. It is where Jesus said, "I am come that they may have life, and may have it more abundantly" (St. John 10:10). Jesus is life and there is no life until He is present. Everything is second rate, second best, or an imitation until the "Real Presence" is there.

Living in the light of the gospel brings us hope. In every home and on every continent is the longing of basic instincts of man—faith, hope, and love. The 20th Century closed with wars and rumors of wars. Fear was everywhere. For peace in our homes and elsewhere, man must discover a spirit of trust and hope. This is not merely a false optimism, it is a hope nurtured "in that inner sanctuary of conscience where 'man is alone with God' and thus perceives that *he is not alone* amid the enigmas of existence."[11] "Optimism is a matter of psychology; hope was a theological virtue informed by faith. In order to conquer fear 'at the end of this century of sorrows,' even politicians and diplomats had to 'regain sight of that transcendent horizon of possibility to which the soul of man aspires.'"[12]

A person will hopefully get to the point in his life where Jesus Christ reveals the face of God, for the true meaning of human life is to be found in self-giving, not self-assertion. This is where Heaven intersected time in the Person of Jesus Christ, as this is precisely the conversion point when it is realized. For some people, it may be a short road to conversion, others a longer one. For some others it goes fairly smooth as the gift is realized and the seed takes root easily. For many, the seed never takes root as the seed falls on thorny or rocky ground. The Law of the Gift written into the human heart is an expression of the self-giving love that constitutes the interior life of the Triune God—Father, Son and Holy Spirit. To live the Law of the Gift is to enter, by way of anticipation, into the communion with God for which humanity was created from the beginning. The fulfillment of this destiny is greater than the soul can imagine. It is all ours for the asking—all we need to do is die like the grain of wheat, for it is only when we die that we obtain a new and greater life. The entire history of mankind has been a fight against the dying process. Only at this point does a new life emerge. It is that turning point that is the most important, a combination of the will and grace, as when a train enters a switch where an inch forward decides its future direction. It is when a person's fiat is "yes" to God's Divine Will that the angels rejoice and history is thus altered. The heavenly battle is waged by Satan so the answer for some remains "no." The choir of Angels and the Church Triumphant encourage the "yes."

Suffering Is Redemptive

Suffering has the therapeutic capability to alter a person's views to realize that only God is in control of our life, liberty and pursuit of happiness. Suffering has redemptive qualities. Free will sufficiently predisposed by Divine grace can steer a suffering soul to the eternal 'yes', or if God's grace is refused it can harden the heart.

The Canticle of Tobit in the Old Testament makes it clear that those who do good, above all opening their hearts to the needs of their neighbor, are pleasing to the Lord, and He will eventually come to the aid of those who are tested. The hymn of Tobit is understood in this perspective. Punishment appears thus as a sort of divine pedagogy in which the final word is reserved for mercy. One can therefore trust absolutely in God, Who never abandons His creatures. Suffering takes on a mysteriously positive meaning when it is lived in a spirit of abandonment to God's plan. Our reference point can only be the Cross of Christ in which the mystery of the world's suffering finds a profound response. For sinners who are punished for their injustices, Tobit's hymn addresses a call to conversion and opens the marvelous perspective of a reciprocal conversion to God by man. Here lies the heart of the matter where many from the natural mind do not understand God's mercy. Sin is a tragedy not so much because it draws on us the punishments of God, but because it pushes us away from His heart. The Canticle directs our gaze to God the Father, inviting us to blessing and praise. Then in Jesus, the face of Heaven will shine and His limitless mercy will be revealed. Suffering can only be understood if Heaven's perspective is introduced.

A joyful heart rooted in God's plan possesses an eternal gaze. Those not moving in the light of redemption miss the Divine Plan and see events in their lives with the eyes of carnal man, only seeing the immediate physical realm in front of them. It is only in silence and prayer that we will find life's answers. Today's society refuses this answer. The deepest meaning of prayer can be understood by reflecting on a passage from Saint Paul to the Romans: "For the expectation of the creature waits for the revelation of the sons of God. For the creature was made subject to vanity, not willingly, but by reason of him that made it subject, in hope: Because the creature also itself shall be delivered from the servitude of corruption, into the liberty of the glory of the children of God. For we know that every creature groans and travails in pain, even till now. And not only it, but ourselves also, who have the firstfruits of the Spirit, even we ourselves groan within ourselves, waiting for the adoption of the sons of God, the redemption of our body. For we are saved by hope. But hope that is seen, is not hope. For what a man sees, why does he hope for" (Romans 8:19–24)?

The verse above is about the connection of the very existence of what it means to be born into a sinful world and affirm *the value of existence, the value of creation and of hope in the future life.*[13] In the world there is undoubtedly evil, but one can also learn the joy of the Christian experience by knowing "Christ's ultimate victory over evil will intensify one's awareness of evil's enduring power in the world."[14] Herein lies the very essence of a life lived joyfully in a sinful world. The Christian is to bring the world's suffering before the Lord in prayer, knowing that all roads to the truth eventually wind to Calvary and to the Cross. As much as Calvary remains a lonely place, it seems in the end for all of us to be inescapable.

In today's world, everyone appears to be off course. The problems in the West seem to be rooted in an affluence that has dulled our senses of spiritual truth. What the West has lost in affluence, the East has lost in state-sponsored suffering. Both have missed the mark. Modernity with all of its technological sophistication has placed science on the altar and worshipped it. With the increase in gadgets and marvels, man today, as previous civilizations in front of him, has said, "Do we really need God anymore?" Where for years the admirable characters in history were the men and women of biblical patronage, and heroes in the classical sense, today they are on the football field, or parading on a stage in Hollywood with the figure of a model to accept an award. Their personal lives will most probably be manifested in a public image of drugs, sex, and nervous breakdowns. There is very little for youth to emulate. We have the wrong heroes.

Because there is a yearning for the absolute built into the human condition, people are attracted to things and other people, something concrete. "When fragments of truth are absolutized by pagans, the world's suffering begins to take on the aspect of the demonic."[15] This is what happens when man is only viewed as a public utility—to be used and not valued as a soul, a person. This is why the Nazi death camps happened in World War II, along with Stalin's camps, Mao's and other tyrants' of the 20th Century. When utility is the sole measure of human life, man loses an identity in the Divine Plan. Christ teaches a higher standard of personal responsibility rooted in Christian humanism. By demonstrating that Jesus Christ in you is the light of the world Who transforms, faith can be restored to the world. As long as the media pushes an agenda of flesh and lewd conduct, the civilization will continue to deteriorate. Only with people of genuine Christian character coming onto the world scene and walking among us, can we expect change. People do not gravitate to ideas as much as they gravitate to people. This is why the transforming agents of civilization remain centuries after they are long gone, people like Saints Francis of Assisi, Benedict, Dominic, Ignatius of Loyola, Francis de Sales, Anthony of Padua, Catherine of Siena, Theresa of Avila, and others. Observing a person who has overcome obstacles is a powerful inspiration. There is good and there is evil, and their respective cohorts battle in the physical and spiritual world.

14

Are America's Wings about to Be Clipped?

This used to be a helluva country. I can't understand what's gone wrong with it.
— Jack Nicholson, *Easy Rider*

It is important to appreciate that prophecies add nothing to the revelations and truths revealed in Scripture and Tradition. It is all there for the faithful. Nevertheless, God in His infinite mercy communicates to mankind throughout history through the Holy Spirit and those blessed souls who have attained eternal happiness in the presence of God. The purpose is obvious: mankind needs continual guidance because by nature we are flawed through Original Sin and are susceptible to evil influences. These special messages from Heaven aren't for the times when people and nations are living by the Gospel, but for the times they're not.

Messengers or prophets typically convey prescient concerns from Heaven about the state of our existence and the possible outcomes based on our response. They are a grace from Heaven to help us along the way. The receivers of the prophetic messages represent a wide spectrum of society, not all of whom are saintly people. As the saying goes, "Don't shoot the messenger." This is one reason why the Church is very deliberate in its approach to approve or disapprove locutions, apparitions and other types of possible supernatural communications. Another reason concerns how the devil disguises himself, using prophecy to fool or confuse people, or half-truths to convince an audience of the authenticity of the messenger. That is why it remains important for the clergy and the laity to test the message over time and see what 'fruits' such information generates. For Christ assures us that a bad tree does not bear good fruit.

With this in mind, we have an opportunity to review carefully the significance of a select group of prophecies and current analyses and commentaries that appear relevant to our modern day and our future. It will become evident from the information presented that the Red Dragon, that is communism, is alive and well and is preparing for a worldwide confrontation with the last remaining super-power, the

202

United States. It is unfortunate that the media in general and the public at large are deluded by the appearance of the demise of the Soviet Union. The data presented demonstrates otherwise. To quote Soviet dissident Alexandr Solzhenitsyn, "As far as I can judge, two strongly held opinions are widely shared in the West: that during the last few years democracy has unquestionably been established in Russia, albeit one under a dangerously weak national government, and that effective economic reforms have been adapted to foster the creation of a free market, to which the way is now open. Both views are mistaken."

For America and the civilized world to prevail over the forthcoming events, we need to address first of all our present spiritual malaise. One aspect of our review of prophecies unfolding will be on the state of the clergy. Before God purifies a nation, He purifies the House of Israel, the Church—a long and painful process. The clergy are the sentinel on the 'watchtower' that Jesus forewarned are held responsible for the protection of His flock. They have neglected their duties and there is confusion in the pew. This underscores the famous Third Secret of Fatima. Where the first secret warns of the reality of Hell, where poor sinners go, such as those corrupted by rationalism and materialism; and the second secret the outbreak of the Second World War, the worldwide spread of communism and the total annihilation of nations; the third secret deals with the persecution of the Church, the culpability of the clergy, and the general, worldwide loss of faith. Zephaniah 3:4 concurs: "Her prophets are senseless, men without faith: her priests have polluted the sanctuary, they have acted unjustly against the law." History over the last 80 years verifies the truth of the Fatima messages. Unfortunately, we remain stubborn in our ways and the errors spread by communism will ultimately cause the loss of many poor souls with the corresponding destruction of many nations, including quite possibly the United States.

Prophecy Pertaining to Our World Today

St. Nilus was a student of a great Father and Doctor of our Church, St. John Chrysostom, and he remains a leading ascetic writer from the 5th Century. The prophecy attributed to him below is remarkably accurate in its portrayal of our society today.

After the year 1900, toward the middle of the 20th Century, the people of that time will become unrecognizable. When the time for the Advent of the Antichrist approaches, people's minds will grow cloudy from carnal passions, and dishonor and lawlessness will grow stronger. Then the world will become unrecognizable. People's appearances will change, and it will be impossible to distinguish men from women due to their shamelessness in dress and style of hair. These people will be cruel and will be like wild animals because of the temptations of the Antichrist. There will be no respect for parents and elders, love will disappear, and Christian pastors, bishops, and priests will become vain men, completely failing to distinguish the right-hand way from the left. At that time the morals and traditions of Christians and of the Church will change. People will abandon modesty, and dissipation will reign. Falsehood and greed will attain great proportions, and woe to those who pile up treasures. Lust, adultery, homosexuality, secret deeds and murder will rule in society.

At that future time, due to the power of such great crimes and licentiousness, people will be deprived of the grace of the Holy Spirit, which they received in Holy Baptism, and equally of remorse.

The Churches of God will be deprived of God-fearing and pious pastors, and woe to the Christians remaining in the world at that time; they will completely lose their faith because they will lack the opportunity of seeing the light of knowledge from anyone at all. Then they will separate themselves out of the world in holy refuges in search of lightening their spiritual sufferings, but everywhere they will meet obstacles and constraints. And all this will result from the fact that the Antichrist wants to be Lord over everything and become the ruler of the whole universe, and he will produce miracles and fantastic signs. He will also give depraved wisdom to an unhappy man so that he will discover a way by which one man can carry on a conversation with another from one end of the earth to the other. At that time men will also fly through the air like birds and descend to the bottom of the sea like fish. And when they have achieved all this, these unhappy people will spend their lives in comfort without knowing, poor souls, that it is the deceit of the Antichrist. And, the impious one!—he will so complete science with vanity that it will go off the right path and lead people to lose faith in the existence of God in three hypostases.

Then the All-good God will see the downfall of the human race and will shorten the days for the sake of those few who are being saved, because the enemy wants to lead even the chosen into temptation, if that is possible...then the sword of chastisement will suddenly appear and kill the perverter and his servants."[1]

As if to substantiate further St. Nilus' prediction, here are prophetic words communicated by the Blessed Mother to the Venerable Sister Marianne de Jesus Torres in the 17th Century in Quito, Ecuador. "Moreover, in these unhappy times there will be unbridled luxury which, acting thus to snare the rest into sin, will conquer innumerable frivolous souls who will lose themselves. Innocence will almost no longer be found in children, nor modesty in women, and, in this supreme moment of need of the Church, those whom it behooves to speak will fall silent." Later the "child Jesus" appeared saying, "...My Justice will be tried to the limit by the evils and sacrileges of the 20th Century." On another occasion, God the Father said, "This punishment will be for the 20th Century" and a vision of three swords appeared over the head of a crucified Christ saying, "I shall punish heresy, blasphemy, and impurity."[2]

Born in Germany in the 17th Century, the Venerable Bartholomew Holzhauser prophesied about man's future misuse of conscience. "During this period many men will abuse of the freedom of conscience conceded to them. It is of such men that Jude, the Apostle, spoke when he said: 'These men blaspheme whatever they do not understand; and they corrupt whatever they know naturally as irrational animals do... They feast together without restraint, feeding themselves, grumbling, murmurers, walking according to their lusts; their mouth speaketh proud things, they admire people for the sake of gain; they bring about division, sensual men, having not the spirit.... Everyone will be carried away and led to believe and to do what he fancies, according to the manner of the flesh.... They will ridicule Christian simplicity; they will call it folly and nonsense, but they will have the highest regard for advanced knowledge, and for the skill by which the axioms of the law, the precepts of morality, the Holy Canons and religious dogmas are clouded by senseless questions and elaborate arguments." Who today has not had ample opportunity to personally witness such behavior within one's community, workplace and home?

In 1846 at La Salette, France, (the message became public in 1858) the seer Melanie Calvat listened to the Blessed Mother's concerns that, "Evil books will be abundant on earth and the spirits of darkness will spread everywhere and a universal slackening in all that concerns the service of God.... The chiefs, the leaders of the people of God have neglected prayer and penance, and the devil has bedimmed their intelligence.... All civil governments will have one and the same plan, which will be to abolish and do away with every religious principle, to make way for materialism, atheism, spiritualism and vice of all kind.... They will abolish civil rights as well as ecclesiastical, all order and all justice would be trampled underfoot and only homicides, hate, jealousy, lies, and dissension would be seen without love for country or family."[3] How many times have the American people heard from our political leaders regarding the advent of the "New World Order"? Over the last generation, America has abdicated its Judeo-Christian ethics in the name of tolerance, removing the Decalogue from our government facilities and our schools, promoting everything from adultery to homosexuality with a growing antagonism towards Christians and Christian ideals. This is an engineered movement to unite America and the nations under a new system of government and jurisprudence. Our moral collapse has not just happened, it has happened through an open agenda of corrupted elites.

Over the last one hundred and thirty years, a very select group of top Masonic leaders created an ultra-secret, worldwide sect in the 1870's called the New and Reformed Paladian Rite. It was led by its creators Albert Pike (United States) and Giuseppi Mazzini (Italy) with the stated goal of the destruction of Christianity and the establishment of a 'New Age' that in Pike's own written words would be "maintained in the purity of the Luciferian doctrine." Pike professed that Lucifer is the God of Light and of good struggling for humanity against 'Adonay,' the god of darkness and evil. To achieve their goal, Mazzini devised a strategy whose purpose was to embroil every nation in a conflict so bloody and chaotic that eventually these nations would surrender their national sovereignty to an international, world government directed by this Luciferian order. This strategy is composed of three world wars. The first would be the downfall of the remaining strongholds of Christian monarchies in Europe, namely Austria-Hungary, Germany and Russia, with the establishment of a foundation in Central or Eastern Europe to promote civil unrest throughout the world with a particular emphasis in the nearer term to Europe. The direct result of World War I included the toppling of the Russian Tsarist government, establishing an 'Illuminized' communist dictatorship, and the downfall of the German and Austrian-Hungarian monarchies.

The second world war would allow the new political entity, that is, the Russian government (Soviet as it turns out), to spread its atheistic ideology worldwide with particular emphasis on the destruction of any remaining nationalism in Europe. This was accomplished somewhat successfully with the loss of the colonial empires of the western European nations and the establishment of the 'Eastern Communist Bloc,' thanks to the Yalta Agreement. Further success is abundantly evident today in the many and varied forms of socialist states throughout Europe and the escalating post war de-emphasis of nationalistic sovereignty, manifested by the evolution from the European Common Community to the establishment of a pan-Euro government and the 'Euro' currency.

The third world war required the establishment of a Jewish state promoted by Masonic Zionists, which would cause sufficient enmity between Moslems and Jews to initiate a regional conflagration that would quickly escalate between two world factions, Moslems and Christians. The horror of a worldwide conflict between Christian and Moslem nations would ensue with the atheist nations allying themselves with the Moslems. Pike predicted that as a result, "We, the Illuminati, shall unleash the Nihilists and Atheists, and we shall provoke a formidable social cataclysm which in all its horror will show clearly to the nations the effect of absolute atheism, origin of slavery and of the most bloody turmoil. Then everywhere the citizens, obliged to defend themselves against the world majority of revolutionaries, will exterminate those destroyers of civilization, and the multitude, disillusioned with Christianity, whose deistic spirits will from that moment be without compass, anxious for an ideal, but without knowing where to render its adoration, will receive the pure light through the universal manifestation of the pure doctrine of Lucifer, brought finally out in the public view...which will follow the destruction of Christianity and atheism, both conquered and exterminated at the same time."[4] To think that moneyed forces of evil would not want to control the destiny of nations through social, financial, and economic policy, one would have to have lived the last generation on an island with Rip Van Winkle. Evil and vice have an agenda, as do virtue and goodness.

The plan for control and its enactment are the fruit of generational thinking by socialist doctrinaires, such as Antonio Gramsci, and sympathetic moneyed interests. The openly stated goal of the Alta Vendita, the summit group of Italian Masonry in the 19th Century, is the destruction of the Catholic Church through Masonic lodges. Blessed Pius IX was informed of this and wrote warnings of this plot during his papacy. The goal has been achieved to a great extent because it has been done so masterfully and stealthily, and the Christian body fell asleep. Those who believe that institutions are being demolished purposely are often labeled as nuts by those who do not believe in God. Actually, it is the other way around, for those who do not believe in God do not understand how Satan works. They are naïve to the Evil One's ways.

This confirms what Bishop George Michael Wittman predicted in the 19th Century when he said, "Secret societies will wreak great ruin, and exercise a marvelous monetary power, and through that many will be blinded, and infected with the most horrible errors: however, all this shall avail naught."

To interdict this Luciferian strategy the Mother of God appeared to the three seers in Fatima, Portugal in 1917 offering God's mercy through a program of prayers, devotion to her Immaculate Heart and the collegial consecration of Russia by the pope with the bishops throughout the world. If we did not heed this request, she warned, Russia would spread her error (communism), a greater war would occur under the future Pope Pius XI, and the Church would suffer severely. Unfortunately, mankind did not heed the Blessed Virgin's request. At the end of the war in 1945, Jesus appeared to four children in Heede, Germany. He gave the following ominous message, "Humanity has not heeded My Blessed Mother, who appeared in Fatima, to exhort everyone to penitence. Now, I have come, in this last hour, to admonish the world. The times are grave. Men should do penance for their sins...I am near. The earth will tremble and will suffer. It will be terrible. **A minor judgment. For those who are not in a state of grace it will be frightful.** The angels of My justice are now scattered all over the world. Men do not listen to my calls. They close their ears, resist My graces and refuse My mercy, My love and My merits. They will agonize in the blindness of their faults. Hatred and greed fills the hearts of men. All this is the work of Satan. The world sleeps in a dense darkness. This generation deserves to be annihilated, but I desire to show Myself as merciful. Great and terrible things are being prepared. That which is about to happen will be terrible, like nothing ever since the beginning of the world."[5]

In 1961, Sister Lucia, the last remaining seer from Fatima, affirmed Heaven's disappointment that mankind chooses to ignore Mary's advice when she said to Fr. Augustin Fuentes, "Father, our Lady is very unhappy because they have not taken Her message of 1917 seriously. Neither the good nor the bad have paid any attention to it. The good continue their way without preoccupying themselves with it, they do not heed Her celestial request. The bad walk through life swollen with perdition, not taking into account the punishment that threatens them. Believe me, Father, God will chastise the world very soon. Think, Father, about all the souls who will fall into hell. This will happen because no one prays, because they do not do penance [the first secret—this author's emphasis].... Father, tell everyone that our Lady has, frequently, announced to me that many nations will disappear off the face of the earth. Russia is the scourge chosen by God to punish mankind [the second secret—this author's emphasis].... The devil

208

knows that when religious and priests fail in their beautiful vocations they carry along with them many souls into hell" [the third secret—this author's emphasis].[6] (This comes from conversation between the prophetess, Sister Lucia, and Father Augustin Fuentes, postulator of the Cause of Beatification of the two little prophets of Fatima, Francisco and Jacinta, reported in 1961.)

It is clear that all of the above warnings pertain to our generation today. A review of relevant 20th Century historical facts verifies the prophecies noted above and the success of the Pike and Mazzini strategy to date. We must remind ourselves that this hideous strategy continues to be played out by secret societies throughout the world, the most notable being the Masonic lodges, Council of Foreign Relations, and the Bilderbergers, to name a few. As fraternal networks, these groups perpetuate an agenda. The vast majority of members join for career ambitions and advancement. They merely follow humanistic doctrines. (To substantiate the prophecies regarding the coming third world war, additional analyses of strategic capabilities pertaining to war preparations by the communistic/atheistic nations based on qualified analysts and Soviet defectors are included in this book.)

Given Heaven's exhortations, what is the response of our clergy? We will see below that the failed role of our clergy in helping us face the confrontations of our modern era is unfortunately only making matters worse.

The Silence of the Shepherds

It is important to state up front that it is not the intent here to condemn the clergy on a wholesale basis. By far, most are men who suffer under cloud of scandal, and many of these have often lacked the courage to speak up. That notwithstanding, God's dissatisfaction with the religious is explicitly conveyed from Heaven through the prophets. It also must be stated that aside from the growing secularization of the Church at the parish level, the Church hierarchy is infiltrated quite effectively by 'Ecclesiastical Masons' who are determined to remove the dogmas and precepts of the One, Holy, Catholic and Apostolic Church and replace them with Masonic 'New Age' philosophies and rituals. There is no mystery to why seminaries are empty. Members of the laity who are not informed often ask why so few men are entering the priesthood. The answer is quite simple: Those holding orthodox views are being disqualified. If priests and seminarians do not subscribe to liberal views, they are often sent for psychological evaluation to behavioral science centers, like the one in Cincinnati,

Ohio. In Cincinnati, Dr. Joseph Wicker, whose evaluation was needed for admission to seminary, was turning away men because, "Although the applicant is an intelligent person who scored high on the mental ability tests, he is deficient in emotional and personality areas that would make him a suitable candidate for ordained ministry." A report was written on a candidate that was highly critical despite glowing recommendations from those who knew him well, including his own pastor. Who is this Dr. Wicker who has turned away so many men from the priesthood? To reach his position, he had to first be assessed and approved by the Worshipful Master of Mt. Washington Masonic Lodge 642. When Catholics found out and complained, Archbishop Daniel Pilarczyk defended Wicker. Is there any wonder there are so many problems in the Church?[7]

Historian James Hitchcock of St. Louis University endorses these findings saying that one cannot understand what has happened in the Church unless one understands what has happened in the seminary. Speaking of Michael S. Rose's *Goodbye! Good Men*, a book which exposes much of the recent scandal in the Catholic Church, Hitchcock says, "Few books in the last 30 years have shed more light on the continuing crisis in the Church." Notre Dame philosopher, novelist, and editor Ralph McInerny said the book helps explain that the artificial priest shortage was created by "keeping good candidates out, and admitting effete and unorthodox ones."[8] The prophecies of La Salette and Akita will be fulfilled in this scandal of "cardinals against cardinals, bishops against bishops, and priests against priests." Many sacred traditions that have been the glue of civilizations have crumbled in the last generation. Enemies are not just trying to change celibacy in the priesthood; they want to change the very nature and image of the Church.

We need to exhort the clergy and the remaining faithful to be brave, to persevere, and to right their ship for mankind's sake as well as their own. Historically, when the Church is at a moral low point, people finally begin to say that enough is enough, and they move back to what works. The Church is on the precipice of evangelization.

As stated earlier, the clergy serve as our sentinels and shepherds. Their responsibility is to gather, watch, and nurture. In these difficult times the Catholic Church's clergy (as well as any other Christian denomination) are compromised severely and failing their prime mission. This was prophesied well in advance by a number of Blessed and Venerable Saints.

At La Salette, the Blessed Virgin Mary gave the following admonishment, "The priests, ministers of my Son, the priests, by their wicked lives, by their irreverence and their impiety in the celebration of the holy mysteries, by their love of money, their love of honors and pleasures, the priests have become a cesspool of impurity. Yes, the priests are asking for vengeance, and vengeance is hanging over their heads. Woe to the priests and to those dedicated to God who by their unfaithfulness and their wicked lives are crucifying my Son again! The sins of those dedicated to God cry out towards Heaven and call for vengeance, and now vengeance is at their door, for there is no one left to beg mercy and forgiveness for the people. There are no more generous souls, there is no one left worthy of offering a stainless sacrifice to the Eternal God for the sake of the world."

The term "cesspool of impurity" created a firestorm when the message was released to the world in 1858. Questions of authenticity broke out and the Church released a sanitized version with that term removed. For a period of years the message was suppressed by the Church, but it was later re-released with that original term back in. Few terms in the history of private revelation have been as controversial. The fact remains that it was said. In chapters eight and nine of Ezechiel and other places in Scripture, the purification of nations started with the clergy. This is what we are witnessing today as the Church is being stripped naked for the world to see. It is not a good thing, but it is necessary for a revitalized Church to emerge.

In the 19th Century, Elizabeth Canori-Mora conveyed Christ's warning, "Woe to the religious who does not observe his rule! I say the same to the secular clergy and to all the people in the world who give themselves to a life of pleasure and who believe in the false maxims of modern ideas."[9] St. Nicholas of Flüe lived in 15th Century Switzerland as a husband, father, hermit, prophet and warrior. He made a number of prophecies regarding the state of the Catholic Faith. One pertaining to the future and specifically to the clergy says, "The Church will be punished because the majority of her members, high and low, will become so perverted. The Church will sink deeper and deeper until she will at last seem to be extinguished, and the succession of Peter and the other Apostles to have expired. But, after this, she will be victoriously exalted in the sight of all doubters."[10]

This perversion encompasses both spiritual and temporal attributes. It is seen in the false intellectualism of contemporary theologians who are wedded to humanism, materialism, modernity without boundaries, and who spread age-old heresies previously condemned by the Church. This perversion also manifests itself by the number of dispensations requested by priests to get married and the infiltration of homosexuals, pedophiles, communists, masons and satanic cults even into the upper hierarchy of the Church. They have reached the very summit of leadership.

Blessed Sister Anne Katarina Emmerick was an Augustinian nun who lived in Germany from the late 18th Century up to 1824. She was a 'victim soul' who bore the stigmata and received many visions and prophecies of the future state of the Church. She specifically forewarns us of the secret sects that plan to undermine the Church. On one occasion in May of 1820 our Lord revealed to her, "I saw how baleful would be the consequences of this false church. I saw it increase in size; heretics of every kind came into the city of Rome. The local clergy grew lukewarm, and I saw a great darkness... Once more I saw that the Church of Peter was undermined by a plan evolved by the secret sect, while storms were damaging it." She continues, "I saw all sorts of people, things, doctrines and opinions. There was something proud, presumptuous, and violent about it, and they seemed to be very successful. I did not see a single angel nor a single saint helping in the work. But far away in the background, I saw the seat of a cruel people armed with spears, and I saw a laughing figure which said: 'Do build it as solid as you can; we will pull it to the ground.'"

In June of 1821, she further stated, "Among the strangest things that I saw were long processions of bishops. Their thoughts and utterances were made known to me through images issuing from their mouths. Their faults towards religion were shown by external deformities. A few had only a body, with a dark cloud of fog instead of a head. Others had only a head, their bodies and hearts were like thick vapors. Some were lame; others were paralytics; others were asleep or staggering." Yves Dupont, author of *Catholic Prophecy* offers suggestions about the imagery. The "Heads like fog" could mean errors in thinking. A "Lame" bishop could mean performance of duty in a half-hearted way. "Paralytics" could mean powerless to do anything yet knowledgeable of what should be done. "Asleep" could denote unawareness or disinterest in the critical issues facing the Church. "Staggering" could mean that the burden of responsibility is overwhelming.

"I saw what I believe to be nearly all the bishops of the world, but only a small number were perfectly sound. I also saw the Holy Father—God fearing and prayerful. Nothing left to be desired in his appearance, but he was weakened by old age and by much suffering. His head was lolling from side to side, and it dropped onto his chest as if he were falling asleep. He often fainted and seemed to be dying. But when he was praying, he was often comforted by apparitions from Heaven. Then, his head was erect, but soon as it dropped again onto his chest, I saw a number of people looking quickly right and left, that is, in the direction of the world." This appears to be a very accurate depiction of Pope John Paul II. His illness is asserted by many to be Parkinson's disease. The comment that his "head was lolling from side to side" could easily be believed to allude to the visible effects of disease. The commentary about his appearance and "seemed to be dying" certainly reflects the public opinion of many that our current pope is too ill and should abdicate. Lastly, many faithful Catholics are concerned today regarding the worldly views offered by many in the Vatican bureaucracy, who quietly undermine the pope's authority. This seems to be substantiated by the next vision: "Then, I saw that everything that pertained to Protestantism was gradually gaining the upper hand, and the Catholic religion fell into complete decadence. Most priests were lured by the glittering but false knowledge of young school teachers, and they all contributed to the work of destruction." In light of the abuse to the pastoral teaching of Vatican II by heretical Catholic theologians and Masonic hierarchy, this vision appears to validate what many traditional Roman Catholics perceive as the protestantization and auto-demolition of the Church in preparation for the New Age. The new world religion of the universal church of the United Nations cannot be fully implemented until the Catholic Church and the papacy are disabled and destroyed.

This is verified by a prophecy from St. Anthony of the Desert in the 4th Century who wrote, "They will say that if they had lived in our day, Faith would be simple and easy. But in their day, they will say, things are complex; the Church must be brought up to date and made meaningful to the day's problems. When the Church and the World are one, then those days are at hand. Because our Divine Master placed a barrier between His things and the things of the world."[11]

In September 2002, Mikhail Gorbachev met at the U. N. World Conference on Sustainable Development in Johannesburg, South Africa, furthering the Earth Charter program. In October 2002 in New York City, he is to introduce to the world the "Universal Church of the United Nations." There are presently 200 church denominations scheduled to participate in this new global church village under the aegis of a one-world church. In time, you will have to be a member of this globalist church to be involved in U. N. activities. Those who are not members would be considered rogue religious groups. There has been an agenda to destroy the Roman Catholic Church because of its world influence, and scandals have given the promoters of this agenda a green light and an open door. To succeed the Papacy and the Eucharist would have to be destroyed. The present scandals and their lasting effects will further confuse and divide the American people from Rome. In all likelihood, a new American church will emerge.

In October 1973, the Blessed Virgin Mary appeared as Our Lady of All Nations to Sister Agnes Sasagawa in Akita, Japan. Mary confirmed the sad state of affairs within the Church, saying, "The work of the devil will infiltrate even the Church in such a way that one will see cardinals opposing cardinals, bishops against other bishops. The priests who venerate Me will be scorned and opposed by their confreres...the Church will be full of those who accept compromises and the demon will press many priests and consecrated souls to leave the service of the Lord. The demon will be especially implacable against souls consecrated to God. The thought of the loss of so many souls is the cause of my sadness. If sins increase in number and gravity, there will be no longer pardon for them."

When we look at all the homosexual scandals that have rocked the Church in recent decades, we can clearly see that these external signs are truly the culmination of prophecies and warnings given by Heaven throughout history. Yet, we should listen to the words of our Lord spoken to the children of Heede saying, "**Be not afraid!**" His message continues, "All those who have suffered, in these last times, are My martyrs and they prepare the newly converted of My Church. That which will shortly happen, will greatly surpass everything that has ever happened until now. The Mother of God and the angels will intervene. **Hell will believe that victory is theirs, but I will seize it from them.** Many blaspheme Me and, because of this, I shall allow all kinds of misfortunes to rain upon the earth for, through this, many will be saved. Blessed are those who suffer everything in reparation for those who offend Me... Blessed are those who prepared. Blessed are those who hear Me."

Later we will view specific prophecies regarding how the Church will lose its property and wealth and its clergy and laity will be persecuted for keeping the faith. As the Church's economic base dramatically deteriorates, there will no longer be a comfortable and complacent neutrality, and those who act like the turtle on the fence post will need to make decisions. People will need to choose sides. Will they join the American catholic church under the guidance of the Universal Church of the U. N., or will they stay with the Magisterium? As the old order in the Church disintegrates, it will be cardinal against cardinal, bishop against bishop, and priest against priest. This is the prophecy told at Heede, Germany; La Salette, France; Fatima, Portugal; and Akita, Japan; and it is happening before our very eyes.

The Move to One-World Government

In the 12th Century Bishop Christianos Ageda specifically predicted that the 20th Century would usher in the downfall of nobility, the rise of Hegelian dialectic of right versus left, of capitalism verses communism, and the impoverishment of the southern hemisphere to the benefit of the northern hemisphere. "In the 20th Century...there will be wars and fury which will last long; provinces divested of their people and kingdoms in confusion... In diverse places the ground shall be untilled, and there shall be great slaughters of the nobility... There shall be great mutilations of kings and rulers. The right hand of the world shall fear the left and the north shall prevail over the south."[12]

Here is a partial list of world tragedies of the 20th Century from data in the public domain[13] that illustrates that the move towards one-world governance, as was mentioned earlier, is proceeding forward:

❖ For World War I, including the Armenian massacres, the estimated casualty list of civilians and military is fifteen million.

❖ Three Christian monarchies tumble, Germany, Austria-Hungary and Russia.

❖ The Spanish Civil War, a conflict essentially between Christianity and communism, inflicted over 365,000 military and civilian casualties.

❖ During the Mexican Revolution and Cristeros civil wars, there were over 1.25 million Mexican casualties including thousands of Catholic religious.

❖ Stalin and Soviet Russia murdered tens of millions of Christian Ukrainians during the forced collectivization of their farms in the early 1930's.

❖ An estimated additional fifty-five to seventy-five million people were effectually murdered in the various Soviet concentration camps over a seventy-year period. Of these more than 200,000 Christian clergy were murdered by crucifixion, scalping and as the Commission on the Rehabilitation of Prisoners phrased it, by "beastly torture" according to Alexander Yakovlev, Russian diplomat-intellectual and trusted advisor to Mikhail Gorbachev.

❖ World War II had a total estimated civilian and military casualty list of over 30 million.

❖ Hitler and Nazi Germany murdered between four and six million Jews alone throughout Western Europe—and three to five million gentiles.

❖ The various persecutions in Red China, especially during the Cultural Revolution, have accounted for the murder of over two hundred million people—a number admitted by Mao Tse Tung, and labeled "Hsao Mei" [deprived of existence].[14]

❖ The mass murders in communist-supported coups and wars in Africa in the middle to later part of the 20th Century cost over ten million lives. This includes the Nigerian-Biafran revolt, the Congolese Civil War, Ethiopia Civil War, Mozambique Civil War, Rwanda Civil War, French-Algerian Wars, Angolan Civil War, the two Somalia Civil Wars and the Sudanese Civil War (supported by the P. R. C.). For more than ten years, the Muslim controlled government of Sudan has waged a cruel war against its own Christian citizens. The war has claimed nearly two million lives and displaced an additional four million people.[15]

❖ As portrayed in the movie "The Killing Fields," the communists in Cambodia under Pol Pot murdered over 1.65 million people in less than a decade.

❖ There were over 5.5 million military and civilian deaths due to wars in Korea, Vietnam, Laos and Cambodia, primarily involving indigenous communist and U. N., French and American armed forces. In Korea, Soviet fighter pilots engaged in armed conflict with U. S. fighter pilots.

❖ The Pakistan-Bangladesh war and subsequent famine cause the loss of over 1.2 million lives.

❖ The Iran-Iraq War is estimated to have caused over one million casualties.

❖ In the 1990's, we witnessed the "ethnic cleansing" of several hundred thousand Bosnian Muslims by Bosnian Christian Serbs.

❖ Abortions worldwide average about 46 million per year or approximately 126,000 per day.

❖ In the United States, abortions average over 1.3 million per year (4,000 per day), with over 42 million since 1973. This does not include the toll in lives and sickness wrought by the birth control pill, which is an abortifacient that causes infertility and cervical and breast cancer.

❖ In September of 2000, the Peoples Republic of China boasted publicly of the success of their programs to control the growth of their population, announcing in the press, for example *The South China Sea Post*, that their 'One Child per Couple Program' has effectively precluded the lives of over 250 million souls.

With the increasing secularization of the clergy and the infiltration of secret societies within the Church, it is not surprising that the growing corruption has and continues to accelerate the chastisement of mankind throughout the world. This culpability is verified by a message from the Child Jesus to Sister Marianne de Jesus Torres. "Know, moreover, that Divine Justice releases terrible chastisements on entire nations, not only for sins of the people but for those of priests and religious persons. For the latter are called, by the perfection of their state, to be the salt of the earth, the masters of truth, and the deflectors of the Divine Ire."[16]

"Straying from their divine mission, they degrade themselves in such a way that, before the eyes of God, they are the ones who quicken the rigor of the punishments. Because, detaching themselves from Me, they end up living only a superficial life of the soul, maintaining a distance from Me that is unworthy of My Ministers. With their frigidity and lack of confidence, they act as if I were a stranger to them."[17] So, the question is, does the world deserve judgment?

The New Road to Emmaus

Certain events will happen whether we approve of them or not, and whether we think they will roll out as we perceive they should. Events are ordained to happen in the near future which will rattle our comfort zone—and whether we realize they will happen is the key issue. Most everyone is walking around virtually clueless to the "signs of the times." A new springtime is coming to the Church and the birth pangs preceding it are fast and furious. The Church will be renewed and enlightened, made humbler and stronger, poorer and more evangelical through her purification, so the glorious reign of Jesus will shine forth for all to see. Those who believe today do so in spite of many obstacles. The Church is sprouting branches with many new buds, which are entrusted to a heavenly agenda. The tares are being separated from the weeds as the present spiritual environment has caused people to choose a camp. The so-called reformers and modernizers are one group, and the traditionalists who speak of restoring holiness and discipline are the other. Faithful disciples are desirous of a spirit of contempt for the world and of living in spiritual poverty, humility, in silence, prayer and mortification, in charity and in union with God, while at the same time being unknown and scorned by the world.

If one looks at the story of Jesus on the road to Emmaus, Our Lord provides the information to the men walking with Him that His death was preordained. "And behold, two of them went, the same day, to a town which was sixty furlongs from Jerusalem, named Emmaus. And they talked together of all these things which had happened. And it came to pass, that while they talked and reasoned with themselves, Jesus himself also drawing near, went with them. But their eyes were held, that they should not know him. And he said to them: What are these discourses that you hold one with another as you walk, and are sad? And the one of them, whose name was Cleophas, answering, said to him: Are you only a stranger to Jerusalem, and have not known the things that have been done there in these days? To whom he said: What things? And they said: Concerning Jesus of Nazareth, who was a prophet, mighty in work and word before God and all the people; and how our chief priests and princes delivered him to be condemned to death, and crucified him. But we hoped, that it was he that should have redeemed Israel: and now besides all this, to day is the third day since these things were done. Yea and certain women also of our company affrighted us, who before it was light, were at the sepulchre, and not finding his body, came, saying, that they had also seen a vision of angels, who say that he is alive. And some of our people went to the sepulchre, and found it so as the women had said, but him they found not. Then he said to them: *O foolish, and slow of heart to believe in all things which the prophets have spoken. Ought not Christ to have suffered these things, and so to enter into his glory? And beginning at Moses and all the prophets, he expounded to them in all the scriptures, the things that were concerning him.* And they drew nigh to the town, whither they were going: and he made as though he would go farther. But they constrained him; saying: Stay with us, because it is towards evening, and the day is now far spent. And he went in with them. And it came to pass, whilst he was at table with them, he took bread, and blessed, and brake, and gave to them. And their eyes were opened, and they knew him: and he vanished out of their sight. And they said one to the other: Was not our heart burning within us, while he spoke in this way, and opened to us the scriptures" (St. Luke 24:13–32)? When one looks at the above conversation it is a very casual one. In verse 26, Jesus says that the Son of Man must suffer and die to fulfill prophecy— enter into His glory. While walking, Jesus spoke about Himself, which was spoken in the Scriptures beginning with Moses.

Painful and bloody hours are in preparation for the believing church. These gut instincts are coming from people of faith in many denominations. After the time of great suffering, it will be a time of the great rebirth and the church will blossom again. Humanity will become again a garden of life and beauty, enlightened by truth, nourished by grace all the while consoled by the presence of the Holy Spirit. We will see a new Heaven and a new earth. The Divine imprint of the hand of God will be on all as they worship Jesus in spirit and truth. The new reign will be a universal reign of grace, of beauty and harmony, of communion, holiness, justice, and of peace. The new mercy will come as a burning fire of love brought by the Holy Spirit as at the first Pentecost. The Holy Spirit will come down as fire, but in a manner different from His first coming: It will be a fire that will burn and transform everything, which will sanctify and renew the earth from its foundations.

It is all in the Scriptures for those wishing to know. As Jesus talked to the men on the road to Emmaus expounding the truth of the Scriptures, so today we too can come to conclusions on many generalities about the seasons and the signs of the times. Satan with the cup of lust has seduced the nations and led them astray with modern-day idols by many names, names like pleasure, money, amusement, power, pride, and impurity. The new springtime will bring many changes to a hate-filled world. Those who would remain faithful during these troubling times must be humble, yet resolute; militant in spirit, yet forgiving in their hearts; living life to the fullest, yet accepting suffering with patience, appreciative of its worth before God.

The Red Dragon Confronts America

A people without religion will in the end find that it has nothing to live for.

—T. S. Eliot, 1939

The Florentine Niccolo Machiavelli taught, "For the great majority of mankind is satisfied with appearances as though they were realities...and are often more influenced by the things that seem, than by those that are." Despite the general worldwide acclaim of the Soviet Union's demise, Americans should be alarmed by the continued deception being foisted on us by the Russian military and its government leaders. Russia and its republics and satellite governments remain under the control of leaders thoroughly indoctrinated in atheistic communism. The military and political strategies taught in the Russian war colleges, and made operational in their economic and military budgets, specifically indoctrinate their officers and servicemen to prepare and win a first-strike nuclear war with the United States. Their hardened and mobile nuclear missiles remain targeted at the U. S. They have violated every test ban and nuclear arms treaty, especially the Anti–Ballistic Missile (ABM) Treaty. The internal resources and economic infrastructure over the past fifty years continues to direct strategic investments in the vast accumulation of raw materials and precious food supplies in sufficiently 'hardened' facilities to sustain an adequate percentage of trusted military troops indefinitely after the initiation of the war with any retaliation by the U. S. or any of our allies. To complicate matters, Russia is allying itself with China and a host of terrorist nations and sects to overextend America's military and economic capacity, while increasingly portraying America in a negative light to developing nations and our historical allies. This is especially the case regarding American versus European interests in the Middle East.

These assertions are supported by a number of Catholic prophecies and current expert analyses by renowned subject matter experts, including but not limited to, Jeffrey Nyquist, Christopher Ruddy, Kenneth Timmerman and Jean-Francois Revel, along with recent high-level defectors to the West including the incredibly reliable Anatoly Golitsyn (*New Lies for Old*), Colonels Lunev and Gorievsky, and various U. S. dignitaries and media journalists. They all assert that America suffers from a potentially fatal illusion on the current international balance of power and has a distorted picture concerning diplomatic and Cold War history. They further question America's ability to offer a sufficient deterrent and conclude that most Americans are naïve and so alien to the concept of such a war that we can't even imagine it, much less try to stop it.

Why do Americans, especially our political leaders, suddenly believe that Russia and China are our friends? These are the same two countries that over the past decades are directly responsible for hundreds of millions of deaths worldwide through civil wars, genocide, mass murder, massacres, abortions and assassinations. Author Jean-Francois Revel is astonished by the West's gullibility. He is reminded of the story of Demosthenes in 341 B. C., who tried to open the Athenians' eyes to the "peace offensives" of Philip of Macedon: "Our adversary, with arms in hand and supported by a strong force, covers himself with the word 'peace' while committing acts of war..." Peace, peace, where there is no peace. Revel asserts that Russia and China have openly declared their future plans of war with America, as history teaches that "Totalitarians are obliging: they declare and put in writing in advance everything they plan to do. The democracies normally make the same mistake they made with Hitler in refusing to take these detailed programs seriously because they seem so horrendous.... But how could we Westerners have been so willfully blind to Soviet expansionism? Because all our notions about soviet communism rest on the same [false] supposition: that everything will straighten itself out."[1]

Mother Russia

True to communist strategies, the Russians have broken or violated every treaty ever entered into with the West. One particular and alarming concern for Americans ought to be the ABM Treaty. Today Russia has over 10,000 ABM missiles, all nuclear, operational and at their disposal. America recently has conducted testing of its Ground-based Midcourse Defense (GMD) system as a part of President George W. Bush's modified strategy to provide our nation sufficient protection from weapons of mass destruction. This change in strategy has caused both Russia and the Peoples Republic of China to publicly warn the U. S. on July 18, 2000, of "The most grave adverse consequences" for proceeding ahead with its plans for a national missile defense system. That warning was issued at a one-day summit meeting between President Jiang Zemin and his visiting Russian counterpart, Vladimir Putin, in which the two countries also pledged to bring Chinese-Russian ties to a "new" and "higher" level, while focusing on what they described as a shared preoccupation with the role of the United States as the world's only superpower. The statement also called the 1972 Anti–Ballistic Missile Treaty banning national missile defenses "the cornerstone of global strategic stability and international security," and said, "Any damage to the ABM will trigger a new arms race." This is utter nonsense since the Russians have already built a massive ABM infrastructure. To complicate matters further, there is growing concern that both Russia and the P. R. C. continue to export intellectual property and materials pertaining to weapons of mass destruction to their Moslem allies and terrorists abroad.

All this and more supports what many experts assert is Russia's continued preparations for a surprise nuclear attack. Defectors claim that the Russian general staff members are beyond deluded. They are diabolical. Their first objective is the elimination of our strategic weapons. Their second objective is the preservation of sufficient nuclear strength and biological weaponry after the first strike to blackmail American allied nations or surviving countries. They reason that Britain, France and Israel have relatively small and vulnerable nuclear weapons. Even if used, these remaining arms would only be bombing cities already destroyed to rubble (deemed expendable by the Russians themselves).

As preparation for such an event, Russia's military and industrial complex requires sufficient stockpiling of strategic supplies, raw materials, food, fuel and machine tools for rebuilding vital industries with an extensive disinformation campaign to mask such preparation. A typical excuse would be the creation of some form of phony internal crisis as the reason for such preparative actions. Nyquist provides ample evidence in his report, "Russia's Economic Moves and What They Portend,"[2] demonstrating that Russia's communistic tendencies to fabricate lies continues in their disinformation campaign publicizing severe internal shortages and financial instability to hide the fact that they are massively stockpiling strategic supplies for military purposes. This stockpiling includes:

❖ Precious metals: Russia, a historical major producer, has curtailed most exports of gold, platinum and palladium. Nyquist notes that in the first ten months of 1999 Russia's central banks bought approximately 50 metric tons of gold compared to 34 metric tons for all of 1998. Former CIA analyst Peter Vincent Pry, cited by Nyquist, believes that Russia's general staff watches for large U. S. gold purchases as a strategic sequential signal for a preparation of a surprise attack. Russia claims it is financially strapped but is buying and hoarding gold! Who's lying here? Russia also announced it is minting $1.5 billion in gold and silver coins. The government abolished taxes on the sale of gold coins and ingots, giving citizens a strong incentive to buy gold. These actions are counter-intuitive for a government with a major currency crisis. It would typically do everything it can to prevent citizens from dumping the national currency and buying foreign currencies or gold. But in a war time economy gold and other precious commodities are the most stable currency.

❖ Copper: Production continues to increase significantly, with an entirely new copper industry created in the Urals that spans from mining ore to producing cables and cathode copper (production capacity of over 360,000 metric tons annually).

❖ Oil: Russia has dramatically cutback exports of its oil (as much as 26-plus percent in one year) and continues to heavily import Iraqi oil, as much as 35 percent of Iraq's exports (over 100 million barrels in the first six months of 1998 alone)—this despite significant capital investment from the West in modernizing its oil production capabilities. Russia also continues to cut back its exports of refined fuel oil, gasoline, jet fuel and diesel fuel. This is confirmed by the fact that Kremlin officials have suggested that Russia is increasing its reserves. But for what purpose? The only time the Russians seem to export a lot of oil, as they did after the 9/11 attacks, is when they want to drive down the price of oil in an effort to bankrupt the oil-dependent, Western-leaning emirates of the Persian Gulf. By destabilizing these Arab monarchies, they increase the chances of an Islamist terrorist takeover in the area, which would deprive the West of oil supplies.

❖ Russian Prime Minister Putin claimed in 1999 that Russia "succeeded in achieving industrial growth....," yet annual retail sales in Russia plummeted fourteen percent in the first nine months of 1999. Nyquist suggests that the expansion is all attributable to industries in the Urals and the Far East, where Itar-Tass reported freight haulage increased by over 40 percent. Russia warehouses most of its tanks, artillery and other military equipment east of the Urals.

❖ In Christopher Ruddy's report, "Russia and China Prepare for War—Part 6: Eleven Signs of a Russian Surprise Attack,"[3] Richard Starr, a Reagan administration arms control expert, writing in *The Wall Street Journal*, claims that Russia has stockpiled some 362 million metric tons of wheat, perceivably enough to feed the current population of Russia for three years. This is occurring while Russia intentionally misinforms the world that its nation is experiencing a famine; in response, Europe is sending approximately $550 million in food and the U. S. is shipping $625 million in food, including 1.5 million metric tons of wheat gratis. The U. S. also agreed to 'lend' 1.5 million tons of other food commodities. In October of 1998, Prime Minister Primakov announced that Russia allocated $600 million to purchase food stocks for "special consumers," which the Associated Press reported really refers to "soldiers." Meanwhile the West is unable to monitor the distribution of its food aid.

❖ Why during a supposed famine is Russia dramatically reducing the number of acres to be planted with crops? Why is the head of the Russian Security Council placed in charge of crop production? If America had a severe crop shortage, would we place its management in the hands of the Pentagon?

❖ While Russia is acquiring meat and other food commodities from the West, it is slaughtering its cattle and sheep at an alarming rate. Nyquist believes the Russians are canning the meat from their herds because they know that grazing herds, such as sheep and cattle, will be less valuable after a nuclear war begins.

Further deceptions and preparations for war with the West include:

❖ Even the U. S. S. R.'s Gulags—the concentration camps that were the epitome of totalitarian communism—remain and have grown. Avraham Shifrin, author of The First Guidebook to Prisons and Concentration Camps of the Soviet Union, stated in 1996: "Basically the situation in the camps of Russia, the Ukraine has not changed. As a matter of fact, the Russian authorities have had to transform their entire industry and base it on forced labor of prisoners; for this purpose, the camps—within the last few years—

have been gradually enlarged.... The West believes the Russians lies, as it wants to believe there will be a quiet life, but there won't be."

❖ As a means to avoid demilitarization under the 1990 Treaty on Conventional Forces in Europe, the Russians conveniently moved 20,000-plus modern main battle tanks east of the Ural Mountains to avoid converting such tanks to "peaceful uses." Whereas, NATO has vastly shrunk its armored components, selling many of them to developing nations. Worse still, Russia kept most of its advanced armored fighting vehicles in huge reserve depots in Russia, while demilitarizing second and third-level equipment in Eastern Europe.

❖ In 1993, a secret agreement was signed between Russia and Germany for the establishment of a future set of "spheres of influence" similar to the Yalta Agreement. This agreement was cited by Hal Lindsey in his best-selling book, *Planet Earth—2000 A. D.*, who referenced an article in the respected journal, *Intelligence Digest.* To the detriment of other western democracies, both parties agreed that the Czech Republic and Slovenia would become part of the German sphere with regional political incorporation into Germany within twelve to fifteen years. Hungary would be allowed to pursue regaining territories lost after World War I. This includes Transylvania, the area of the Danube west of Czechoslovakia, parts of the Ukraine and portions of Yugoslavia ceded by Hungary. What remains unclear is what type of military cooperation and support would be given by Germany to Russia should a military confrontation ensue. Yet, Catholic prophecies specifically cite military alliances and collaboration between "Prussians" and "Russians" during the third world war. For example, Brother Anthony of Aachen (19th Century) predicted that "The Russians made common cause with the Prussians" and marched their armies together. And the Curé of Ars, St. John Vianney in the 19th Century warned that "The enemy (the Prussians) will allow the burning of Paris and they will rejoice at it..."

The Russian government and their military chiefs remain convinced that a successful first strike nuclear exchange (though it causes wholesale slaughter and destruction), followed by blackmail of the rest of the world, would usher in a new world atheistic order wrapped in communistic totalitarianism. They are quite aware that notwithstanding expansion of NATO alliances into Eastern Europe, aggregate defense budgets of European NATO nations have declined from $184 billion in 1995 to approximately $159 billion in the year 2001. Throughout NATO, politicians accept the outward appearance of the Soviet Union's demise and have successfully pressed for the realization of a 'peace dividend' through disarmament.

This only reassures the Russian military that the European nations have no stomach for a nuclear or conventional confrontation. This reinforces the education of the Russian generals who are inundated with Marxist-Leninist theories on war, including the assertion that future war will be "missile-nuclear." Russian military strategists insist that this is a decisive fact, and with such foresight politicians and soldiers can deliberately prepare the armed forces, the economy and the people for the inevitable. To quote Colonel Skirdo of the General Staff Academy, "A nuclear missile war will serve as a harsh, merciless test of economic, military, moral and political potential of the belligerent states." As 20th Century history shows, no political state, including Nazi Germany, has been as belligerent as Russia and China, who are prepared to offer tens, even hundreds, of millions of lives as nuclear fodder to achieve their aims.

Another indication of Russia's preparations for war is the over 200 recently upgraded, secret and deep underground nuclear war-fighting sites in Russia that analysts claim can house up to 150,000 people. The investment in the past decade alone exceeds billions of U. S. dollars. The core of these complexes is called Yamantau Mountain ("Death Mountain" in the local dialect), the ultra-secret underground site in the Ural Mountains. Author Kenneth Timmerman, in a report posted on WorldNetDaily.com titled "Can Moscow Be Trusted? Inside Russia's Magic Mountain,"[4] documents Russia's vast scale of nuclear deception including the over-400-square-mile complex beneath Yamantau where a gigantic underground military and industrial facility spans the size of the city of Washington, D. C. Analysts believe over $6 billion has been invested in this facility alone since 1991. Timmerman notes that it is located close to one of Russia's remaining nuclear weapons labs, Chelyabinsk-70. Neither our President, the Congress, the military, our intelligence community, nor any foreigner is allowed to visit the site or gain access to any specific knowledge regarding its use. It is believed the complex can house up to 60,000 people indefinitely with sufficient food, water and air, and can withstand a nuclear, chemical or biological attack. A handful of U. S. Congressmen monitoring developments are convinced that the site's purpose is "post–nuclear war." KGB defector Colonel Oleg Gordievsky claims that the KGB maintains the facility as well as the entire network of underground command bunkers for the Russian leadership, saying, "And what is interesting [is that Russia's new 'democratic' leaders] are using those facilities, and the same service [KGB] is still running the same facility, like it was ten, fifteen years ago."

While Russia cannot feed its civilians, pay or house its military, service its international space station or dismantle its nuclear warheads in support of the arms limitation treaty, START II, it continues to acquire billions in aid from the West (over $112 billion as of the Year 2000).[5]   Additionally, Russia has recently developed a road-mobile ICBM, the most advanced ICBM in the world, called the Topol-M missile. The launch of the Topol-M, with its reputed ultimate range of more than 6,000 miles, is the latest in a series of recent alarming military moves in Russia—and to what purpose?[6]

Keep in mind that our war-fighting centers, *all three of them* (Cheyenne Mountain, Colorado; Fort Richie, Maryland; and Mount Weather, Virginia), are vintage facilities from the 1950's designed to withstand first generation atomic weapons. One should question why America is aiding and abetting Russia while our military facilities become dated.

Supposedly under START II, America and Russia would each reduce their respective number of nuclear warheads to 2,500. Being unable to inspect Russian underground facilities like Yamantau or gain credible knowledge specifically about them places in question whether, like the ABM Treaty, Russia is violating START II as well. Even more alarming are the ongoing negotiations with Russia on START III with the potential to reduce warheads supposedly on each side to 1,500. Aside from Russia's enormous ABM missile infrastructure, analysts for the CIA and the Joint Chiefs of Staff are very concerned that the 200 deep underground sites are a "weapons sink" requiring multiple warheads each.   This would create an insufficient stockpile of remaining U. S. warheads for other strategic targets as a deterrence to Russia from attacking U. S. cities where 80 percent of our population resides (only 25 percent for the Russians). This is a dilemma that according to some analysts the Russians would not face.

This calls to mind the prophecy from Sister Elena Aiello who lived in Italy, died in 1961 and was a 'victim soul' who bore the stigmata as a visible sign of her suffering. During one vision of Jesus Christ, He stated, "The world is flooded by a deluge of corruption. The governments of the people have arisen as demons in human flesh and even though they speak of peace they prepare for war with devastating weapons that can annihilate peoples and nations...if people...do not return to God with truly Christian living, another terrible war will come from the East to the West. *Russia with her secret armies will battle America, will overrun Europe.* The river Rhine will be overflowing with corpses and blood. Italy will also be harassed by a great revolution, and the Pope will suffer terribly."

Communist China: Understanding the Oriental Patience

Napoleon Bonaparte once remarked, "When China awakes, it will shake the world." Since Nixon went to Peking in 1972 and opened what was called Ping Pong Diplomacy, America's apparent strategy is to placate the People's Republic of China with capitalistic overtures of investments and technology and political overtures (the de-emphasis of Taiwan as a member of the international political community in support of a "One China Policy"). All this effort is to persuade the P. R. C. be to at least indifferent between America versus Russia, while building a community of capitalist interests within the P. R. C. who would eventually promote democratic ideals. Yet just last year, the Chinese made an international incident out of a collision with an American plane. They took the plane and held the crew until they were satisfied that the U. S. had been sufficiently humbled. They wanted the technology inside so they simply knocked it down and stripped the plane. What was our response? The Congress voted to grant the Chinese "permanent normal trade relations," a position the Chinese needed in order to be awarded membership in the World Trade Organization (WTO). The P. R. C. won membership in November 2001. A month earlier, *The Washington Post* reported that the U. S. was thinking about waiving the sanctions imposed on China following the 1989 crackdown on Tiananmen Square demonstrators. Does this one event not at least put into question the merits of America's strategy with the P. R. C. over the last forty years? Is the U. S. being taken for a fool as the patience of the Chinese oriental mindset waits the two, three, or five generations it may take for China to be ready to take on the U. S.? Or are the globalists giving it all away to bring into fruition the New World Order?

Presently, many political and defense analysts have expressed concern about 'hyped assessments' of the Chinese communist's nuclear threat or espionage activities. They maintain that there is no reason to believe communist China is any more of a threat today than yesterday, or will be in the foreseeable future, and the charges of espionage should be viewed merely as standard operating procedures within the international community of nations "where gentlemen read each other's mail whenever possible." Our defense scientist community even discounts the W-88 missile espionage activity, asserting that the P. R. C. cannot catch up to the U. S. inventory of ballistic missiles ('a Herculean task'), has stopped nuclear testing, has essentially relied on an antiquated, liquid-fueled inventory of intercontinental ballistic missiles simply for retaliation and could not take advantage of W-88 technology which is designed specifically for America's Trident submarines, of which the P. R. C. lacks an equivalent platform. Additionally, the U. S. satellite makers justified their use of the communist Chinese to launch their communications satellites because the U. S. program, which had relied on the success of the space shuttle, was scuttled after the Challenger disaster. As one of Stanford's missile experts, Lewis R. Franklin, notes: "...it was not a bad outcome for the People's Republic of China to have more reliable commercial space launching rockets, as they mostly launch U. S.–built satellites.... By taking advantage of the P. R. C. launch capabilities over the 1990–1998 period, one French and eight U. S. satellites were successfully launched...resulting in U. S. commercial dominance of the Asian communications satellite market."

What all this espionage suggests is that Americans should be concerned that the P. R. C., an atheistic nation, remains antagonistic towards the U. S. Like Russia, the Chinese are prepared to make monumental sacrifices to achieve their pan-Pacific regional hegemony. In February 2000, *Der Spiegel* magazine reported various details regarding a secret document produced by the military sub-committee of the Chinese Communist Party's Central Committee, called Document 65. This secret document indicates that the P. R. C. is prepared to initiate a war with the U. S., even nuclear conflict, should fighting break out over Taiwan. The document emphasizes speed in tactical maneuvers related to a Taiwanese war. "We would have to make a military intervention as early as possible, before the American troops are fully operational..." Faced with U. S. bombardment of key sites and military installations, the document stresses that the mainland has roughly the same level of conventional forces and would benefit from a fight close to its own territory. While arguing that the U. S. would have little interest in starting a nuclear war over Taiwan, Document 65 states that the P. R. C. would be ready to use its nuclear arsenal should circumstances demand. This supports the attitude of a number of the People's Liberation Army chiefs of staff. Regarding the threatened use of nuclear weapons against China and North Korea during the Korean War, in October 1995, General Xiong Guankai said, "You could do that then because you knew we couldn't retaliate. Now we can. In the end,

you care a lot more about Los Angeles than you do about Taipei."
Whatever weapon man devises he will ultimately use against himself.

As if to reaffirm this view, in March of 2000, UPI reported that the
Chinese People's Liberation Army have outlined plans for the
liberation of Taiwan with a two million strong invasion force and an
advanced laser weaponry system to disable guidance instrumentation
aboard aircraft. The Chinese communists declared, "The United States
will not sacrifice 200 million Americans for twenty million Taiwanese
and eventually they are going to back down."

The P. R. C. also is willing to collude with Russia to achieve their
strategic goal. An example of this is their recent formalization of a
five-year military alliance with Russia. In all likelihood, this includes
military and industrial espionage. If the P. R. C. has no need for W-88
intelligence, the communist Russians do. The P. R. C.'s espionage
history over the past ten years illustrates demonstrable success in a
number of areas of vital strategic interest to the U. S. and to Russia.
These include:

❖ The transfer of the so-called Legacy Codes containing data on 50
   years of U. S. nuclear weapons development, including over 1,000
   nuclear tests;

❖ The sale and diversion to military purposes of more than 600 high
   performance computers enabling China to enhance its development
   of nuclear weapons, ballistic missiles, and advanced military
   aviation equipment;

❖ The compromise of nuclear warhead simulation technology which
   could enhance either party's ability to perfect miniature nuclear
   warheads without actual testing;

❖ The compromise of advanced electromagnetic weapons technology
   useful in the development of anti-satellite and anti-missile systems;

❖ The transfer of missile nose cone technology enabling either party
   to substantially improve the reliability of its intercontinental
   ballistic missiles;

❖ The transfer of missile guidance technology enabling either party to
   substantially improve the accuracy of its ballistic missiles;

❖ The compromise of super-secret space-based radar technology giving either party the ability to detect our previously undetectable submerged submarines; and

❖ The compromise of some other "classified thermonuclear weapons information" which the Clinton administration "has determined...cannot be made public."[7]

Other recent developments firmly establish Russia's collusion with the P. R. C. to bolster the latter's capabilities to confront the U. S. China constitutes Russia's biggest arms market. In 2000, it is believed to have signed an estimated $1.5 billion worth of weapons contracts, accounting for around 40 percent of Russian arms exports. Total trade between the countries was $8 billion in 2000 and is expected to hit $10 billion in 2001.

This includes the P. R. C.'s purchase of SU-30 jet-fighters from Russia and the first two Russian-built guided-missile destroyers (*Sovremenny*-class destroyer) that enhance the P. R. C.'s ability to threaten American aircraft carriers in any future encounters over Taiwan. Russia also delivered the ship's most formidable weapon, the state of the art Sunburn anti-ship missiles specifically designed to penetrate American carrier battle group defenses. The Russian version of the sea-skimming supersonic missile can carry nuclear or conventional warheads. One may question whether Russia will deliver nuclear warheads with these missiles, but one should not question the likelihood that the PLA could develop technology that would enable these missiles to deliver a Chinese nuclear warhead. All this, plus a 17.7 percent boost in the army's budget—for what purpose in a 'peacetime' economy? We are told by analysts that a few dozen Chinese missiles targeted at the United States do not alter the world strategic balance. The idea that a country might seek to steal our military secrets is neither particularly new nor especially shocking.

The P. R. C. has also declared publicly its intent to conduct 'unrestricted warfare,' exploring the use of computer viruses, information warfare and stock market manipulation as non-traditional "weapons" against the U. S. The strategy is aimed directly at the extreme reliance by the U. S. on high-tech computer and communications infrastructure and weaponry. Perhaps this explains why the P. R. C. was so reluctant to return the U. S. spy plane. The aircraft is a gold mine of information about how the U. S. military gathers, processes and transmits surveillance data, and insights into how such a system could jam or manipulate an adversary's communication and computing network. Given the P. R. C.'s public position in this matter, the U. S. Congress should exclude investors from Hong Kong (investment front for PLA) from gaining effective control of Global Crossing and its vast worldwide communications network.

If, in fact, the P. R. C. is an inevitable challenger to U. S. strategic interests, giving it broad access to international markets appears to be helping its long-term goals. Would America not be wise to constrain that access in any way we can? But such a step would require a full reversal of our long-standing support for liberalization of trade and investment, and that would cause considerable adverse publicity and pressure from U. S. and foreign business interests as well as economic consequences. This would mean not just denying China access to American markets but also urging the Europeans and the Japanese markets to cooperate with this strategy as well. Any containment policy against China would also dictate a search for powerful allies. India would clearly be an obvious candidate. India's support would likely require America's acceptance of Delhi's membership in the world's "nuclear club." This could only cause great anxiety with the Moslem world, particularly Pakistan, traditionally an ally of the P. R. C. Additionally, India has gone to war over border disputes with the P. R. C. and with Pakistan on multiple occasions in the last half of the 20th Century.

Recall earlier the Masonic strategy for a third world war pitting Moslems against Christians. One is hard pressed to find anyone who is not concerned presently with the state of unrest in the Mideast, especially between Israel and the Palestinians. Followers of world events should always keep their eyes on Jerusalem, the place where the match will light the fuse. Could a U. S. military initiative into Iraq be the spark? If Israel and the Palestinians are unable to resolve their differences and the violence gets out of hand, and America extends itself further by attacking Iraq, the Russians might perceive that moment as an appropriate time to initiate a preemptive strike against the U. S. Russia would align itself openly with the Moslem community, and encourage the P. R. C. to attack Taiwan immediately, sensing America's inability to adequately fight a global war after a first strike. Only a fool would say that it could never happen.

America Is Ill-Prepared

Dr. Edward Teller, the former director of Lawrence Livermore National Laboratory and best known as "the father of the hydrogen bomb," remarked to Christopher Ruddy of Newsmax that in 1992 the chance of the United States becoming involved in a global war was at most one in a hundred. Now, thanks in large part to the military policies and directives implemented during the Clinton administration, including the infamous Presidential Decision Directive (PDD) of November 1997, the U. S. has a much greater chance of entering into a global nuclear war. Portions of this particular PDD leaked to the *Washington Post* indicated that the **U. S. would accept a first strike and only retaliate after millions of our citizens had been killed.** Robert Bell, senior director for defense policy and arms control at the National Security Council, confirmed in an interview with *Arms Control Today* that "we direct our military forces to continue to posture themselves in such a way as to not rely upon launch on warning—to be able to absorb a nuclear strike and still have enough force surviving to constitute credible deterrence... Our policy is to confirm that we are under nuclear attack with actual detonations before retaliating." Think about it. Ignore all our investment and expertise in early warning systems and a complete arsenal of weaponry, implementing instead a strategy based on a very compressed period of time after a detonation! This means that critical minutes of time are lost. Two-thirds of our strategic defense triad, land-based ICBM missiles and strategic bombers could be wiped out before we can retaliate. The Defense Department estimates that only fifteen percent of Russia's ICBM's would need to be launched at our U. S. silos to destroy up to 85 percent of our land based ICBM's. At any given time, six of our eighteen ballistic missile submarines are in port. If wiped out, that is 50 percent of the 400 megatons required under Mutually Assured Destruction (MAD), a policy that has kept America safe in the nuclear age. Compare this to Russia, which has at least 42 ballistic missile submarines. In addition, Russia also maintains a fleet of nearly 50 active attack submarines centered on a core force of twenty nuclear-powered Akula and Victor attack boats, which are tracking our naval and submarine fleets. Also note that Russia is presently moving a huge number of their land-based, strategic nuclear weapons into naval ships, which are less vulnerable to attack. In the event of a first strike by Russia, how would we expect our nuclear allies to react?

In our collective delusion that MAD is intact and that the Russians and Chinese care, the Federal Government is ignoring the obvious need to strategically direct a sufficient amount of its resources to protect our nation. We have virtually no civil defense system, no anti-ballistic missile system deployed (National Missile Defense and Ground-based Midcourse Defense systems under development), and defense spending was dramatically reduced from 28 percent of the federal budget in 1988 to seventeen percent in 1999. The Bush Administration's proposed defense budget for fiscal year 2003 is seventeen percent of the total federal budget, nearly a percentage point higher than fiscal year 2002. According to Casper Weinberger in his book *The Next War*, since 1985 America is embarking on massive disarmament. Military budgets have declined 35 percent, research and development 57 percent and procurement of new weapons a whopping 71 percent. Defense Department records show that our naval ships have decreased from over 600 in 1991 to 336, the lowest total since the 1930's. What Ronald Reagan built up, Bill Clinton dismantled. These remaining ships have been effectively stripped of their tactical nuclear weapons during the Clinton administration, making them very vulnerable, if not sitting ducks, to Russian and Chinese tactical nukes. The substantial decline in U. S. military preparedness confirms Anatoly Golitsyn's warning to the West in his 1984 book, *New Lies For Old*, that "A Soviet-socialist European coalition, acting in concert with non-aligned movement in the United Nations, would create favorable conditions for communist strategy on disarmament. The American military-industrial complex would come under heavy fire. 'Liberalization' in the Soviet Union and Eastern Europe would provide additional stimulus to disarmament. A massive U. S. defense budget might be found no longer justified..."

Today, analysts believe that Russia has a huge advantage in tactical nuclear weapons, over 20,000 compared to a few remaining thousands, which is the result of significant reductions by the Clinton administration. Under President Clinton, virtually our entire inventory of cruise missiles was depleted with no plans for restoration. Remember that these missiles were primarily built to deliver strategic nuclear warheads deep into Russia.

To make matters even worse, according to Christopher Ruddy,[8] GAO reports to Congress in 1998 present some grim statistics about our national preparedness for a second wave of an overseas war by our ten Army divisions. For example:

❖ 1st Infantry Division: The 1st brigade had only 56 percent of personnel needed to fill its armored vehicles. Many brigades were only partially filled or had no personnel.

❖ 254h Infantry Division: 52 of 162 infantry squads were "minimally filled or had no personnel assigned."

❖ 1ˢᵗ Armored Division: sixteen of 116 tanks had full, battle-qualified four-man crews.

❖ 4ᵗʰ Infantry Division: thirteen of 54 squads in the engineer's brigades either had no personnel assigned or fewer personnel than required.

Meanwhile Russia's military growth continues to outpace the U. S. A Defense Department report in 1988 shows that Soviet to U. S. weapons procurement ratios between 1978 and 1987 are: submarines 2:1, tanks 3:1, other armored vehicles 4.5:1, bombers 4:1, ICBM's/SLBM's 4.5:1, SAM's 6.5 to 11, artillery, mortars, multiple rocket launchers 8.5:1. Additionally, according to the 1998 *World Almanac*, Russia could field 1.2 million troops and has an incredible twenty million reservists. With the P. R. C. entering into a global war on Russia's side, the P. R. C. has 2.9 million active troops, 1.2 million reservists and about one million militia (national guard) troops. (This was in 1988. Thanks to Clinton, those number are now much worse.) This compares to about one million total U. S. troops. Lastly, while the Clinton administration halted all underground testing of nuclear weapons, Russia in 1998 alone conducted no less than five such tests in an attempt to develop a new generation of 'superweapons.'

Compounding America's decline in military preparedness for war is the fact that our current forces are spread too thin, bearing the additional load of conducting policing actions and counter-terrorism worldwide. Things are so severe that our military leaders, for example Army General William F. Kernan, commander in chief of the U. S. Joint Forces Command, assert that their troops and equipment are "overextended and exhausted," leaving dangerous shortages that ultimately could hurt Americans. Congress presently is questioning these commanders regarding the ability of their current operations to engage in a military action in Iraq. Their response, according to Missouri Democrat, Representative Ike Skelton, was "very troubling." General Kernan advises that the services need over 51,000 additional people in the near term alone.[9]

Navy Admiral Dennis Blair has informed the House Armed Services Committee that should the Afghanistan operation continue at its current levels, his command does not have adequate forces to carry out its missions for the Pacific region. Admiral Blair told the Congressional committee that due to the Afghan operations, his command was without a carrier battle group in the Western Pacific. He explained, "So we can mitigate for a while...but there are shortages of naval forces, of intelligence, surveillance and reconnaissance forces, in particular, that have to be made up for if we are to continue the current level of operations in the Central Command." When asked of the impact of another aircraft carrier being retired, the admiral said, "I'm already at zero. With one less, I can't be any worse than zero."[10]

Air Force General Joseph W. Ralston, commander in chief of the European Command, gave a quite similar response regarding the state of his team's mission. Ralston oversees military operations in 91 countries with eight percent of the military's total active personnel (115,000). His command presently lacks even a marine amphibious ready group to evacuate Americans in the event of a NATO operation in one of the 91 countries. He also commented on the redeployment of surveillance aircraft (AWACS) to Southwest Asia having an impact on his operations.[11]

This all confirms Anatoly Golitsyn's prediction that the communist strategy to orchestrate an apparent collapse of the Warsaw Pact and the Soviet government as an incentive for the West, particularly America, to disarm, thus giving the Russians an added advantage, has come to reality. Golitsyn and Czech defector General Jan Sejna call this a grand deception on an unprecedented scale. Regarding the West's refusal to even consider the possibility of this plan, Sejna explained, "One of the basic problems with the West is its frequent failure to recognize the existence of any Soviet 'grand design' at all. Those rejecting this concept unwittingly serve Soviet efforts..." Golitsyn warned that as the West disarms, Russia would form a military partnership with China. Americans hardly noticed when Russia sealed a military alliance with China, negotiating a combined arm sales package with China valued up to $15 billion over a five-year period.

America, steeped in immorality and materialism and ill-prepared to fight a global confrontation, is ignoring the truth because our selfish interests preclude our deluded intelligence from recognizing that evil knows no bounds and has been dedicated to humanity's destruction since the days of Adam and Eve. It is the centuries-old strategy of speaking peace but arming for war. This is confirmed by a message from Our Lady of America who told the late Sister Ephrem (also known as Mildred Neuzil), *"It is evident that the Forces of Evil are enveloping the world. Their hatred, however, is now particularly focused on the United States because of the Divine Mandate given to it to lead the world to peace."* America is the key to world peace and Satan knows that if the U. S. is not a dominant player, the world will resort to more violence. So Satan's goal is to reduce the U. S. to rubble.

If the reader cannot comprehend all the of the numbing detail, a grasp of at least the grand design of Russia will make it better understood. Russia has fulfilled the qualified prediction of Our Lady of Fatima that it would spread its error worldwide. Socialism is pandemic across western societies and governments. Where communistic totalitarianism doesn't reign, social prejudice and intolerance, plus the persecution of Christians, run rampant. Just look at the Sudan, the Moslem Mideast, P. R. C. or India where Christians and their missionaries are jailed or murdered. In Russia, Catholics and many Protestants are openly prohibited from promoting the Bible and are either deported or prosecuted to the fullest extent of the law. Turkey wants to become a member of the European Union, but try to erect a Christian church in Istanbul and watch the reception you get. As the number of Moslems in Europe and the U. S. increases due to the West's free immigration policies, ethnic divisions and animosity will increase.

America is becoming increasingly paganized each passing year. Today we equate the one, true God with every other type of god violating the First Commandment. When we cease to worship God in accord with the First Commandment, the other Commandments fall quickly. Our sentinels, the clergy, are disengaged and absorbed in materialism, or worse still, heresy and apostasy. The Mother of God has warned us that the next step would be the annihilation of nations and the increased persecution of the Church on earth. Yet, when the Blessed Virgin appeared as "Our Lady of America" to the late Sister Ephrem, She implicitly followed God's methodology of the conditional "if...then" clause and gave specific instructions for all of us that we should take to heart. *"I desire, through my children of America, to further the cause of faith and purity among peoples and nations.... My beloved daughter, what I am about to tell you concerns in a particular way my children in America. Unless they do penance by mortification and self-denial and thus reform their lives, God will visit them with punishments hitherto unknown to them."*

16

Where's the Hope?

For what glory is it, if sinning and being buffeted you suffer it: But if doing well you suffer patiently; this is praiseworthy before God.

—1 St. Peter 2:20

We have examined the state of America and based on what we found, in all likelihood before God's eye, it is wanting. There exists documented and substantial proof of the collusion, cooperation and common interest among secret societies, cults, transnational businesses and governments wedded to secular humanism. In many cases there has been outright Satanism with the common objective of enslavement of mankind to the benefit of a small, select group, ultimately causing the eternal damnation of many souls. The writings of Antonio Gramsci have shown that this type of diabolical system works. Although it is orchestrated by Satan on the highest level, for the masses it is simply an ideology of thinking on a humanistic and natural level of man devoid of God. One of the visions and associated messages of Our Lady of Fatima in 1917 presented to the three Portuguese shepherd children included the veritable blizzard of souls falling into Hell. One must understand that this vision is for each and every one of us today. Our generation is no different than the lost generation of Jews that wandered the desert with Moses for 40 years. With disobedience come repercussions. For a generation, people have likewise wandered aimlessly, not knowing or caring what God intends. By the time Moses and Joshua finally approached the outskirts of the Promised Land, many of the original generation that left Egypt had died. That generation of Jews failed to heed God's conditional blessing and curse, therefore suffering the consequences of their sin. What was to have been a journey of several weeks turned into a forty-year odyssey.

With this in mind, recall 1960 when the Catholic world waited with hopeful anticipation for the disclosure of the Third Secret of Fatima. The worst of all scenarios happened. Not only was the secret not disclosed, but the Roman Catholic hierarchy failed to appreciate the Mother of God's exhortation to prepare for the Church's Calvary.

Currently the Church's ecclesiastical Masons are wittingly causing the "auto demolition of the Church" as foreseen by Pope Paul VI. Look at the state of the Church today, inebriated by the size of the collection boxes, corrupted by scandals, homosexuality, and Black Masses, afraid of losing its wealth, property, or 501c tax status. It seems that Pope Paul VI was right in realizing that the smoke of Satan has entered the sanctuary.

What has ensued in the last 40 years? If you are blinded by pride and aspirations of material prosperity and power, then you will have one answer. If you are honest with yourself and rooted in the Gospel, you are weathering the storm, having many concerns and praying often. This is no accident. God's Divine Grace is preparing His 'faithful remnant' for the coming tribulation. That is why Pope John Paul II exhorts his flock to pray the Rosary daily and wear the Brown Scapular as protection. For Americans what will the tribulation be? Simply put, it will be the demise of our nation. Unless there is a reversal of what is happening in America, it will know the humiliation of poverty beyond the scope of the 1930's, and the defeat by an outside enemy made possible by moral decline from within—just like previous great civilizations. We are at the point of irreversible damage due to Biblical indifference and the false pride of our nation.

A key element in the demise of America is the means to manipulate our country by institutionalizing division, corruption, greed, idolatry and perversion. This is all wrapped in a blanket of false pride, freedom and misguided patriotism, with the sole purpose of exhausting our collective will to live by our Founding Fathers' Constitution and intents. As in the days of the Roman Empire, we will be satisfied merely with circus and bread. The patrician Romans knew they needed to keep people content, so they kept the general population well fed in order to keep them under control. Today the bread and circuses of the masses are driven by credit and government-sponsored redistribution of income. Give the people enough of what they want, that is, easy commercial credit. This access to government funds becomes the means of control that furthers the process of social and language engineering. It is a rare individual who willingly walks away from a lifestyle of ease and comfort. Over time, the system of the world gives us what we want, and we go along. The Gospel is incrementally pushed out. In our desire for material wealth, Americans have become modern-day 'Pavlov's dogs,' addicted to credit and government handouts.

After peering into the abyss, how do we fight and win? One must remember that in the end God is victorious. Recall Jesus' promise to

Peter that the gates of Hell would not prevail against the Church—no matter how small the Church will be. The Blessed Virgin Mary promised at Fatima that at the end of this present battle there would be an "Era of Peace." So how do we get there? Simply by living the Gospel, we shall overcome. It begins with the fear of the Lord. It is all fine and dandy to talk about the love of God, but American Christians are myopic, eliminating the healthy fear of God from our hearts. We are foolish to think that it is passé to fear the Almighty God and the consequences of sin. On the contrary, it is a great enabler of faith and the first step towards salvation. We must appreciate that God both blesses and punishes nations and individuals. Do parents not love children when they punish them? Look at what happens to a nation that refuses to heed God's will, for example, Sodom and Gomorrah. God tests mankind with trials and tribulations, not only as Holy Justice but as an act of Holy Mercy, to convince sinners to repent. Therefore, Americans need to stop ignoring the responsibility to pursue publicly and privately, with the highest priority, what is morally right in God's sight, not our own. To paraphrase President Kennedy, fear not what your fellow men can do to you, but fear what God can do to you and your country.

Americans must understand that the fight needs to be directed at kingdoms, principalities and dominions that are not of this world. Satan, the fallen angel, is out to destroy every one of us. He has an army of fallen angels with powers given by God that are extraordinary and beyond our comprehension, all for the purpose of testing us and leading us from God's ways. These fallen angels enlist evil and powerful men to achieve their goals. The only way to defeat Satan is with spiritual weapons, but today they are largely ignored. Catholics should recall the revelation to Pope Leo XIII that Satan would be granted a reign of 100 years to test humanity.

There is a strong presence of evil in the world today. Satan is prowling freely for the destruction of souls. In many respects, it is his finest hour because he roams undetected. Satan is mentioned 51 times in the Bible, "devil" and "devils" 104 times, and evil in its many forms 598 times. Those three forms alone total 753 times the Scriptures give notice to the fact that there is an evil presence among us. Evil's presence in other forms is mentioned hundreds of times as well. Because Satan goes undetected, people have forgotten how to fight him, let alone use the armor necessary for day-to-day living. When an entire generation of people doesn't think he exists, there is an opportunity for Satan's free reign.

There are five stages of evil that have always existed in the world:

1) Man sins;
2) Man rationalizes sin;
3) Man boasts about sin;
4) Man attacks goodness; and
5) God chastises man.

Evil presents itself with false enticements, then offers bitter disappointments. Where there is rampant sin, the destruction is even greater, as there is no ability to fight off temptation. The deceitful action of the evil one is constant. To combat him, it is necessary to use the armor of God: the Sacraments—especially Communion and Confession—Penance, the Scriptures, Prayer—especially the Rosary—and other fundamental aspects of the Faith. Coaches in any sport will tell their athletes when things are not going as well as they ought to, "Get back to the fundamentals." People, families, and the nation of America need to get back to the fundamentals of the faith to reverse the present moral slide. There is no other option because a faith-based society is the only hope.

In these difficult times, the faithful remnant in America must become a strategic weapon of the Church. For the common good and the eternal salvation of our souls, we must be prepared to "lift high the Cross." In a time of such trials, one should realize Satan may destroy the religion of some, but he will never defeat the Cross. We must not accept any compromise or anesthetic offered by anyone who wishes to change the way Heaven ordains us to live. The watering down of faith has brought us to where we are today. With confidence and hope, we must prepare ourselves and our loved ones to always be faithful.

This is not a call to violence. On the contrary, Christians must prepare to walk Calvary in faith, hope and love just as Jesus Christ did 2000 years ago and as many of the apostles and disciples of Jesus did during the early days of the Church. It is no coincidence that historically Christian civilization achieved significant progress on the back of Christian fortitude and martyrdom. The blood of martyrs waters the seed of the Church. O people of God, now it is your time. Get up, take a stand, drive a stake in the ground and move "not one foot back." Not to put the monster Josef Stalin or communism in a good light, but at the Battle of Stalingrad in 1942, Stalin had the order passed to the Soviet troops, "Not one foot back or you will be shot." Likewise, we should feel the same sense of urgency. We must not retreat even one foot.

Spiritual Warfare

We are in a battle of Christianity versus paganism and barbarism. There are many well-dressed pagans in suits and ties. Any contemporary debate on this is nothing more than useless questions and elaborate arguments designed to distract and divide us. Pray that the clergy will challenge the laity to appreciate the severe and eternal consequences of dying outside the State of grace. Hell is real. It is eternal. It is the ultimate manifestation of despair and doom. If we sufficiently understand what Hell is, we will be more inclined to forgive our neighbors as ourselves, encourage conversions and pray for our enemies. With the scandals deeply rooted into the interior of the Church, and with the significant numbers involved, it is no wonder there is rarely a strong word coming from many of the pulpits across America.

We must affirm our faith and the Church's teachings publicly and repeatedly, for the sake of our family's well being, and to our neighbors and especially to those who lack faith or are stubborn sinners uncomfortable with public declaration of Christian faith. People of faith have become so disillusioned with the demolition of the Church that they are in despair, going to other churches, and not giving financially. Why would someone tithe to the Church when it would go to paying an attorney for a sex-scandal settlement? This is the mood in America, and the donation plate is down twenty to fifty percent in many dioceses because of scandal.

A key objective of this strategy is the reintroduction of Christian morals and beliefs in an explicit way into our public institutions and commercial enterprises. It starts with the discriminating use of our accumulated wealth and influence in a collective fashion. Vote with your dollars. Better yet, vote with your feet. It is time to root out the weeds from the wheat. Make a sacrifice and live a simpler life refusing to buy products and services marketed by companies or institutions which lack Christian morals. For example, an issue today in education is charter schools. Parents are fed up with mediocrity in education and want a choice of where to send their children. Parents often get nothing back from their investment in churches and schools, and if there is false doctrine, or no doctrine, simply don't give financially. Find a worthy cause and tithe to a place where the money will be used wisely. Vote against corrupt politicians and judges who violate God's Decalogue. Aggressively encourage bishops to publicly reprimand, shun and deal with public officials, businessmen, educators and other leaders who defy Church teachings, whether they are practicing Christians or not. Christians need to relentlessly hold our leaders accountable in a material way. Would it ever have been possible for stridently pro-choice officials to be elected if the Christian hierarchies taught the Scriptures? There is no move here being advocated to choose party lines, but the former Speaker of the House of Representatives, Tip O'Neil, a prominent Boston politician in his day, was proud of saying, "I am a Democrat, Irish, and Catholic in that order." That mentality is carried throughout our government and is a reason why we are where we are today. That's the problem in a nutshell.

Roe v. Wade was in 1973, and it has taken the leaders of the Church nearly that long to recognize the problem. They should have had the wisdom and the foresight to see that what we have become was inevitable thanks to godless policies, but they have been saddled with a lack of courage that so often comes from a life of easily-won comfort. If the bishops had walked down Pennsylvania Ave. each year on January 22, the anniversary of *Roe v. Wade*, every aspiring Catholic politician in America would have had to conform.

To build fortitude, we as Christians must discipline ourselves with daily exercises of prayer and devotions, especially participation in the Holy Sacrifice of the Mass. Accepting the fact that the Holy Eucharist is the body, blood, soul and divinity of Jesus Christ, we need to promote and attend Eucharistic Adoration as frequently as possible and deluge the pastor and priests with phone calls and letters when they remove the Tabernacle from the inner church. More can be accomplished in one day of intense prayer than in a year of discussions. Who better than Jesus, Who experienced humiliation, suffering and death on the Cross, to understand our daily trials and concerns? The practices of fasting or abstinence as a penance or in conjunction with prayer to request God's direct help need to regain popularity. Christians need to practice self-denial. The purification of the world must start in the Church and spread on a grand scale.

We will need all the Divine Grace that God is prepared to give us. Particularly, Catholics need to believe in the power of, and take advantage of, sacramentals, for example, the Miraculous Medal, the Rosary, Brown Scapulars, as added armor to resist temptation and encourage initiative where any doubts may arise. The Rosary is especially effective in these troubled times and should be prayed daily, as should the Chaplet of Divine Mercy. We are told by Popes and prophets that the Holy Rosary and Brown Scapular are our primary spiritual weapons during the difficult times ahead. Christians need to realize that the Blessed Virgin Mary is rallying the "Church Triumphant," that is, the saints along with the angels, to fight the evil kingdoms, principalities and dominions on a spiritual plane which we are unable to fathom. As part of that battle, Our Lady presents our humble petitions conveyed through prayers, especially the Rosary, to our Savior, Jesus. She is the intercessor before the throne of God as Esther was in the Old Testament. The Holy Bible reveals to us that her Son denies her nothing. Think about it. Who on earth could rally all the saints to petition Jesus Christ like Mary in Heaven with such empathy, continuously, over and over again?

All Christian families must build a daily lifestyle that reinforces Christian ideals and aspirations. This goes beyond Bible reading and private acts of charity, as it focuses on the sanctification of our souls. Given our perverted age, parents must be scrupulous and tenacious in eliminating any potential avenues of influence that could corrupt children, neighborhoods and communities. From television to video games, computers, music, the internet and the use of drugs, parents must first appreciate that the companies marketing these products and services care nothing about the well-being of the family or society. These companies care only about profits and power. They want our children's generation to become addicted, even obsessed with their products and services. Therefore, parents must filter the marketing message, severely question the purported benefits, and reduce if not totally eliminate the use. To follow Christ is not to embrace the world. To offset any lifestyle change that may arise from this type of action, parents must devote far more substantial time personally to educate, recreate and discipline their children. Potential complaints from the children (especially those heavily influenced by their peers) might well be prevented or reduced by sharing the truth with them in simple language; most children can understand and accept an explanation that in today's world, followers of Jesus must take extra (and sometimes difficult) steps to preserve their faith. Since the stakes are high, priorities need to be reorganized, reengineering what our family members currently perceive as temporal and spiritual well being. This requires personal sacrifice, including career and material gain. A healthy offensive position is necessary to turn things around.

Christians need to promote vocations aggressively to our children. We need an army of religious where few exist today. In parallel, we need to hold the Church hierarchy accountable for promoting a chaste and holy life among the religious and remove bad shepherds who corrupt the flock. Jesus said that the harvest is great but the laborers are few. Times will be tough for the clergy who will be persecuted for being faithful. If the tax exemption is removed, Americans must rally behind the Church to either restore it or contribute sufficiently through whatever means to offset the loss. Unfortunately, especially over the last two centuries, history is replete with examples of governments ransacking churches and confiscating property. It has already sold off property in the inner cities to pay legal bills, and whole dioceses will cease to exist as they go broke. If good priests have nowhere to go, then the laity should house them. Given circumstances today, it would be a wise and faithful servant who initiated prayer cenacles building a network of Christians who are capable of sheltering a religious for the purposes of maintaining a remnant Church. Recall in the Old Testament Daniel's reference to the abomination of desolation where "the victim and the sacrifice shall fail..." The Church is crossing the threshold of hope to the promised Era of Peace. This should be our hope—the new springtime.

A New Springtime

Unless Jesus went to the Cross, there would have been no redemption. Unless America and the Church are purified, we cannot have a new beginning. When He was with the apostles just before Calvary, "Jesus said to them: But whom do you say that I am? Simon Peter answered and said: You are Christ, the Son of the living God. And Jesus answering, said to him: Blessed are you, Simon Bar-Jona: because flesh and blood have not revealed it to you, but my Father who is in heaven" (St. Matthew 16:15–17). Peter spoke through grace and grace responded. Jesus knew what He was asking and Peter answered. This conversation took place immediately before Jesus was handed over by Judas. Unless a person is able to say, "Jesus is Lord and Master of my life," then that person will fall short of what God intends. Grace will never flow nor will the response be adequate unless we say, "You are Christ, the Son of the living God." As Peter proclaimed Who Jesus was in the true unobstructed form of the truth, only if we too are unencumbered by man's views can we respond as Peter did. Until that answer is "yes," then we will stumble to the extent we say no. The fact remains that Jesus had to go to the Cross, and no one at the time understood the prophetic words of Jesus when He said, "Destroy this temple; and in three days I will raise it up" (St. John 2:19). In other words, Jesus was announcing specifically what would happen to Him, but no one else had a frame of reference or the ability to understand exactly what Jesus meant. The same is true today. We know for certain we are in unique times and some sort of sea change or decisive event is near, an epiphany of some sort. From the Old Testament, one could clearly see Heaven warns through its prophets. A general indication through the written word is there, but how events will unfold is not certain. There are numerous Scripture passages in the Old Testament foretelling a Messiah to be born, but nowhere does it tell about the specific circumstances and events pertaining to the coming of Jesus and the exact nature of His ministry.

When the time comes, and we are called to defend our Faith, many Americans will need to sacrifice many things they hold dear. We should be prepared to offer such sacrifice as a just penance for our collective and individual errors. We should take joy that our pain, suffering and blood will be collected by the angels and offered to God as atonement. St. Paul sums it up best, "Being justified therefore by faith, let us have peace with God, through our Lord Jesus Christ: By whom also we have access through faith into this grace; wherein we stand, and glory in the hope of the glory of the sons of God. And not only so; but we glory also in tribulations, knowing that tribulation works patience; and patience trial; and trial hope; and hope confounds not: because the charity of God is poured forth in our hearts, by the Holy Spirit, who is given to us" (Romans 5:1–5).

Hope is to be found in the fact that after Good Friday there is an Easter Sunday. Unless Jesus walked the road to Calvary, there would be no redemption. Americans must prepare to walk to Calvary. As we enter deeper into this struggle, we must hold on to our possessions lightly so as to keep our eye on what this earthly existence is all about—the eternal prize. All else is fleeting. Trials and tribulations can lead us to holiness and thus closer to God. So, lift up your heads for your redemption is near.

17

The Correct Response to Scandal

*Have confidence in the Lord with all your heart, and
lean not upon your own prudence. In all your ways
think on Him, and He will direct your steps.*
                                —Proverbs 3:5–6

The Church in Boston and other places throughout the U. S. is
reeling from sex scandals and sordid laundry of every kind. The dirty
little secret is now out in the open, and enemies of the Church who
loaded guns long ago are now firing away. The real problem is that the
shepherds didn't care enough to address the problem when they knew it
existed. They thought they were above the law. Many clergy have lost
their faith along the way, and the sex scandal is merely symptomatic of
shepherds not doing their jobs. They have fallen asleep in luxury and
sin, and have taken many souls with them. The Lord is cleaning house.
The shepherds' sense of the sacred was lost long ago. Power ceased to
come from the pulpits because clergy ceased to believe.

When you love something you want to be near it. Seminarians
making ice cream sundaes in a Chalice is but one example of many that
shows us the depth of unbelief and disdain for the sacred. The Lord has
always had traitors with Him, and today is no different than when Judas
betrayed the Lord. Jesus had trained the apostles, performed miracles
in front of them, raised people from the dead, walked on water, and
spent three years doing signs and wonders, yet when circumstances got
tough, Judas betrayed Jesus by a false gesture of love, and for 30 pieces
of silver. "Do you betray the Son of man with a kiss" (St. Luke 22:48)?
Sometimes God's chosen betray Him. If all the disciples left after
Judas had betrayed Jesus, the Church would have failed to grow.
Instead, the Church did grow, not from the sins of traitors, but from the
blood of martyrs. The early Church focused on the other eleven
apostles and spread throughout the world. Of the eleven remaining, ten
went on to become martyrs. I suspect the "media" of the day devoted
more scrolls to Judas than the other eleven. It's the same today. There
is no doubt a stench in many rectories, and more in some seminaries.
These scandals fracture the faith of many of the faithful. From the

beginning the Evil One has sought to undermine the Church with a particular focus on the destruction of the Liturgy, the role of the Blessed Mother in Tradition, and the Real Presence. During the past century he has expanded his assault by especially targeting the priesthood and the family. Destroy the priesthood and there will be no Eucharist.

During the Last Supper the apostles were stunned by Jesus' statement that "one of you will betray me." Judas moved so well among the apostles that even then they could not comprehend that one of their own would betray Him. Judas represents 8.3 percent of the apostles and he had the unique grace of walking with the Lord and observing all He did for nearly three years; yet he fell. Should we not think that Satan is capable of the same today? Can he not infiltrate as he did in Christ's time on earth? At the time of Calvary, all of the remaining eleven apostles, but one, deserted Jesus, yet all came back. They became the first bishops of the Church and all went on to become saints. Our pillar of strength in times of trial must be Jesus Christ. All men will be inadequate and ultimately fail us. The apostles were men with faults, just as the shepherds today have faults. With the bad news of the arrest of Jesus, they scattered. His best friend, Peter, openly denied him three times. We are all weak. As the poet Oscar Wilde said, "All of us are in the gutter, but some of us are looking at the stars."

Scandal is nothing new for the Church. There have been many times in the Church's history when it was much worse off than it is now. The history of the Church is like a cosine curve, with ups and downs throughout the centuries. At each of the times when the Church hit its low point, God raised up tremendous saints to bring the Church back to its real mission.[1] It's almost as if in those times of darkness, the Light of Christ shone ever more brightly.

St. Francis de Sales was one saint God raised up after the Protestant Reformation. The Reformation was not principally about theology or the faith—although theological differences came later—but about morals. There was an Augustinian priest, Martin Luther, who went to Rome during the papacy of the most notorious pope in history, Pope Alexander VI. This pope never taught anything against the faith—the Holy Spirit prevented that—but he was simply a wicked man. He had nine children from six different concubines. He put out contracts against those he considered his enemies. Martin Luther visited Rome during his papacy and wondered how God could allow such a wicked man to be the visible head of his Church. He went back to Germany and saw all types of moral problems. Priests were living in open relationships with women. Some were trying to profit from selling spiritual goods. There was a terrible immorality about lay Catholics as well. He was scandalized, as anyone who loved God might have been, by such rampant abuse. So he founded his own Church. Eventually God raised up many saints to address the malaise within the Church.

St. Francis de Sales was one of them. At the risk of his life, he went through Switzerland, where the Calvinists were popular. Oftentimes he was beaten up on his way and left for dead. Once he was asked to address the situation of the scandal caused by so many of his brother priests. What he said is as important for us today as it was for his listeners then. He didn't pull any punches. *He said, "Those who commit these types of scandals are guilty of the spiritual equivalent of murder," destroying other people's faith in God by their terrible example. But then he warned his listeners, "But I'm here among you to prevent something far worse for you. While those who give scandal are guilty of the spiritual equivalent of murder, those who take scandal—who allow scandals to destroy their faith—are guilty of spiritual suicide."* They're guilty, he said, of cutting off their life with Christ, abandoning the source of life in the Sacraments, especially the Eucharist. He went among the people in Switzerland trying to prevent their committing spiritual suicide on account of the scandals.

Those who are not rooted in the Faith will drift from the Church, or join somewhere else. Over time many will leave Christianity altogether. If a person's faith is based on the activity of others, it is a faith that is built upon loose sand and thus easily shaken. Our gaze can only be on Christ because man by his very nature will always fail us. At this time of stress, the clarion call is to stand firm. Now is not the time to ponder; now is the time to drive the enemy out.

At the hierarchical level, there has been an institutional stench and rot at all times in the history of the Church. It's simply the nature of man. The relative degree of health within the Church's clergy is typically a reflection of the nations that they serve. When the clergy is silent, Scripture tells us that they fail their job on the watchtower. That is why when a nation is purified, it always starts first within the Church. This is precisely what we are seeing as scandals of a very serious nature consume today's clergy. The call today is the cry of Saint Francis de Sales, "do not commit spiritual suicide by tossing out what is good and holy because it has been abused by Judas."

Another great saint who lived in a tremendously difficult time can help us further. St. Francis of Assisi lived in the 1200's, which was a time of terrible immorality in central Italy, a dark age culturally and spiritually. Priests were setting a terrible example. Lay immorality was even worse. St. Francis himself, while a young man, gave some scandal to others by his carefree ways. But eventually he was converted back to the Lord, founded the Franciscans, helped God rebuild His Church and became one of the great saints of all time. Once one of the brothers in the Franciscans, who was very sensitive to scandals, asked him a question. "Brother Francis," he said, "What would you do if you knew that the priest celebrating Mass had three concubines on the side?" Francis, without missing a beat, said slowly, "When it came time for Holy Communion, I would go to receive the Sacred Body of my Lord from the priest's anointed hands." What was Francis getting at? He was pointing to a tremendous truth of the faith and a tremendous gift of the Lord. No matter how sinful a priest is, provided that he has the intention to do what the Church does—at Mass, for example, to change bread and wine into Christ's body and blood, or in confession, no matter how sinful he is personally, to forgive the penitent's sins—Christ Himself acts through that minister in the sacraments. Whether Pope John Paul II celebrates the Mass or whether a priest with a felony celebrates Mass, it is Christ Who Himself acts and gives us His own Body and Blood. So what Francis was saying in response to the question of his religious brother—that he would receive the Sacred Body of His Lord from the priest's anointed hands—is that he was not going to let the wickedness or immorality of the priest lead him to commit spiritual suicide. Christ can still work and does work even through the most sinful priest. And thank God! If we were always dependent on the priest's personal holiness, we'd be in more trouble than we are now. Priests are chosen by God from among men, and they're tempted just like any human being and fall through sin as well. But God knew that from the beginning. Eleven of the first twelve apostles scattered when Christ was arrested, but they came back. One of the twelve sinned in betraying the Lord and sadly never came back. But God has essentially made the sacraments "priest-proof," in terms of their personal holiness. No matter how holy they are, or how wicked, provided they have the intention to do what the Church does, then Christ Himself acts, just as He acted through Judas when the Iscariot expelled demons and cured the sick.

Lessons from the Boy Scouts

What should the response of the Church be to these deeds? Does the Church have to do a better job in making sure no one with any predisposition toward homosexuality gets ordained? Absolutely. But that would not be enough. Does the Church have to do a better job in handling cases when they are reported? The Church has changed its way of handling these cases, and today the response is much better than it was in the 1980's, but a lot more can still be done. The situation may not be as bad as reported, though, as the press exaggerates the numbers. Phillip Jenkins noted in an Oxford University book in 2001 that pedophilia is extremely rare in the priesthood, with only 0.3 percent of priests being guilty of the crime. The most extensive study of priests over a thirty-year period found only one case of pedophilia, and in that case, the abuse occurred among members of the priest's extended family.[2] The scandals are a legitimate concern in the Church. However, now that they perceive an opening, the enemies of faith will attack relentlessly.

There is virtually no doubt that the priesthood attracts many great men who are faithful to the call. Their lives are often marked by heroic sacrifices as they serve and love selflessly. However, I would expect that the percentage of priests involved in immoral behavior is probably higher in the United States and the West because we are a culture virtually consumed with and saturated by sex. Television is like it is because we have not only invited it in, but have paid cable companies to install it. We have allowed the enemy in. Many of us choose to watch football on Sunday from 11:00 a. m. to 11:00 p. m. rather than be involved with family life.

John Adams, in 1774, wrote a commentary entitled, *Novanglus: A History of the Dispute with America, from Its Origin, in 1754, to the Present Time.* In it Adams admonished the clergy to speak out regarding public errors, saying:

> It is the duty of the clergy to accommodate their discourses to the times, to preach against such sins as are most prevalent, and recommend such virtues as are most wanted. For example, if exorbitant ambition and venality are predominant, ought they not to warn their hearers against those vices? If public spirit is much wanted should they not inculcate this great virtue? If the rights and duties of Christian magistrates and subjects are disputed, should they not explain them, show their nature, ends, limitations, and restrictions, how much soever it may move the gall of Massachusetts.[3]

Asherah has not only taken over the West, it has worked its way deeply into the seminaries. As the seminaries moved further into liberal Modernism, there was a wholesale abandonment of much that for centuries was considered sacred and good. This heresy propagated a false intellectualism, which brought senseless and elaborate arguments to attack the traditional teachings of the Church. The fruit of this Modernism, in its secularized version, is found in nearly every classroom in America.

The Church's leaders should go to a Boy Scout meeting, because the Scouts had it right when they rejected homosexual troop leaders. Having homosexuals around young boys cannot produce anything good. The Boy Scouts of America felt so strongly about it, they took a case to the Supreme Court. When members of the Church hierarchy invited homosexual men to enter seminaries, what did they think would happen? If it looks like a duck, walks like a duck, and quacks like a duck, there's a good chance it's a duck. The scandals that are now out in the open will change the Church. Nearly everyone feels it is time for a thorough housecleaning. Liberals see the scandals as a huge opportunity to challenge the Church's teachings on many issues, such as married priests, women's "ordination," and contraception. The head of the Jesuit Seminary in Cambridge, Mass., sees this as a time for open discussion because so many people are behind these changes. He said, "Rome will be forced to change now."[4]

Pope John Paul II responded to the Church's critics on March 21, 2002, when he spoke on the sex scandal involving priests. In his annual Holy Thursday message to priests, he said it was a "grave scandal that was casting a dark shadow of suspicion over all priests. As priests we are personally and profoundly afflicted by the sins of some of our brothers who have betrayed the grace of ordination." He continued by saying "the Church shows concern for the victims and strives to respond in truth and justice to each of these painful situations. There are many fine priests who perform their ministry with honesty and integrity and often with heroic self-sacrifice."[5]

Little will be seen in the press about homosexuality as it relates to the sex scandals in the Church. The press is making it an issue of celibacy because many in the press are pro-homosexual. By attacking the Magisterium, the Church's teaching on women's "ordination," the Real Presence, contraception, and a host of other issues will come under assault. Theological dissent will increase to the point where the public will be sufficiently confused that it won't know where to turn. As the problems play out, the American catholic church will show itself to be distinct from the Roman Catholic Church. A lot of Church "reformers" now believe they have a green light for wholesale changes. When all is said and done, many in the Catholic Church in America will leave and be in official schism.

A few bad apples cause the infection to spread. The priesthood has so many good men throughout the world. We will now see a war in the sanctuaries between liberal and conservative. In the end, it will be a question of whom do you follow: the Magisterium in its truth and splendor, or a modern teaching fashioned to appease American filth and impurity? The changes will be radical, and the fight will be fierce.

For the American public, the genie is out of the bottle. For many who love the Church in all of its grandeur, it will be painful to watch the Church's economic demise through the selling off of its property to pay litigants. The fact is that an appendage must often be cut off to save the body. There is cancer in the body and it must be cut out. To the dismay of the faithful, there is a homosexual underworld in which promiscuity and sexual harassment are rampant, contrary to popular belief. There is not a shortage of men in the priesthood, but there is a shortage of places that will accept doctrinally correct heterosexual men. Straight men, even if admitted to the seminary, are marginalized to the point of being forced out. If they do not leave of their own volition, they are sent to 'retreats' for psychological evolution and asked "why they suppress sexual tendencies." Many who leave become disillusioned with the Church and subsequently desert the faith altogether.

What atmosphere fosters sexual promiscuity? Many seminaries resemble "gay brothels"[6] with no oversight and a blind eye from the hierarchy. The problem is not isolated, but is a systemic and institutional contagion. The proliferation of the homosexual agenda allowed by the rectors of the seminaries produced an environment where homosexual men could find each other in a secure economic and social setting. In the 1960's, a papal pro-nuncio in Washington, D. C.— the man responsible for submitting to the Vatican the names of candidates to become bishops—was homosexual. Over the years, many homosexual bishops were thus appointed in the United States. This is the reason for the openly gay agenda of many ranking clergy. The problem is not pedophilia, it is homosexuality. Because the media in America are heavily in favor of the homosexual agenda, they will not sound alarms over the homosexual molestation, but will rather attack the Catholic Church and her doctrine of celibacy. The deviant American catholic church will flourish as the Roman Catholic Church will be condemned for not being open to reform.

Americans have been taught to obey their clergy as men of God bringing the gospel and sacraments to the people. However, many of the faithful have a right to feel betrayed as many of the clergy have intentionally misled them. People feel betrayed for putting their trust in shepherds who have abandoned their responsibilities to teach correct doctrine and instruct the youth. Devastation has often resulted when parents have placed their children under the protection of the clergy. They had a right to trust the Church, even a responsibility to do so, but some in the Church let them down by lying to them. The errors have been across the board. From seminary formation to theological dissent and doctrinal error, the Church has been scandalized, often with assent from many in the hierarchy. A blind eye is a sign of agreement. The faithful have been worn out by the fragmentation in society and the Church and they have lost the will to fight for something seen as so corrupt. They seem to be saying that it just doesn't seem to be worth it anymore—they are tired. As a result, funds will dry up, buildings, schools, rectories, chanceries, and parishes will be sold to pay off debt from litigation and settlements. There is rot and stench now oozing out of an open wound.

There is open dissent with Rome from ranking clergy in the world. They now believe they have an open door through which they will lead many Catholics who are unaware of true Church doctrine. All issues will be put on the table for assessment, and people will believe themselves to be the final arbiters of what is good and true because absolute truth is obscured. When Pope John Paul II visited Boston in 1979, he was asked if he would address the issue of sex in America. He said, "No, because America has a hang-up on sex."

It is extremely important for the reader to realize the ease of bashing the clergy, as they are visible targets. The people who often bash the clergy for their views are the same ones promoting sex education in schools, who are not monitoring their children, and who are not teaching them the faith. They have been very lax in personal cultivation of *any* spiritual values. It's always easy to blame someone else for what ails us. There are only 300 bishops in the United States, yet over 63 million Catholics. It's time to be more personally aware and introspective of the problems we face. The abdication of spiritual responsibility is pandemic across America. We get the leaders we deserve. When was the last time your family took an hour of prayer and actually prayed for the priests and the shepherds as Scripture ask us to? If one believes Satan exists, would you not believe that Satan would also attack the Generals? So, when we point our finger at someone, three are pointing back at us. The clergy is merely a reflection of the general moral state of society—just like the Supreme Court of the United States.

The Answer

The adequate response to scandal, the only true Catholic response to scandal—as St. Francis of Assisi recognized in the 1200's, as St. Francis de Sales recognized in the 1600's, and as countless other saints have recognized in every century—is HOLINESS! Every crisis that the Church faces, every crisis that the world faces, is a crisis of saints. Holiness is crucial, because it is the real face of the Church. There are always people—a priest meets them regularly, you probably know several of them—who use excuses for why they don't practice the faith, why they slowly commit spiritual suicide. It can be because a nun was mean to them when they were nine years old, and they like to hold onto a petty grievance. Or because they don't understand the teaching of the Church on a particular issue—as if any of these reasons would truly justify their lack of practice of the faith, as if any of them would be able to convince their consciences not to do what they know they should. There will doubtless be many people these days—and you will probably meet them—who will say, "Why should I practice the faith, why should I go to Church, since the Church can't be true if God's so-called chosen ones can do the types of things we've been reading about?" Scandals give some people justification for not practicing the faith. That's why holiness is so important. They need to find in all of us a reason for faith, a reason for hope, a reason for responding to the love of the Lord. Do priests have to become holier? They sure do. Do religious brothers and sisters have to become holier and give ever-greater witness of God and heaven? Absolutely. But all people in the Church do, including lay people! We all have the vocation to be holy and the crisis is a wake-up call.

The Lord Wins

It's a tough time to be a priest today. It's a tough time to be a Catholic today. But it's also a great time to be a priest and a great time to be a Catholic. Jesus says in the beatitudes, "Blessed are you when they shall revile you, and persecute you, and speak all that is evil against you, untruly, for my sake: Be glad and rejoice, for your reward is very great in heaven" (St. Matthew 5:11, 12). It's a great time to be a Christian, because this is a time in which God really needs us to show off His true face. Only a generation ago, the Church was respected. Priests were respected. It's not so any more. One of the greatest Catholic preachers in American history, Bishop Fulton J. Sheen, used to say, that he preferred to live in times when the Church has suffered rather than thrived, when the Church had to struggle, when the Church had to go against the culture. It was a time for real men and real women to stand up and be counted. "Dead bodies float downstream," he used to say, pointing that many people can coast when the Church is respected, "but it takes a real man, a real woman, to swim against the current." How true that is! It takes a real man and a real woman to recognize that when swimming against the flood of criticism, you're safest when you stay attached to the Rock, on whom Christ built his Church. This is one of those times.

Is the Church on the verge of disaster? The French emperor Napoleon was swallowing up countries in Europe with his armies bent on total world domination. He then said to Cardinal Consalvi, "I will destroy your Church." "Je detruirai votre église!" The Cardinal said, "No you won't." Napoleon, all 5'2" of him said, "Mais oui, je detruirai votre eglise!" The Cardinal said with confidence, "No you won't. If bad popes, immoral priests and thousands of sinners in the Church haven't succeeded in doing so from the inside, how do you think you're going to do it?" The Cardinal was pointing to a crucial truth. Christ will never allow His Church to fail. He promised that the gates of hell wouldn't prevail against His Church, that the barque of Peter, the Church sailing through time to its eternal port in heaven, will never capsize, not because those in the boat won't do everything sinfully possible to turn it over, but because Christ, who is in the boat, will never allow it to happen. Christ is still in the boat and He'll never leave it. Never lose trust in Him! It's His Church. Even if some of those He chose have betrayed him, He will call others who will be faithful, just as after Judas' death, the eleven apostles convened and allowed the Holy Spirit to choose someone to take Judas' place; St. Matthias, who was selected, thereupon proclaimed the Gospel faithfully until his martyrdom.

Are the scandals today a prelude to an even worse situation in the future? Maybe. If they are, then it will be up to the faithful to rely even more on the wisdom of the saints who preceded us in dark periods of the Church's history. As there is further deterioration more people will fall away. The heel is the lowest point on the body and supports all its weight. The remnant is the heel. Scripture warns that the devil will strike at the heel, but promises that he will not be successful. It will be up to the remnant Church to bring light to a dark world much in the same way that Gideon won with a small army (Judges 7). What started out with an army of 32,000 was whittled down to 300 men. The Lord makes it very clear to Gideon that it was He Who wins the battle on His terms—not Gideon's might, wisdom, or military prowess. The Lord always wins on His own terms. For over forty years, there has been a gradual chipping away at the faith to the point where it is unrecognizable from times past. Isn't it now time to turn it around? In the last generation, Catholics were too docile when it came to the Church. It's time to take it back.

Peace, Justice, and Forgiveness

After the September 11 events, Pope John Paul II addressed the issues facing the world. The following is a synopsis of the words of His Holiness on January 1, 2002, in a speech titled, "No Peace without Forgiveness."

In a few brief hours, thousands of innocent people of many backgrounds were slaughtered. Since then, people throughout the world have felt a profound personal vulnerability and a new fear of the future. The Church testifies to her hope, based on the conviction that evil, the *mysterium iniquitatis*, does not have the final word in human affairs. The history of salvation, narrated in Sacred Scripture, sheds clear light on the entire history of the world and shows us that human events are always accompanied by the merciful Providence of God, Who knows how to touch even the most hardened of hearts and bring good fruits even from what seems utterly barren soil. Peace is the work of justice and love. The persistent question in such a presence of evil is, "How do we restore the moral and social order subjected to such horrific violence?" Pope John Paul II's reasoned conviction, confirmed in turn by biblical revelation, is that the shattered order cannot be full restored except by a response that combines justice and forgiveness. The pillars of true peace are love and that form of love which is forgiveness.

But in the present circumstances, how can we speak of justice and forgiveness as the source and condition of peace? We can and we must, no matter how difficult this may be—a difficulty which often comes from thinking that justice and forgiveness are irreconcilable. But forgiveness is the opposite of resentment and revenge, not of justice. In fact, true peace is "the work of justice" (Isaiah 32:17). As the Second Vatican Council put it, peace is "the fruit of that right ordering of things with which the divine founder has invested human society and which must be actualized by man thirsting for an ever more perfect reign of justice" (Pastoral Constitution *Gaudium et Spes*, 78). For more than fifteen hundred years, the Catholic Church has repeated the teaching of Saint Augustine of Hippo on this point. He reminds us that the peace which can and must be built in this world is the peace of right order—*tranquillitas ordinis*, the tranquillity of order (cf. *De Civitate Dei*, 19,13).

True peace therefore is the fruit of justice, that moral virtue and legal guarantee which ensures full respect for rights and responsibilities, and the just distribution of benefits and burdens. But because human justice is always fragile and imperfect, subject as it is to the limitations and egoism of individuals and groups, it must include and, as it were, be completed by the forgiveness which heals and rebuilds troubled human relations from their foundations. This is true in circumstances great and small, at the personal level or on a wider, even international scale. Forgiveness is in no way opposed to justice, as if to forgive meant to overlook the need to right the wrong done. It is rather the fullness of justice, leading to that tranquillity of order which is much more than a fragile and temporary cessation of hostilities, involving as it does the deepest healing of the wounds which fester in human hearts. Justice and forgiveness are both essential to such healing.

It is precisely peace born of justice and forgiveness that is under assault today by international terrorism. In recent years, especially since the end of the Cold War, terrorism has developed into a sophisticated network of political, economic and technical collusion which goes beyond national borders to embrace the whole world. Well-organized terrorist groups can count on huge financial resources and develop wide-ranging strategies, striking innocent people who have nothing to do with the aims pursued by the terrorists.

When terrorist organizations use their own followers as weapons to be launched against defenseless and unsuspecting people they show clearly the death wish that feeds them. Terrorism springs from hatred, and it generates isolation, mistrust and closure. Violence is added to violence in a tragic sequence that exasperates successive generations, each one inheriting the hatred which divided those that went before. Terrorism is built on contempt for human life. For this reason, not only does it commit intolerable crimes, but because it resorts to terror as a political and military means it is itself a true crime against humanity.

It must be firmly stated that the injustices existing in the world can never be used to excuse acts of terrorism, and it should be noted that the victims of the radical breakdown of order which terrorism seeks to achieve include above all the countless millions of men and women who are least well-positioned to withstand a collapse of international solidarity—namely, the people of the developing world, who already live on a thin margin of survival and who would be most grievously affected by global economic and political chaos. The terrorist claim to be acting on behalf of the poor is a patent falsehood.

Following the teaching and example of Jesus, Christians hold that to show mercy is to live out the truth of our lives: we can and must be merciful because mercy has been shown us by a God Who is Love (1 St. John 4:7–12). The God Who enters into history to redeem us, and through the dramatic events of Good Friday prepares the victory of Easter Sunday, is a God of mercy and forgiveness (Psalm 103:3–4, 10–13). Thus Jesus told those who challenged his dining with sinners: "Go then and learn what this means, I will have mercy and not sacrifice. For I am not come to call the just, but sinners" (St. Matthew 9:13). The followers of Christ, baptized into his redeeming Death and Resurrection, must always be men and women of mercy and forgiveness.

The Need for Forgiveness

But what does forgiveness actually mean? And why should we forgive? A reflection on forgiveness cannot avoid these questions. Returning to what I wrote in my Message for the 1997 World Day of Peace ("Offer Forgiveness and Receive Peace"), I would reaffirm that forgiveness inhabits people's hearts before it becomes a social reality. Only to the degree that an ethics and a culture of forgiveness prevail can we hope for a "politics" of forgiveness, expressed in society's attitudes and laws, so that through them justice takes on a more human character.

Forgiveness is above all a personal choice, a decision of the heart to go against the natural instinct to pay back evil with evil. The measure of such a decision is the love of God who draws us to himself in spite of our sin. It has its perfect exemplar in the forgiveness of Christ, who on the Cross prayed: "Father, forgive them, for they know not what they do" (St. Luke 23:34).

Forgiveness therefore has a divine source and criterion. This does not mean that its significance cannot also be grasped in the light of human reasoning—and this, in the first place, on the basis of what people experience when they do wrong. They experience their human weakness, and they want others to deal leniently with them. Why not therefore do towards others what we want them to do towards us? All human beings cherish the hope of being able to start all over again, and not remain for ever shut up in their own mistakes and guilt. They all want to raise their eyes to the future and to discover new possibilities of trust and commitment.

Forgiveness therefore, as a fully human act, is above all a personal initiative. But individuals are essentially social beings, situated within a pattern of relationships through which they express themselves in ways both good and bad. Consequently, society too is absolutely in need of forgiveness. Families, groups, societies, States and the international community itself need forgiveness in order to renew ties that have been sundered, go beyond sterile situations of mutual condemnation and overcome the temptation to discriminate against others without appeal. The ability to forgive lies at the very basis of the idea of a future society marked by justice and solidarity.

By contrast, the failure to forgive, especially when it serves to prolong conflict, is extremely costly in terms of human development. Resources are used for weapons rather than for development, peace and justice. What sufferings are inflicted on humanity because of the failure to reconcile! What delays in progress because of the failure to forgive! Peace is essential for development, but true peace is made possible only through forgiveness.

Forgiveness, the High Road

Forgiveness is not a proposal that can be immediately understood or easily accepted; in many ways it is a paradoxical message. Forgiveness in fact always involves an apparent short-term loss for a real long-term gain. Violence is the exact opposite; opting as it does for an apparent short-term gain, it involves a real and permanent loss. Forgiveness may seem like weakness, but it demands great spiritual strength and moral courage, both in granting it and in accepting it. It may seem in some way to diminish us, but in fact it leads us to a fuller and richer humanity, more radiant with the splendour of the Creator.

The present troubled international situation prompts a more intense call to resolve the Arab-Israeli conflict, which has now been going on for more than fifty years, with alternate phases of greater or lesser tension. The continuous recourse to acts of terror and war, which aggravate the situation and diminish hope on all sides, must finally give way to a negotiated solution. The rights and demands of each party can be taken into proper account and balanced in an equitable way, if and when there is a will to let justice and reconciliation prevail. Once more I urge the beloved peoples of the Holy Land to work for a new era of mutual respect and constructive accord.

Dialogue

Religious leaders have a responsibility to work together to eliminate the social and cultural causes of terrorism. This can only be done by teaching the greatness and dignity of the human person, and by spreading the clearer sense of the oneness of the human family. The prayer for peace is of the very essence of building the peace of order, justice, and freedom. To pray for peace is to pray for freedom, especially for the religious freedom that is a basic human and civil right of every individual. To pray for peace is to seek God's forgiveness, and to implore the courage to forgive those who have trespassed against us. There is no peace without justice, and there is no justice without forgiveness.

O Ye of Little Faith

The abortion battle will not be won on a legislative basis or in a political arena. Pro-life leaders of Christian denominations, who have attempted this since the 1973 Supreme Court *Roe v. Wade* decision legalizing abortion, have fought the battle on worldly terms. There is an element of the physical battle as we will see from the below passage in the story of David and Goliath, but the battle is most deeply a spiritual one where we wrestle "against principalities and power, against the rulers of the world of this darkness, against the spirits of wickedness in the high places" (Ephesians 6:12). Only in the last two or three years have pro-life leaders and senior-ranking clergy decided to begin fighting the battle on a spiritual level. As much as this is now a very good thing, the question remains, "What took them over twenty-seven years to figure this out?" If a young boy with no weapon other than a slingshot can kill a giant, should we realize we may need different strategies and tactics? Are our weapons to be the weapons of Heaven—namely, humility, prayer, fasting, and penance? The only possible answer is yes! Americans must take courage, have faith, and confront the Culture of Death with the help of Heaven's divine weapons and strategy. There is no better example of this type of faith than where David acknowledges the battle is the Lord's:

And when he was brought to him, he said to him: Let not any man's heart be dismayed in him: I your servant will go, and will fight against the Philistine. And Saul said to David: You are not able to withstand this Philistine, nor to fight against him: for you are but a boy, but he is a warrior from his youth. And David said: The Lord who delivered me out of the paw of the lion, and out of the paw of the bear, he will deliver me out of the hand of this Philistine. And Saul said to David: Go, and the Lord be with you. And he took his staff, which he had always in his hands: and chose him five smooth stones out of the brook, and put them into the shepherd's scrip, which he had with him, and he took a sling in his hand, and went forth against the Philistine. And the Philistine came on, and drew nigh against David, and his armourbearer before him. And when the Philistine looked, and beheld David, he despised him. For he was a young man, ruddy, and of a comely countenance. And the Philistine said to David: Am I a dog, that you come to me with a staff? And the Philistine cursed David by his gods. And he said to David: Come to me, and I will give your flesh to the birds of the air, and to the beasts of the earth. And David said to the Philistine: You come to me with a sword, and with a spear, and with a shield: *but I come to you in the name of the Lord of hosts, the God of the armies of Israel, which you have defied. This day, and the Lord will deliver you into my hand*, and I will slay you, and take away your head from you: and I will give the carcasses of the army of the Philistines this day to the birds of the air, and to the beasts of the earth: that all the earth may know that there is a God in Israel. And all this assembly shall know, that the Lord saves not with sword and spear: for it is his battle, and he will deliver you into our hands. And when the Philistine arose and was coming, and drew nigh to meet David, David made haste, and ran to the fight to meet the Philistine. And he put his hand into his scrip, and took a stone, and cast it with the sling, and fetching it about struck the Philistine in the forehead: and the stone was fixed in his forehead, and he fell on his face upon the earth. And David prevailed over the Philistine, with a sling and a stone, and he struck, and slew the Philistine. And as David had no sword in his hand, he ran, and stood over the Philistine, and took his sword, and drew it out of the sheath, and slew him, and cut off his head. And the Philistines seeing that their champion was dead, fled away" (1 Samuel 17:32–33, 37, 40–51).

The rock in the sling of David today is a strong faith and trust in the Lord. It is accompanied by the Sacraments—especially Confession and Communion—Eucharistic Adoration, and the humbling of the believing Church. We must plead with God for our own good to end the scourge which harms us. If a boy with faith in his slingshot can slay a giant warrior, so much more can the Eucharist, the Body and Blood of God made Man, strengthen the souls of the faithful and lead them to victory. We have the answer; it needs to be utilized. Do we have sufficient faith to trust in the Lord and let His will be done?

18

Coming Prophesied Events

When the Round Table is broken man must follow
Galahad or Modred: middle things are gone.
                                    —C. S. Lewis, *God in the Dock*

There are two curses in life when it comes to private revelations: those who believe in everything and those who believe in nothing. There are many false locutions and apparitions in the world today with messages that appear to be good. The forces of Satan are most cunning and clever at weaving slight untruths into words that appear to be holy. It takes a long period of careful discernment by holy priests well-versed and knowledgeable in how Satan and his cohort operate, who understand the wiles the devil is capable of performing—which are quite a few—and who understand what is Catholic doctrine and what is not, before a sober and proper decision can be rendered on whether or not a given locution or apparition is of God. We must seek the "salt from Heaven" rather then the "sugar from hell." As wrote St. Margaret Mary Alacoque, to whom Our Lord entrusted the Sacred Heart devotion, "Jesus warned me to be on guard and said my greatest defense was obedience. 'Don't believe easily,' He said, 'in every inspiration, and don't be too sure of it. Satan is furiously bent on deceiving you. So don't do anything without the approval of those who are guiding you. As long as you have the sanction of obedience, he can never delude you. He is completely powerless over those who obey.'"

In this light, it is proper for people to be extremely careful when it comes to alleged private revelations. We should keep in mind, however, that it typically takes a very long period of time to reach a proper decision regarding private revelation. For example, regardless of the fact that from 70,000 to 100,000 people were on hand to witness the Miracle of the Sun on October 13, 1917, it took nearly fourteen years before the local bishop approved the apparitions at Fatima, Portugal. Although Fatima was not yet approved, were those people who attended the event wrong in being at the apparition? After the apparitions ended, were those who believed that Our Lady had appeared at Fatima and who spread devotion to Her and to what She had asked for—reparation to Her Immaculate Heart and penance for the countless grievous sins calling to Heaven for judgment—were they wrong? The same must be asked about locutions and apparitions in our times. Are people in error because they believe and spread devotion to apparitions or believe in locutions whose authenticity has not yet been determined by proper ecclesiastical authority? A serious impediment to Heaven's desires and calls is the lack of faith of the clergy. Ranking clergy are often the first to discourage what Heaven wants. With the myriad problems in sanctuaries, rectories, and seminaries, is it a wonder that so few announce what the Holy Spirit is asking us to do? With so much error and theological dissent in the Church today, the voice of Heaven is crying for our attention—and it is largely lay apostolates that have taken up the charge of spreading messages as the Blessed Mother is asking. The number of locutions and apparitions is great because the times we are now living demand it. Our times are urgent. It's really that simple.

In an age when the Church and world seem to be falling apart in every possible way because people have wandered away from God, would not God in His infinite mercy do all in His power to warn His children and help them avert greater trials and tribulations? It is in this light that the charitable Christian should look at modern private revelations: as a means of miraculous intervention to show people that God does exist and that He wants to spare the world the catastrophes due it because we have turned our backs on Him. The stories of the Bible and history show that God purifies and chastises His people because of sin. At the same time, people must be constantly vigilant and discerning, for as most of the world chooses sin over goodness, so the messengers of Satan vastly outnumber the messengers of God.

With this said, we present below a relatively brief list of private revelations that give the reader a glimpse of the potentially ominous future ahead for America, the world and the Church. While reading these prophecies, keep in mind that America's history is interwoven in the historical events of the rest of the world, particularly in the last 100 years. To understand the possible or likely outcome for America, and our generation in particular, one must also look at what the prophets say regarding the entire world. America's security, prosperity and peace rest somewhat on the nature of our relationship with our allies and the strength and strategies of our enemies—notwithstanding our response to Divine Truth.

The Handwriting Is on the Wall

The events of 9/11 certainly appear to represent a divine warning. The date of September 11 was not an arbitrary date chosen by Osama bin Laden. It was on that date in 1683 outside Vienna that King Jan Sobieski led an army of the Church—combined Papal, Polish, Austrian, and German forces—to defeat a massive Turkish army led by Kara Mustapha. This was the culminating defeat of the Islamic forces in Europe who from this point on would be in steady retreat. If you think this is simply a coincidence, note that the U. S. government launched its attack against bin Laden's forces in Afghanistan on October 7, 2001, the anniversary of the Battle of Lepanto, when a combined Catholic fleet annihilated the Turks in 1571, thus ending any Muslim seaborne threat to Christendom. Dates do have meaning.

If Americans insist on being stubborn and hard-hearted, we can rest assured that God will judge us more harshly. Recall the words from the Old Testament in the Book of Daniel: "You also his son, O Baltasar, have not humbled your heart, whereas you knew all these things: But have lifted yourself up against the Lord of heaven: and the vessels of his house have been brought before you: and you, and your nobles, and your wives, and your concubines have drunk wine in them: and you have praised the gods of silver, and of gold, and of brass, of iron, and of wood, and of stone, that neither see, nor hear, nor feel: but the God who has your breath in his hand, and all your ways, you have not glorified. Wherefore he has sent the part of the hand which has written this that is set down. And this is the writing that is written: MANE, THECEL, PHARES. And this is the interpretation of the word. MANE: God has numbered your kingdom, and has finished it. THECEL: you are weighed in the balance, and are found wanting. PHARES: your kingdom is divided, and is given to the Medes and Persians" (Daniel 5:22–28).

Worldwide Economic Chaos

As a prelude to a third world war, we are told, a worldwide severe economic collapse will occur. The Ecstatic of Tours in the 1880's wrote: "Before the war breaks out again, food will be scarce and expensive. There will be little work for the workers, and fathers will hear their children crying for food."[1] Bishop George Michael Wittman also of the 19th Century wrote: "Woe is me! Sad days are at hand for the Holy Church of Jesus Christ. The Passion of Jesus will be renewed in a most dolorous manner in the church and in her Supreme Head. In all parts of the world there will be wars and revolutions, and much blood will be spread. Distress, disasters and poverty will everywhere be great, since pestilential maladies, scarcity, and other misfortunes will follow one another." More recently, The Blessed Virgin Mary, appearing as Our Lady of All Nations, presented multiple visions and messages to Ida Peerdeman over the course of second half of the 20th Century. Ida Peerdeman confirms the prophecies above, based on a message she received from the Lady of All Nations in 1951 that says, "Economic and material disaster will strike the world. I have said disaster will come, disasters of nature...the material world is rushing into economic ruin...." In 1953, the Lady reaffirmed this prophecy saying, "I said great powers will be overthrown; a political and economic struggle will arise;...be on the lookout for the meteors; there will be disaster: there will be catastrophes of natures." The worldwide economic calamity will set the stage for greater armed conflicts worldwide between the East and the West. In bad economic times, good people can do horrible things.

Conflict with Russia and China

During one vision in 1946, Ida saw a stretch of map and heard the Lady say, "Judea," and then saw written, "Jerusalem." Then, she suddenly saw two lines, each with an arrow at the end; on the one it said, "Russia" and on the other "America." The Lady then said, "Look carefully and listen...the East against the West. Be on your guard, Europe." In 1947, Ida conveyed the following vision given to her by our Lady: "Now I see something like a cigar or a torpedo flying past me so rapidly that I can scarcely discern it. Its color seems to be that of aluminum. All of a sudden I see it burst open. I feel with my hand and have a number of indefinable sensations. The first is a total loss of sensibility. I live and yet I do not live. Then I see faces before me (swollen faces) covered with dreadful ulcers, as it were a kind of leprosy. Then I am aware of terrible diseases (Cholera and so on). Then tiny little black things are floating around me; I cannot distinguish them with my eyes and it is as if I were made to look at them through something (a microscope) and now I see (what the seeress now knows to be) slides of extraordinary brilliancy and upon them those little things enlarged. I do not know how I am to interpret this. "Bacilli?" I ask. The Lady says, 'It is hellish!' I feel my face swelling and it is swollen when I touch it, all bloated and quite stiff. I can no longer move. Then I hear the Lady again saying, 'Just think! This is what they are preparing!' and then very softly, 'Russia, but others as well.'

Finally, the Lady says, 'Nations, be warned.'" Many feel this is biological warfare.

In 1950, the Lady again warned mankind that "A great conflict will arise there—America and Russia; that is approaching." Later that same year, the Lady points at a map and explains the deceit of the communist Chinese who will confront America in Southeast Asia, saying, "That is America." Pointing to another part of a map, "Manchuria; a terrible uprising will happen there." As Ida moved her hands across the map over Formosa and Korea she hears our Lady say, "Child, I told you this is a sham. By this I meant that there will be periods of apparent tranquility. But this will not last long. The Eastern peoples have been roused by a type of humanity which does not believe in my Son."

Later, Ida is allowed to run her hands twice over the image of a cross, which weighs heavily over America. The Lady points to America with a disapproving finger to and fro saying, "Do not push your politics too far." Could this be a reference to America's political and military support for nations worldwide, or perhaps a reference to our exportation of secular humanism and abortion through government funded programs and tax-sheltered foundations? During the vision, Ida saw Russia in a hellish light. It seemed to explode from the ground upwards. The Lady then interjects, "And then you see nothing anymore."

In a broader context, that is regarding the whole world, in Akita, Japan the Blessed Virgin Mary told Sister Agnes Sasagawa on October 13, 1973, the anniversary of the "Miracle at Fatima," that "if men do not repent and better themselves, the Father will inflict a terrible punishment on all humanity. It will be a punishment greater then the deluge, such as one will never have seen before. Fire will fall from the sky and will wipe out a great part of humanity, the good as well as the bad, sparing neither priests nor faithful. The survivors will find themselves so desolate that they will envy the dead."[2]

War and Anarchy in Europe

Western Europe will not be immune from this coming war. In 1847, Sister Rose Asdente of Taggia: "A great revolution will spread over all Europe... A lawless democratic spirit of disorder shall reign supreme throughout all Europe. There will be a general overthrow. There shall be great confusion of people against people, and nations against nations.... The Russians and Prussians shall come to make war on Italy... Priests and religious shall be butchered, and the earth, especially in Italy, shall be watered with their blood."[3]

Several seers have prophesied about the "Prussians" and "Russians" invading Europe primarily through two avenues. Recall that earlier in this book a secret treaty recently completed between Germany and Russia was revealed that looks like a modern day Yalta Agreement. The first avenue would be the northern, Baltic region turning southward towards France and Italy. The second avenue includes the "Mohammedans" joining forces with the Russians and attacking southern Europe through the Balkans. Keep in mind that these wars have the stated diabolical purpose of destroying Christianity and other religions to the ultimate benefit of a universal religion based on Luciferian doctrine. Islam is no exception. Islamic militancy becomes a very important tool of the "Illuminized" elite. That is why the Venerable Bartholomew Holzhauser wrote, "Are we not to fear, during this period, that the Mohammedans will come again, working out their sinister schemes against the Latin Church?"

In addition to the combination of economic collapse, natural disaster and the invasion from the east, civil wars between the "right" and the "left" will break out throughout all of Europe that are so horrible that even fathers will fight their sons and whole cities, including many capitals such as Paris, Prague and Rome, will be entirely destroyed. Again, the Ecstatic of Tours prophesied that "England, too will have much to suffer.... Victims will be innumerable. Paris will look like a slaughter-house."[4]

The Pope Goes into Exile, the Church Is Persecuted Worldwide

As civil war wages in Italy and the Russians come to the aid of the communists, Rome and the Vatican will be under heavy assault. In the 14th Century Brother John of the Cleft Rock foresaw that "At that time, the Pope, with the cardinals will have to flee Rome in trying circumstances to a place where he will be unknown. He will die a cruel death in this exile. The sufferings of the Church will be much greater than any previous time in her history."[5] Supporting this prophecy is St. Pius X, who received the following vision: "I saw one of my successors taking to flight over the bodies of his brethren. He will take refuge in disguise somewhere; and after a short retirement he will die a cruel death."[6]

As early as the 6th Century, St. Caesar of Arles foretells that the Church will be persecuted severely at this time: "There shall be a great carnage...the altars and temples shall be destroyed...the pastors of the Church shall abandon their pulpits and the Church itself be despoiled of all temporalities." A Capuchin Friar 18th Century confirms this prophecy: "All priests, both secular and regular, shall be stripped of their possessions and of every kind of property. They will have to beg from lay people their food and everything necessary for their support and for the worship of God. The Pope shall die during these calamities, and the Church will be reduced to the most painful anarchy as a result."

The vision from the Third Secret of Fatima, given to Sister Lucia in Tuy, Spain in March of 1944 and finally released in the year 2000, clearly substantiates these earlier prophecies and appears to apply to our times. Specifically, it cites: "...a Bishop dressed in White—'we had the impression that it was the Holy Father.' Other Bishops, Priests, men and women Religious going up a steep mountain, at the top which there was a big Cross of rough-hewn trunks as of a cork tree with the bark; before reaching there the Holy Father passed through a big city half in ruins and half trembling with halting steps, afflicted with pain and sorrow, he prayed for the souls of the corpses he met on his way; having reached the top of the mountain, on his knees at the foot of the big Cross he was killed by a group of soldiers who fired bullets and arrows at him, and in the same way there died one after another the other Bishops, Priests, men and women Religious, and various lay people of different ranks and positions. Beneath, the two arms of the Cross there were two Angels each with a crystal aspersorium in his hand, in which they gathered up the blood of the Martyrs and with it sprinkled the souls that were making their way to God."

America's Fate Teeters on the Brink

Most prophecies regarding the ultimate outcome of these future events tend to focus primarily on areas outside of America. These prophecies provide specific details on civil wars, invasions, and persecutions, but also describe the introduction of a great and victorious leader for Christianity. This leader is referred to as the Great Monarch. He will be appointed by arguably one of the greatest popes of all history. With direct divine intervention, orchestrated by the Blessed Virgin Mary, these two leaders will help usher in "The Era of Peace" foretold at Fatima. As promised by St. John Bosco in the second half of the 19th Century, the New World Order will not be Lucifer's victory. God has deemed that the New World Order will be Christian, resting on the pillars of the Immaculate Heart of Mary and the Holy Eucharist. All heresy will end. There will be only one, Holy Catholic and Apostolic Church as faiths will be united together again in truth. Justice will be based again on natural law and God's Decalogue. God has reserved this victory for Mary ever since the fall of Eve. Recall

Genesis Chapter 3, where God said that He would put enmity between the woman and the serpent and that she will crush the serpent's head (Genesis 3:15 and Revelation 12). To not understand Revelation 12 is to not understand the times in which we live.

What about America's future? Little is known directly from prophecy. However, the implications are that the center of temporal power in the world will shift to the Great Monarch, who will reside in Europe. It appears that our era as the "Last Great Superpower" may come to an end. This does not necessarily mean that the U. S. is finished as a nation. If we return to God, we can take confidence that there will be a place for America in the Era of Peace. If we refuse to listen and repent, we can be assured that our nation will be humbled and become irrelevant in the eyes of the world. America is much more culpable than other nations because we have been blessed so greatly. We have had the resources, the riches, opportunities like no other nation on earth, and free will—and still we have turned our backs on God. Perhaps this is the reason why the prophecies are few—because our nation is stubborn and teetering on the brink of collapse. God is awaiting our answer to His warning on 9/11. Will we, like Lucifer, say, "I will not serve," or will we bend our knees in obedience to God? This is our last remaining choice.

One must learn that the Lord is in total control. Commit to heart and mind the five L's:

LOVE,
LEARN,
LISTEN,
LAUGH,
&
LET GO.

Ted Flynn is President of MaxKol Communications. He has worked in government, not-for-profits, real estate development, and management consulting. MaxKol is a book publishing and film production company. He has travelled to nearly 50 countries on business and pleasure. He has degrees from the University of Massachusetts in Amherst and the American University in Washington, D. C. He has also attended the University of Fribourg in Switzerland, and the London School of Economics in England.

Endnotes

Chapter 1

[1] Barbara Walters ABC television special on a ten-day trip to Saudi Arabia, March 29, 2002.

[2] George Archibald, "U. S. to Help U. N. Redefine 'Families,'" *The Washington Times*, April 22, 2002, pp. A1 and A12.

[3] Gerald Atkinson, "What Is the Frankfurt School?" August 1, 1999, p. 2, www.newtotalitarians.com/FranfurtSchool.html, as in Patrick Buchanan, *The Death of the West* (New York: Saint Martin's Press, 2002), p. 76.

[4] Arnold Beichman, "In Search of Civil Society," *The Washington Times*, February 3, 1993, p. G4, as in Buchanan, *Death*, p. 77.

[5] Charles Reich, *The Greening of America* (New York: Bantam Books, 1971), p. 2, as in Buchanan, *Death*, p. 77.

[6] Aldous Huxley, *Brave New World Revisited* (New York: Bantam Books, 1958), p. 115.

[7] Story from the World Communist Congress of 1931 held in Moscow, U. S. S. R., as told by Frank Buchman of Moral Re-Armament.

[8] Abraham Lincoln, First Inaugural Address, March 4, 1861, as in William J. Federer, *America's God and Country* (Saint Louis: Amerisearch, Inc., 1999), p. 378.

[9] Charles Habib Malik, 1958, as in Federer, p. 414.

Chapter 2

[1] United Nations "Declaration of Principles on Tolerance," October 25 to November 16, 1995.

[2] Richard Dawkins, "Is Science a Religion?" *The Humanist*, January/February 1997.

[3] *The Lambs of Christ* newsletter, P. O. Box 20203, Rochester, N. Y. 14602-0203.

[4] *Legislating Morality: There Oughta Be a Law!...*, VHS copies of Today's Life Choices, Series 1106, The Films for the Humanities and Sciences.

[5] Josh McDowell and Bob Hostetler, *The New Tolerance* (Tyndale House Publishers, 1998).

[6] McDowell and Hostetler, *The New Tolerance*.

[7] Chuck Colson, "Why Christians Are Losing the Culture War," *Christian Research Journal*, Summer 1996.

[8] Wernher von Braun, "Applied Christianity," *Bible Science Newsletter*, May 1974, p. 8, as in Federer, p. 69.

[9] National Association for Research and Therapy of Homosexuals, Why NARTH, "The Three Myths about Homosexuality," www.NARTH.com.

[10] *Bartlett's Familiar Quotations* (Boston: Little, Brown and Company, 1855, 1980), p. 825, as in Federer, pp. 67–68.

[11] David Yout, "Decline in Churchgoers Concerns Sociologists", *The Washington Times*, December 4, 2001, p. A2.

[12] Hilaire Belloc, *Essays of a Catholic* (Rockford, Ill.: TAN Books, 1931 and 1992), p. 8.

[13] Ibid., p. 12.

Chapter 4

[1] Will and Ariel Durant, *The Lessons of History* (New York: Simon and Schuster, 1968), p. 78.

[2] Foster Bailey, *Things to Come* (New York: Lucis Publishing Company, 1974), p. 116.

[3] Robert Waite, *The Psychopathic God: Adolf Hitler* (New York: Basic Books, 1977), p. 271, as in Richard Terrell, *Resurrecting the Third Reich* (Lafayette, La.: Huntington House, 1994), p. 26.

[4] Robert Nisbet, *History of the Idea of Progress* (New York: Basic Books, 1980), p. 278–82, as in Terrell, p. 24–26.

[5] Nisbet, p. 277, as in Terrell, p. 27.

[6] William Hubben, *Dostoyevsky, Kierkegaard, and Kafka: Four Apostles of Our Destiny* (New York: Collier Books, 1962), p. 124, as in Terrell, p. 29.

[7] Erich Kahler, *Man the Measure* (Cleveland: World Publishing Company, 1943, 1967), p. 582 as in Terrell, p. 29.

[8] Walter Kaufman, *The Portable Nietzsche* (New York: Viking Press, 1954), p. 570–72, as in Terrell, pp. 29–30.

[9] Terrell, pp. 28–30.

[10] Rev. Heinrich Portmann (1953), translated by R. L. Sedgwick (former British Brigadier General), Cardinal von Galen, 1957, pp. 239–246.

[11] "How Hitler's Forces Planned to Destroy German Christianity," *The New York Times*, January 13, 2002, p. 18.

[12] Federer, p. 83.

Chapter 5

[1] George Washington, "Farewell Address," September 19, 1796, as in Federer, p. 661.

[2] Above points are a rough paraphrase of Don Gobbi, Milan, Italy.

[3] Federer, p. 407.

[4] Don Gobbi, Milan, Italy, a rough paraphrase of Church principles.

Chapter 6

[1] C. S. Lewis, *Mere Christianity* (New York: Macmillan Publishing Company, 1943), p. 111.

[2] Ibid.

[3] Durant, *LoH*, p. 43.

[4] Ernest Renan, *The Apostles* (London: Methuen, n.d.), xxxiii, as in Durant, *LoH*, p. 50.

[5] Jules Lemaître, *Jean Jacques Rousseau* (New York, 1907), p. 9, as in Durant, *LoH*, p. 51.

[6] Will Durant, *The Mansions of Philosophy* (New York, 1929), p. 568, as in Durant, *LoH*, pp. 50–51.

[7] Durant, *LoH*, p. 81.

[8] Durant, *LoH*, p. 83.

[9] Eric Lichtblau, "CIA Warns of Chinese Plans for Cyber-Attacks on U. S.," *The Los Angeles Times* online, www.latimes.com/news/nationworld/world/LA-042502china.story, April 25, 2002.

[10] Will and Ariel Durant, *Our Oriental Heritage* (New York, 1935), p. 1, as in Durant, *LoH*, p. 87.

Chapter 7

[1] Interview with member of the staff of the Governors' Association of the Democratic National Committee, Washington, D. C., March 22, 2002.

[2] Bernard Asbell, *The Voices, the Pill: A Biography of the Drug That Changed the World* (Random House, 1995), Prologue.

[3] Ibid.

[4] www.Widmeyer.com/Widmeyer_wire/pdfs/Pill_timeline.pdf.

[5] Ibid.

[6] Sharon Snider, "The Pill: 30 Years of Safety Concerns," www.fda.gov/ggs/topics/consumer/con00027.html.

[7] "Retailer and Provider Perspective Services," IMS Health and National Prescription Audit Plus, IMS Health.

[8] Pregnancy data from Mary-Louise Kurey (Miss Wisconsin 1999), *Standing with Courage: Confronting Tough Decisions about Sex.*

[9] "Without Respect for Life, Science Will Spawn Monsters, Says Vatican Aide, Academy for Life Proposes New Dialogue Between Faith and Science," Zenit.org, February 26, 2002.

[10] Durant, *LoH*, p. 39.

[11] Abraham Lincoln, in a speech given in Edwardsville, Ill., on September 11, 1858, cited in *Bartlett's Familiar Quotations* (Boston: Little, Brown and Company, 1863, 1980), p. 520, as in Federer, p. 376.

[12] "Human Rights Don't Depend on Majority Consensus, Warns Pope, Democracies Can Become Oppressive, He Says," Zenit.org, March 1, 2002.

[13] Dr. James Dobson *Focus on the Family*, 2000 newsletter, Colorado Springs, CO 80995.

[14] Cited in "Bishops Praise Pope's 'Hymn to Life,'" *The Tablet*, April 8, 1995, p. 467, as in Weigel, p. 759.

[15] See, for example, Richard A. McCormick, S. J., "The Gospel of Life," *America*, 172:15 (April 29, 1995), pp. 10–17, as in Weigel, p. 759.

[16] Steven A. Ertelt, "Dutch Carry Cards that Say: Don't Kill Me, Doctor," *Pro-Life Infonet Digest*, October 20, 1998, as in Weigel, p. 759.

[17] Conversation of George Weigel with Pope John II, March 20, 1997, as in Weigel, p. 759.

[18] See Russell Hittinger's essay in "The Gospel of Life: A Symposium," p. 35, as in Weigel, p. 759.

[19] See "The Pope in Brooklyn, Mass at Aqueduct Racecourse," *L'Osservatore Romano*, English Weekly Edition, October 11, 1995, pp. 4–5, as in Weigel, p. 777.

Chapter 8

[1] Wesley J. Smith, *Brave New World, Here We Come.*

[2] "Furor over Cross-Species Cloning," *The Wall Street Journal*, March 19, 2002, p. B1.

[3] C. Ben Mitchell, "Old MacDonald Had an Embryo, E,I,E,I,Oh?" *Ethics and Medicine*, Volume 17:3.

[4] Nancy L. Jones, Ph.D., "Human Cloning-Embryo Style: Deliverance or Captivity?" The Center for Bioethics and Human Dignity, 11/28/01.

[5] *The Washington Post Magazine*, March 31, 2002.

[6] Federer, pp. 539–540.

Chapter 9

[1] "How Broken Families Rob Children of Their Chances for Future Prosperity," *The Heritage Foundation Backgrounder Executive Summary*, June 11, 1999.

[2] "The Effects of Divorce on America," *The Heritage Foundation Backgrounder Executive Summary*, No. 1373, June 5, 2000.

[3] National Survey of Family Growth, various years (a series of federal studies).

[4] E. Jeffrey Hill, Brent C. Miller, Maria C. Norton, Margaret H. Young, "Religiosity and Adolescent Sexual Intercourse: Reciprocal Effects," Utah State University, unpublished article received from the National Campaign to Prevent Teen Pregnancy.

[5] "National Longitudinal Survey of Adolescent Health," 1995, Center for Data Analysis, The Heritage Foundation.

[6] Edward O. Laumann, et al., *The Social Organization of Sexuality* (Chicago: University of Chicago Press, 1994).

[7] All data is available at the Heritage Foundation's web site, http://www.heritage.org.

[8] Dr. James Dobson, *Focus on the Family*, March 2002 newsletter.

[9] Ibid.

[10] Ibid.

[11] George F. Will, "Broken Families and School Performance," *The Washington Post*, January 6, 2002, p. B7.

[12] "The Paradox of Taliban John," *The Washington Times*, February 4, 2002, p. A2.

[13] "The Nasty Ripples of Divorce," Zenit.org, February 2, 2002.

[14] "Pope Urges Judges, Lawyers to Shun Divorce Cases," Reuters, January 28, 2002. "Lawyers and Judges Must Not Act against Marriage, Pope Says," www.Zenit.org, January 28, 2002.

[15] Diana Lynne, "Schools Sued over Pro-Homosexual Skits: Parents' Orders to Opt-Out Kids from 'Cootie Shots' Overlooked," WorldNetDaily.com, February 6, 2002.

[16] "Largest Pediatricians Group Backs Homosexual Adoption," *The Washington Post*, February 4, 2002, p. A3.

[17] Leslie Berger, "The Therapy Generation," *The New York Times*, January 13, 2002, Education Review section, p. 30.

Chapter 10

[1] Craig A. Anderson and Karen E. Dill, "Video Games and Aggressive Thoughts, Feelings, and Behavior in the Laboratory and in Life," *Journal of Personality and Social Psychology*, Vol. 78, No. 4, 772–790, April 2000, as cited by E. Pooley, "Portrait of a Deadly Bond," *Time* Magazine, May 10, 1999, pp. 26–32.

[2] Edna Gundersen, et al, *"The Osbournes* Find a Home in America's Living Rooms," *USA Today*, April 19–21, pp. 1A–2A.

[3] A. C. Nielsen Co., 1990.

[4] A. C. Nielsen Co., 1990.

[5] A. C. Nielsen Co., 1990.

[6] 1989 study by Larry Tucker at Brigham Young University.

[7] Newton Minnow, former Chairman of the FCC, and Craig LaMay, "Abandoned in the Wasteland: Children, Television and the First Amendment," 1995.

[8] Quote from Abandoned in the Wasteland: Children, Television and the First Amendment, by Newton Minnow, former Chairman of the FCC, and Craig LaMay, 1995.

[9] Educational Testing Service study, 1990.

[10] V. C. Strasburger, "Children, Adolescents, and the Media: Five Crucial Issues," *Adolesc Med: State of the Art Rev.,* 1993, 4:479–493 American Academy of Pediatrics study, 1990.

[11] American Psychological Association.

[12] Compiled by TV-Free America; 1611 Connecticut Avenue, NW, Washington, D. C. 20009.

[13] Ibid.

[14] Ibid.

[15] Ibid.

[16] Ibid.

[17] Ibid.

[18] Ibid.

[19] "Sexuality, Contraception, and the Media," American Academy of Pediatrics Committee on Public Education, January 2001, http://www.aap.org/policy/re0038.html.

[20] John Kiesewetter and Richelle Thompson, "TV's Sex Content Climbs, Study Says," National Coalition for the Protection of Children & Families (NCPCF), http://www.nationalcoalition.org, referencing a news article. *Cincinnati Enquirer* online. http://enquirer.com/editions/2001/02/07/loc_tvs_sex_content.html 2/07/01.

[21] "Internet Usage Reaches Record level," www.USAToday.com, Tech, 11/13/2001.

[22] "An Unbiased Voice in the Word War," *The Washington Post*, November 8, 1995.

[23] 1980 study by the California Department of Education which studied the television habits and test scores of half a million children.

[24] Newton Minnow, former Chairman of the FCC, and Craig LaMay, "Abandoned in the Wasteland: Children, Television and the First Amendment, 1995.

[25] Quote from University of Massachusetts psychology professor Daniel R. Anderson in his 1988 study of television's influence on children's education.

[26] Marie Winn, "The Plug-in Drug, 1985.

[27] Ibid.

[28] Michael Medved, *Hollywood vs. America, Popular Culture and the War on Traditional Values* (Harper Collins Publishers Inc. 1992), page 10.

[29] Medved, p. 245.

[30] Ibid.

[31] Quote from University of Michigan psychologist Dr. Leonard Eron, whose landmark 22-year study of television's effects tracked more than 800 people from age eight to adulthood.

[32] Medved, p. 10.

[33] Ibid.

[34] *Christian Science Monitor*, July 6, 1993.

[35] National Coalition on Television Violence.

[36] Ibid.

[37] Seven-year statistical analysis study by Dr. Brandon Centerwall at the University of Washington.

[38] C. A. Anderson and K.E. Dill, "Video Games and Aggressive Thoughts, Feelings, and Behavior in the Laboratory and in Life", *Journal of Personality and Social Psychology*, April 2000, Vol. 78, No.4, pp. 772–790.

[39] C. Braun and J. Giroux, "Arcade video games: Proxemic, Cognitive and Content Analyses", *Journal of Leisure Research*, 21, 92–105, 1989.

Chapter 11

[1] D. Ackman, "Management & Trends How Big Is Porn?" www.Forbes.com, May 25, 2001.

[2] "Porn.com." *U. S. News and World Report*, March 2000.

[3] E. Moore, "Adult content grabs lion's share of revenue," *Adult Video News Online*, May 26, 1999.

[4] "Alexa Research Finds 'Sex' Popular on the Web…" *Business Wire,* February 14, 2001, as on http://www.nationalcoalition.org.

[5] "Zogby/Focus Survey Reveals Shocking Internet Sex Statistics," Legal Facts: Family Research Council, Vol. 2. No. 20. March 30, 2000, as on http://www.nationalcoalition.org.

[6] "The NetValue Report on Minors Online…" *BusinessWire*, December 19, 2000 (taken from study by NetValue, an internet activity measurement service), as on http://www.nationalcoalition.org/.

[7] Kathleen Parker, "It's Common Sense to Restrict Internet Usage in Libraries," *The Orlando Sentinel* online, http://orlandowsentinel.com/news/031900_parker.htm. March 19, 2000, as on http://www.nationalcoalition.org.

[8] James Harder, "Porn 500," InsightMag.com, http://www.insightmag.com/archive/200101088l.

[9] Brendan I.Koerner, "A Lust for Profits." U. S. News online. http://www.usnews.com/usnews/issue/000327/eporn.htm. March 27, 2000, as on http://www.nationalcoalition.org.

[10] Alvin Cooper, Dana E. Putnam, Lynn A. Planchon, and Sylvain C. Boies, "Online Sexual Compulsivity: Getting Tangled in the Net." Sexual Addiction and Compulsivity, 6:79–104. (Taken from J. Amparano, "Sex Addicts Get Help." *The Arizona Republic*, p. A1. 1999), as on http://www.nationalcoalition.org,.

[11] "Sexuality, Contraception, and the Media." American Academy of Pediatrics Committee on Public Education. 1/2001 http://www.aap.org/policy/re0038.html.

[12] "The Web's Dark Secret" *Newsweek*, March 19, 2001.

[13] Andrea Rock, "Stalkers Online," *Ladies' Home Journal,* March 2000.

[14] Haven Bradford Gow, "Child Sex Abuse: America's Dirty Little Secret," MS Voices for Children, March 2000.

[15] "Kids willing to reveal secrets on Net: study," *The Globe and Mail*, May 17, 2000 referencing a study by the Annenberg Public Policy Center.

[16] R. Kraut et al (Carnegie Mellon University), "Internet Paradox a Social Technology That Reduces Social Involvement and Psychological Well-Being?" *American Psychologist*, September 1998, Vol. 53, No. 9, 1017–1031.

[17] Gloria Goodale, *Christian Science Monitor* online, http://www.csmonitor.com/2002/0201/p13s01-altv.htm, February 01, 2002, edition.

[18] Jan LaRue, Family Research Council, in interview with Bill O'Reilly on "The Corruption of American Youth," Fox Television, March 28, 2002.

[19] *ABC Evening News*, April 16, 2002.

Chapter 12

[1] "Drugs in America", *The Washington Post*, March 29, 2002, p. 1.

[2] Jodie Morse, "Women on a Binge," *Time* Magazine, April 1, 2002, p. 58.

[3] M. S. Wilkes et al, "2000 DTC spend hits $2.28 B led by Vioxx, Prilosec," Med Mark Media, 2001, 36:7, Direct-to-consumer prescription drug advertising: trends, impact, and implications. Health Aff. 2000; 19:110–228.

[4] A. L. Balazs et al, "Direct to Consumer Advertising: An Ad Processing Perspective."

[5] D. J. Mooer, Jr., "Hospital Profits Continue to Nosedive," Modern Healthcare 2000; 3(18):20 and PACE pharmacy group to bypass wholesalers with RxMarketplace.com, FDC Rep. Wkly Pharm. Rep. 2000; 49(19):3.

[6] Ibid.

[7] Ibid.

[8] Ibid.

[9] *Alcohol Advertising: Its Impact on Communities, and What Coalitions Can Do to Lessen That Impact*, Strategizer Technical Assistance Manual, Center for Science in the Public Interest, Community Anti-Drug Coalitions or America.

[10] Ibid.

[11] Ibid.

[12] F. S. Stinson et al, *U. S. Apparent Consumption of Alcoholic Beverages. Alcohol Epidemiologic Data System*, U. S. Alcohol Epidemiologic Data Reference Manual, (Rockville, Md.: National Institute on Alcohol Abuse and Alcoholism, Division of Biometry and Epidemiology, 1997), Vol. 1, 3rd Edition. T. M. Nephew et al, *Surveillance Report #55: Apparent Per Capita Alcohol Consumption: National, State and Regional Trends, 1970–98*, Alcohol Epidemiologic Data System (Rockville, Md.: National Institute on Alcohol Abuse and Alcoholism, Division of Biometry and Epidemiology, 2000).

[13] *Alcohol Advertising: Its Impact on Communities, and What Coalitions Can Do to Lessen That Impact*, Strategizer Technical Assistance Manual, Center for Science in the Public Interest, Community Anti-Drug Coalitions or America.

[14] Ibid.

[15] Ibid.

[16] Ibid.

[17] Michael Reagan, "Why the Drug Statistics Should Come as no Surprise," Michael Reagan Information Interchange, copyright 2001.

[18] "Playing with Painkillers", *Newsweek* cover story, April 9, 2001.

[19] Nilay D. Shah, Lee C. Vermeulen, John P. Santell, Robert J. Hunkler, and Karrie Hontz, Projecting future drug expenditures—2000, American Journal Health-System Pharm. Volume 59, Kam. 15, 2002, page 139, American Society of Health-System Pharmacists, Inc. copyright 2002.

[20] Michael Reagan, "Why the Drug Statistics Should Come as No Surprise," Michael Reagan Information Interchange, copyright 2001.

[21] Interview with Diane Sawyer, *Good Morning America*, March 19, 2002.

[22] Laura Sessions Stepp, "A Wonder Drug's Worst Side Effect," *Washington Post*, February 5,1996, p. A1; Laura Sessions Stepp, "Ritalin: 'In the Wrong Hands, a Dangerous Medication,'" *Washington Post*, February 5, 1996, p. C5.

[23] Linda Ciampa, "Ritalin Abuse Scoring High on College Illegal Drug Circuit", CNN Medical Correspondent, January 8, 2002.

[24] A. Marks, "Bitter Pill—Schoolyard Hustlers' New Drug: Ritalin", *Christian Science Monitor*, October 31, 2000.

[25] Frank Sama, "Decision Resources Study Evaluates the 1999–2009 Market for Drugs to Treat Depression: Emerging and Reformulated Drugs Will Drive Growth in Antidepressant Market," Decision Resource, Inc. November 27, 1999.

[26] Clare Thomson, "Warning: This Wonder Drug Could Seriously Damage Your Health" *The Bulletin*, Brussels' newsweekly in English, reprinted by the Center for the Study of Psychiatry and Psychology June 5, 1997.

[27] CNS Drugs, Adis International Ltd., March 1994.

[28] *Fentress vs. Eli Lilly and Co.* (Cir. Ct, Jefferson County, Ky.) No.90-CI-06033.

[29] *Forsyth vs. Eli Lilly and Co.* (DC Haw) Civ No 95-00185.

[30] Robert Bourguignon, M. D., "Problems with Prozac."

[31] Pfizer Pharmaceuticals' 2001 Annual Report, and a personal conversation with Investor Relations in New York City, April 15, 2002.

[32] Personal M. D., Your Lifeline Online, www.personalmd.com.

[33] Sally Lehrman, "Rx for Sex, SV," *Silicon Valley Magazine*, July 16, 2000.

[34] Randy Dotinga, "Rise in Viagra Abuse Spells Trouble—Gay Men Mixing Erectile Drug with Illegal Substances, Health Officials Say," *Health Scout News Reporter*, August 20, 2001.

[35] *Sexually Transmitted Diseases in America: How Many Cases, and at What Cost?* American Social Health Association (ASHA) (Research Triangle Park, NC: ASHA, 1998), Tables 3 and 4, pp. 24–25.

[36] "International Agency for Research on Cancer, World Health Organization," *The Washington Post*, March 27, 2002, p. A22.

[37] UNAIDS, World Health Organization, AIDS Epidemic Update, December 2001.

[38] Deirdre Wulf et al, eds, "Microbiocides: A New Defense against Sexually Transmitted Diseases (New York: The Alan Guttmacher Institute, 1999), Figures 6 and 9, pp. 18–22.

[39] Evaluate Pharma; MedAd News; Company Info, DH est.

[40] Therapeutic Insight 2001, The first conference focused on therapeutic franchise growth strategies, April 23, 2001.

Chapter 13

[1] Chuck Colson, "What Did Our Founders Think?" Crosswalk.com News Channel, January 10, 2002.

[2] Pope John Paul II, "Address to the 34th Assembly of the United Nations Organization," 5, as in George Weigel, *Witness to Hope* (New York: Harper Collins Publishers, 1999), p. 348.

[3] See Ibid., 48, as in Weigel, p. 841.

[4] Cited in Ibid., 79, as in Weigel, p. 841.

[5] Ibid., 1, as in Weigel, p. 842.

[6] Ibid., 107, as in Weigel, p. 842.

[7] Pope John Paul II, *Fides et Ratio*, 1, as in Weigel, p. 841.

[8] See Ibid., 45–48, as in Weigel, p. 841.

[9] Weigel, p. 841.

[10] Ibid., 17, as in Weigel, p. 776.

[11] Pope John Paul II, "Address to the 50th General Assembly of the United Nations Organization, 16, as in Weigel, pp. 775–776.

[12] Ibid., as in Weigel, p. 776.

[13] Pope John Paul II, *Crossing the Threshold of Hope* (New York: Alfred A. Knopf, 1994), p. 22 [emphasis in original], as in Weigel, p. 862.

[14] See Ibid., pp. 20, 22, as in Weigel, p. 862.

[15] See Balthusar, Hans Urs von, *Theo-Drama: Theological Dramatic Theory—Volume IV: The Action*, (San Francisco: Ignatius Press, 1994), p. 73, as in Weigel, p. 863.

Chapter 14

[1] *Cor Contritum et humilietum Deus non despecies*, The Ron Westernik Library of Sacred Documents in Virginia.

[2] Desmond Birch, *Trials, Tribulation & Triumph* (San Francisco: Queenship Publishing, 1996), pp. 327–330.

[3] Yves Dupont, *Catholic Prophecy: The Coming Chastisement* (Rockford, Ill.: TAN Books), p. 39.

[4] Ted Flynn, *Hope of the Wicked* (Sterling, Va.: MaxKol, 2000), pp. 71–72.

[5] The Last Times, pg.40.

[6] Birch, *Trials*, p. 393.

[7] Michael S. Rose, *Goodbye! Good Men: How Catholic Seminaries Turned Away Two Generations of Vocations from the Priesthood*, as in Phil Brennan, "Anti-Catholic 'Experts' Fuel Church's Scandals," www.newsmax.com, April 4, 2002.

[8] E-mail from MTLaw@Mobiletel.com, April 18, 2002.

[9] Dupont, *Catholic Prophecy*, p. 13.

[10] Dupont, *Catholic Prophecy*, p. 30.

[11] From Disquisition CXIV that was quoted in *Voice of Fatima*, January 23, 1968, and presented in *Catholic Prophecy*, p. 36.

[12] Rev. Richard G. Culleton, *The Prophets and Our Times*, p. 148.

[13] http://users.erols.com/mwhite28/atrox.htm.

[14] Birch, *Trials*, p. 329.

[15] Millard Burr, *Quantifying Genocide in Southern Sudan and the Nuba Moutains, 1983–1988*, U. S. Committee for Refugees, December 1998, pp.74, 75.

[16] Unpublished Manuscript of Life of Sor Marianne de Jesus Torres as in Birch, *Trials*, pp. 398–399.

[17] Ibid.

Chapter 15

[1] Jean-Francois Revel, *How Democracies Perish*, pg 166 and 126.

[2] WorldNetDaily.com, November 18, 1999.

[3] Newsmax.com, March 6, 1999.

[4] Now found at http://www.thefinalphase.com/Primer1.htm.

[5] "House Report Warns of Anti–U. S. Alliance: Panel Says Russia, China Teaming Up," *The Washington Times*, September 25, 2000.

[6] "Russia Launches New Missile as Warning," NewsMax.com, Dec. 15, 1999.

[7] Sen. James M. Inhofe, "Media in Danger of Missing Real Issues in Cox Report," www.senate.gov/~inhofe/coxrpt.html.

[8] Christopher Ruddy, "Russia and China Prepare for War—Part 7: United States Is Unprepared for War," March 11, 1999, www.newsmax.com.

[9] *The Washington Times*, March 12, 2002, p. A10.

[10] Ibid.

[11] Ibid.

Chapter 17

[1] The following is a close paraphrase of a talk given by Father Roger Landry in Fall River, Mass., on February 3, 2002, "Answering Scandal with Personal Holiness." The talk and subject matter were also expanded a great deal.

[2] Statistics from Father Bill McCarthy, "God's Cleansing and Chastisement Always Begin with the Church," Moodus, Conn., My Father's House.

[3] Federer, p. 8.

[4] Interview with Director of the Weston School of Jesuit Theological Seminary, New England Cable News, March 21, 2002.

[5] *The Washington Post*, March 22, 2002, p. 1.

[6] Dr. Richard Sipe, as quoted by Rod Dreher, "Andrew Sullivan's Gay Problem, and Mine," *National Review* online, March 13, 2002, www.nationalreview.com/dreher/dreherprint031302.html.

Chapter 18

[1] Dupont, *Catholic Prophecy*, p. 37.

[2] Ted Flynn, *The Thunder of Justice* (Sterling, Va.: MaxKol, 1993), p. 188.

[3] Dupont, *Catholic Prophecy*, p. 74.
[4] Ibid.
[5] Culleton, *The Prophets and Our Times*, p. 29. as in Birch, *Trials*, p. 313.
[6] Dupont, *Catholic Prophecy*, p. 22.

Notes

Notes

Notes

Notes

Notes

Notes

Notes

Notes

Notes

Notes